Las Vegas Babylon

Las Vegas Babylon

TRUE TALES OF GLITTER, GLAMOUR, AND GREED

Jeff Burbank

M. Evans
Lanham • New York • Boulder • Toronto • Plymouth, UK

Published by M. Evans
An imprint of The Rowman & Littlefield Publishing Group, Inc.
4501 Forbes Boulevard, Suite 200, Lanham, Maryland 20706
www.rlpgtrade.com

Estover Road, Plymouth PL6 7PY, United Kingdom

Distributed by NATIONAL BOOK NETWORK

Library of Congress Cataloging-in-Publication data applied for

ISBN-13: 978-1-59077-136-5 (pbk. : alk. paper)
ISBN-10: 0-1-59077-136-2 (pbk. : alk. paper)

∞ ™ The paper used in this publication meets the minimum requirements of American National Standard for Information Sciences—Permanence of Paper for Printed Library Materials, ANSI/NISO Z39.48-1992.

Manufactured in the United States of America.

For Alessandro and Ansley

CONTENTS

Contents

I will make the land of Babylon an everlasting ruin. . . .
I will repay them for all they have done!

—Jeremiah, chapter 25

ACKNOWLEDGMENTS

$\mathcal{I}$ want first to acknowledge Kenneth Anger, author of *Hollywood Babylon*, whose fascinating and irreverent work inspired this book. I also would like to express my gratitude to my literary agent, Janet Rosen, of the Sheree Bykofsky Associates agency in New York, for her guidance and support.

In Las Vegas, I have to also acknowledge the editors, reporters, commentators, and others I met, worked with, and learned so much from over the years, starting with cartoonist Mike Smith and the rest of the staff of the feisty *Las Vegas Sun*, the newspaper I joined in 1987. Its then-editor, the late Sandy Thompson, hired me as a business reporter and later put me on the local gaming beat, including opening day of the Mirage Hotel in 1989. Next, I must tip my hat to the *Las Vegas Review-Journal*, where I joined the staff in 1990 and where I learned invaluable lessons about Las Vegas through reporting on police, fire, labor relations, and later gaming. The *R-J*'s editors saw fit to assign me some of the choicest stories in town, including the openings of the MGM Grand, Treasure Island Hotel, and Luxor Hotel on the Strip. Though I left that paper back in 1995, I am still indebted to them for their confidence in me.

These and other experiences helped me discover the inner workings of the casino industry, the politics, and the social aspects of what is still a small town for its size. Others whose ideas and thoughts about Vegas have furthered my understandings, big time, include Dr. Michael Green, Las Vegas's Historian to the Stars; Hugh Jackson, one of the important social and political commentators in town and one of its best writers; George McCabe, a former local reporter who knows a lot about what really happens in Vegas, especially for someone who works in public relations; Dr. Jeff Jablonski, of UNLV's English Department, who lets me teach business writing to hundreds of students at that growing university; Flo Rogers, head of KNPR-FM, the area's local public radio outlet, and her crew, for putting me on the air as a commentator, which also expanded my appreciation for the many complicated issues facing this town.

I must also acknowledge my parents, Dr. Rex Burbank, a retired university professor, author, and college testing expert, and Nancy Burbank, a retired R.N., for their lifelong encouragement while I continue to ride my roller coaster. I also want to thank my son, Alessandro, and my daughter, Ansley, for teaching me there are many things to appreciate in life beyond careerism. Also, kudos go out to my sister, Cindy Vandenberg, a writer living in paradise in Carmel-By-The Sea, and my San Francisco Bay Area lawyer brother, Scott. Oh, and I had better mention my ex-wives, Cristina and Andrea.

INTRODUCTION

*D*oes Las Vegas have any redeeming qualities? Let's see. There are blue skies and mostly warm weather about 320 days or more a year. You won't miss shoveling snow, except for the occasional freak storm. If you're kind of lonely, you can sit, drink, smoke, play a video slot, and watch sports all at once, at all hours, and that really comes in handy. And there's the comfortable feeling of freedom you get when you come off an airliner at McCarran International Airport, from anywhere, and you immediately see and hear the slot machines. While other, older large cities appear stagnant and overbuilt, Vegas always has more energy. Since the metro area just grows and grows like no other, it's kind of like post-war America in Vegas all the time. There's a feeling of reinvention here—from fresh money constantly flowing into town—with new entertainment diversions at the hotels and pronouncements of multi-billion-dollar "mixed use" complexes on the Strip, even though many never make it. New career and business opportunities grow on trees, as do good news stories.

When I made the move east to Las Vegas from California back in 1987, it still had a small-town feel, with the novelty of the famous but frayed and out-of-date Strip hotels. These were places where you could go to slum and laugh hysterically at the old-fashioned, third-rate lounge acts and at the forced seriousness of the casino pit bosses in crumbling hotels like the

Thunderbird, Landmark, Sands, and the demented Vegas World. But a number of major trends, in and out of town, were converging in the late 1980s, and things were about to change radically. It started when Deadwood, South Dakota, legalized casino games like blackjack and slots. Then the Mississippi River states started to okay riverboat casinos and Congress gave American Indians the right to open casinos. Gambling was almost everywhere by then. Companies could borrow hundreds of millions to build casinos and pay back the loans with the flowing and growing cash. On the Strip, while most of the big hotels were already building a lot more guest rooms to meet the volume of visitors, in 1989, Steve Wynn and the Mirage started the era Vegas is in now.

It really took off like hell in the 1990s. So many people moved to Vegas so quickly that all of a sudden there were huge new neighborhoods and sections of town that you had no idea about. And yet, you still had the same cast of characters in government and business, the dying fathers and ascending sons of Las Vegas, largely from its old Mormon and Jewish communities. That insular, small-town feel, many Vegas residents will tell you, still exists in the early twenty-first century. Part of the reason is there's so little of that "sense of community" thing here. Vegas, the fun getaway for so many millions of tourists, is the getaway spot for droves of new residents from out of the state, too. You can drive twenty miles from work to your suburban home, open your electronic garage door, and close it behind you. Your yard, if you have one, is so small there's no reason to go outside and see your neighbors (and, it's probably too hot or cold, anyway). You can live for years and never know those who live in the homes beside you, or the parade of neighbors who have rented them and then left town, or the absentee landlords who've flipped them over and over for a profit in faster times, or have had to cover the mortgage payments themselves for months on end when home prices at last got too high from the demand for them. That happened around 2004.

The year of 2005, the 100th anniversary of Vegas's downtown area, started as the valley was earning more money than ever before from hotel rooms, drinks, food, material goods, and casino gambling from its tourists. Four major hotel-casino companies were merging, so that only two might control about three quarters of the guest rooms on the Las Vegas Strip. With so many hotel rooms in town (more than 130,000), the resorts now look at the advance bookings of their pricey guest rooms for how well they're going to do, with gaming regarded more and more as a good side bet. Meanwhile, home and commercial developers are waiting for more federally owned land to become private so that Vegas's suburban sprawl can extend yet further north and south.

To me, Las Vegas is both fascinating and frustrating. Like the writer Michael Ventura once said, you love it and hate it at the same time. Whenever the city's shakers and sappy news media praise something, I wonder what's wrong with it. One image I can't get out of my mind whenever I drive past the "new downtown" area is the 1.3 million square-foot World Market Center on the approach to Interstate 15. Vegas got most of the country's top furniture merchants to bypass North Carolina and San Francisco to come to fun and cheaper Vegas—a theft of such business the town now takes for granted. But when you drive by that building, there, plain as day, fronting downtown Las Vegas, the façade of this eighth wonder wears what looks exactly like the giant frown from the "unhappy face" parody of the 1970s, yellow "Have a Nice Day" happy face. All that's missing is the message: "Shit!"

I wrote this book to convey some of the town's lesser-known popular history, but also to counter the promotional writing about the town that I know would dominate what gets published during the centennial. In Las Vegas, Nevada's legal excesses are magnified by its expanding numbers of tourists and residents, and it is why Nevada ranks the worst or near-worst of the fifty states in a broad variety of social problems, health problems, education, the environment, charitable giving, and on and on. Vegas is an incestuous place where people are tempted to take risks with the worst parts of their nature. Is there a town anywhere where it's as easy to get drunk, at any hour of any day, as Vegas? What is truly real here are grim realities. Vegas encourages its visitors and especially its residents to be what would be considered immoral, greedy, and irresponsible in most towns. For instance, visitors are manipulated into seeking to win millions in a progressive jackpot with only a few coins, then persuaded to forget the thousands of dollars they lost in the process. They're asked if they "had fun anyway" and given a slot club card to facilitate their mindless slot habit, then the casinos trumpet the visitors' losses in their quarterly report. For many who are not up to the task of resisting its devilish seductions, there is retribution, which has long been appreciated in American culture. Like the slot-fevered character who kills himself rather than be haunted by a talking slot machine at the end of an episode of *The Twilight Zone*. Or the guy in *Alfred Hitchcock Presents* who comes to Vegas in the mid-1950s, finds a money belt with hidden skimmed cash dropped by a mobster, drinks himself silly at the tables and gambles it away. He is then taken to the hotel's office where his wife screams frantically on the phone back home that she and their kids are being held hostage, and the mobster in the office demands: "Now give me my money."

The overall premise of this book is based on Kenneth Anger's 1975 work, *Hollywood Babylon*, and his 1984 sequel, *Hollywood Babylon II*. Both books took an irresistibly cynical approach to a place where the truth was often hidden from the public, covered up by studio publicity departments, and glossed over by an extraordinarily reverential mainstream media. Las Vegas and its tourist entertainment/gaming biz has not quite worked on that scale, but there are similarities to Hollywood. Hollywood is now well covered in that regard, but Vegas is not. Its insular, monopolized, and inadequate print and TV media are part of the problem.

Like Anger's books, this one focuses on the celebrities who came to Vegas to perform or play, and found themselves embroiled in its excesses. Vegas has a history of chewing up and spitting out its performers; they are under pressure to work like machines, switched on and off, for some of the highest weekly salaries in American show business. The best, Frank Sinatra and Dean Martin, who also had pieces of the profits at the Sands hotel, could take in $75,000 to $100,000 a week at the height of their Rat Pack years from the late 1950s to early 1960s. Some entertainers who, famously, depended too much on all of the good money to be had in Vegas (Judy Garland and Elvis are obvious examples) regularly risked physical destruction using drugs to sleep and wake up, building up tolerances that required ever-higher doses to work. Hey—read your contract.

Most of the book's chapters are divided into sections. In Chapter One, I sought to sum up in detail the effects that America's most popular tourist destination has had on its people and their environment. For background, I give a brief 100-year history of the town that I decided to break up into three parts: the forty-year "pre-mob years," the forty-year "mob years" and the nearly two decades remaining "post-mob" years. I thought it was necessary to review the history of organized crime in the United States, and its roots in the nineteenth century, in order to give the reader a perspective on a subject that is often misunderstood, and to show just how the mob entered, thrived, and unraveled in Vegas. I decided to write separate chapters on two of the main players in Vegas's history as a one-time haven for the underworld, Ben "Bugsy" Siegel and Moe Dalitz. Though much has been written about Siegel and his Flamingo hotel, I reviewed his 2,421-page FBI file on the agency's website and found much that has not been published in book form before. I did the same with Dalitz, the inside operator of the Desert Inn and other casinos in the 1950s and 1960s who was nicknamed "Mr. Las Vegas" by old-timers but whom many outside of Vegas know little about. My writing on him is also based in large part from facts derived from his 2,729-page digital FBI file.

In "Excess Celebrities," I delve into a long list of famous people whose lives were altered significantly by Las Vegas's temptations, which typically resulted in a fateful reckoning, lessons learned the hard way. The "Vegas Politics" section focuses on the major players, including the Senate's most recent Majority Leader Harry Reid and his controversial tendency to shower public favors on his kids and their spouses. The "Bad Girls, Sad Girls," chapter takes a close look at the many women who've catapulted themselves, some out of nowhere in their first tries at elected office, since the 1990s, only to become caught in ethical or even criminal scandals. In "True Crimes," I centered on the backgrounds of three women caught up in three major recent homicide cases, each of whom fell victim to the town's loose morality and who lived for weeks together in the same Las Vegas jail cell.

"Criminal Refuge" reviews two examples of fugitives who fled to Vegas (as many have, to hide in its critical mass) to avoid murder charges, but were caught thanks to their own folly. Finally, under "Dueling Shills," I talk briefly about how Las Vegas's two money-grubbing daily newspapers—both in an operating agreement fusing the business side and keeping the newsrooms separate—have developed yet another local incestuous relationship by doing business directly with casinos, while leaving their reading public in the lurch and wanting better news coverage.

Above all, I want this to be a fun read. I'd like to say here that I hope that some of the people mentioned here get the joke. I hope that those who might feel skewered here will forgive me for, well, having fun with them, and take it in good humor, or at least in stride. It's just another day in paradise.

—Jeff Burbank

1

Hype and Cold Reality

Behind the stereotype glitter and glamour, Las Vegas is America's version of ancient Babylon, a mixture of eye-catching architecture and sensual excess, where the desires and foolhardiness of its visitors and residents are played out in full, sometimes tragically. For most, it's little more than harmless fun. For others, under the town's encouragement, what comes out of them here stays with them. Its metro area has produced a dazzling $30 billion tourism economy that is the envy of destination resort spots anywhere. But Las Vegas and Nevada, playing the unassuming host to the millions while trying to lure commerce with fewer rules and lower taxes, have produced a seriously malfunctioning society beneath the "It's Vegas, baby!" façade.

The town can be a tempting and disillusioning hellhole for visitors, entertainers, and residents with their unrealistic expectations and destructive vices. Vegas is like Satan, looking on and smiling as people make their thoughtless, selfish choices that may destroy themselves and others.

Take New Year's Eve, 1999. The new millennium was approaching and a record-high number of New Year's partiers crowded the streets of Las Vegas. Police, doctors, and nurses prepared for about 300,000 good-timers for the Las Vegas Strip block party—hobbling, drunken men and women urinating in public or spontaneously vomiting on themselves and others. Five hundred people were to be arrested for throwing glass, fighting, or public nudity. At nine at night, more than a dozen of the 900 Las Vegas police on duty in riot helmets and bullet-proof vests stood atop flat bed trucks as a show of force in front of O'Shea's Casino on the Strip, a notorious spot for New Year's Eve fights. Paramedics a hundred yards away on Flamingo Avenue and the Strip helped ship the injured and sick to one of five special medical treatment centers. At 11:30, they stuck an IV needle into an intoxicated and unconscious sixteen-year-old girl and an ambulance whisked her to a treatment unit set up inside the indoor Fashion Show Mall.

As the minutes wound down on the second two thousand years, the largest number of Vegas revelers that night congregated between the Bellagio Hotel, the one with the big lake out front, and the new Paris-Las Vegas, with the 50-percent scale faux Eiffel Tower, across the street. While thousands hollered and sloshed open beverages, Tod Surmon, a twenty-six-year-old tourist from California, decided to scale a thirty-foot utility pole in front of the Paris. Seconds before the strike of midnight, he grabbed hold of a live wire and his electrocution sent him down head first to the pavement. He became the first death recorded in Las Vegas in the new millennium. As his body lay on the sidewalk, his skull cracked open for all to see, the throng everywhere around him counted down the last ten seconds. At midnight, directly above his lifeless body, an explosion atop the Paris's brightly lit Eiffel Tower fired glitter and confetti into the night to rain onto the Strip below. From The Guess Who concert on Fremont Street downtown to Barbra Streisand's show inside the MGM Grand Arena five miles south on the Strip, people shouted, "Happy New Year!" The brief pause over, people outside wondered what to do next, and gamblers in casinos resumed playing the slots and tables. Five minutes after midnight, paramedics got the call about Surmon.

Only a few months later came the *Twilight Zone* life experience of Cynthia Jay-Brennan. On March 11, 2000, Jay-Brennan put on the brakes of her 1999 Camaro, behind three cars at a stoplight on Boulder Highway. She was pretty, blonde, in her late thirties, and rich. Only six weeks before, after she changed out of her clingy cocktail waitress uniform, she dropped twenty-seven dollars in a dollar slot machine at the Desert Inn casino and won a jackpot (actually a slot machine company's IOU, stretched out over twenty-five years) worth $34.9 million, the largest such payout ever awarded in Nevada. She had played Megabucks, a series of 715 slots linked together and placed in 157 casinos throughout Nevada, knowing that the progressive jackpot had reached its highest level in December. The odds of winning the Megabucks jackpot were far higher than any state lottery: one in 16.7 million. The Desert Inn, enjoying valuable publicity, pampered her with a stay in a three-bedroom luxury suite with private swimming pool, hot tub, dining room, pool table, and twenty-four-hour butler service. Her incredible Cinderella story made national news: Sexy Las Vegas cocktail server becomes instant millionaire. She told the *Las Vegas Review-Journal*: "I don't know what's going to happen for sure. I just want to take care of my family."

She had no idea what was going to happen next that day at the stoplight. In the right passenger seat next to her was her older sister, Lela Ann Jay, forty-five years old, a resident of Las Vegas for two decades. Suddenly a speeding Ford Explorer appeared in Cynthia's rear view mirror and smashed into the Camaro, shoving it forward violently and causing the three cars ahead of her to collide. Lela died right away, but a spinal cord injury rendered Cynthia a paraplegic. The driver of the Explorer was Clark Morse, who was on his way to his mother's house after visiting a bar. He fled the accident scene on foot to hide at Mom's. Child-like and mildly retarded, Morse, fifty-seven years old, already had fifteen drunken driving arrests over nineteen years in Vegas, and was convicted five times. His license had been revoked. A breath test ninety minutes later showed he still had a blood-alcohol level of .18, well above Nevada's standard of the time of .10 to be considered legally drunk.

Then there's Jihad Moukalled, a Muslim from Detroit, who would have shamed himself and ruined his reputation in his tight ethnic community had they known about his gambling addiction. He'd already secretly skimmed a half a million dollars from his printing business and borrowed $111,000 off the home he shared with his wife and three kids. He borrowed another quarter of a million from a friend. Using the money to gamble at blackjack, he'd won and lost large sums, first in the small casinos in Windsor, Canada, Caesars Palace in Atlantic City, the MGM Grand casino in Detroit, and finally the MGM Grand in Las Vegas, the site of his downfall. At one point, a lucky streak put him up $500,000 in Vegas, but it was soon gone. In November 2000, during a four-day whirl on the Strip, Jihad signed markers for $225,000 at the MGM and lost it all. The thirty-six-year-old Lebanese immigrant flew back to Detroit and made a desperate call to a friend. On a piece of paper, he wrote: "There is nothing more destructive to life than gambling. I wonder why there are government agencies to fight drugs and not gambling. A drug addict destroys his life, a gambler destroys his life and the lives of those he cares about." He smothered his three kids and used a gun to kill his pregnant wife and himself.

Perhaps no one exemplifies the pitfalls of Las Vegas like Jenna Jameson, the porn movie superstar who grew up in town with her policeman father. She was a parent's nightmare, in a town that causes many. At sixteen, she befriended bikers in North Las Vegas and moved in with her tattoo artist boyfriend, who showed her how to use methamphetamines. She was raped by her boyfriend's adopted stepfather while on a boat trip on Lake Mead. Jenna graduated from small-time showgirl at Vegas World for a few weeks to topless dancer at the Crazy Horse Too, though still only seventeen. Once hired, she went home and pried the braces off her teeth. She would soon make $2,000 to $4,000 a night. She told her male clients what they wanted to hear—I'm studying to be a real estate agent, etc.—to get them to spring for lap dances. A top local politician, a casino executive, and actor Nicholas Cage were among her regulars. From there, she graduated to modeling (making the cover of *Easy Rider* magazine) and totally nude photography, including an in-the-buff stint at Red Rock Canyon, even as tourists looked on. Then it was on to porn stardom and bisexuality in Los Angeles. One of the few local girls to make it in Hollywood (*Gilligan's Island*'s Dawn Wells was one), and to the *New York Times* Bestseller List, Jenna is biggest of the local girls who made good.

Ah, Las Vegas. Ah, the city of glitz, glamour, neon, feathered showgirls, spinning roulette wheels, adult entertainment! Not to mention hype, pretense, self-interest, cold reality, suicide, dropouts, illiteracy, gambling addiction, slot sections in grocery stores, car washes and laundromats, slot machines programmed to lose, ordinance-sanctioned anal-lap dances, an association of topless dancers headed by a male transsexual, absentee celebrity chefs, a wacky gin-swilling mayor, cartel-like casino mergers, seniors bussed to "locals" casinos, bad planning, poor education system, lousy newspapers, runaway development, blighted downtown, pollution, sleazy land deals, special interest-encrusted leadership, overpaid casino chiefs, underfunded and substandard public schools, blatant nepotism, non-elected incumbents, FBI raids, twenty-first-century political corruption, apathetic public, no public performing arts center, "The Last Honest Place in America."

But 37 million Vegas visitors can't be wrong. It's America's top tourism attraction, the number-one choice for a quick and cheap getaway, or what local tourism czars call a "mini-vacation." And who outside of town can resist the price—a three-day stay at a Las Vegas hotel with roundtrip airfare, comped or discounted meals, and maybe show tickets for a package deal for as little as $500 or $600, or free if you'd rather gamble more money away. But the popularity of Vegas has recently made cost no object, as demand for high-end hotel rooms has pushed rates well above $200 a night in the Strip resorts with the newest attractions. For its millions of fans, Vegas provides the feeling of instant freedom, to party and mill around the casino in the same clothes you might only wear around the house. People who don't drink at home will get wasted, and those who don't even smoke at home will light up a cigarette, which in Vegas is welcomed inside all casinos, and cocktail lounges that closed their restaurants to accommodate slot playing smokers because tavern owners know that smokers always lose the most money. While many visitors still gamble, these days many don't; they come to Vegas to relax in their large suites, by the hotel pools (some permit topless sunbathing), drink to tottering excess in the new nightclubs, dine in the new multi-million dollar, big-name restaurant franchises from New York, Miami, Chicago, Dallas, Los Angeles, visit high-end jewelry and clothing shops from around the world or watch production shows that cost scores of millions more to produce than anything in New York or Europe.

But Vegas is also a preferred place for fugitives from justice (who foolishly believe they can escape among the masses), for scammers, for future politicians with larceny in their veins. It is where faltering celebrities try to jumpstart their careers, with some ending up serving as freak show curiosities, suffering miserably from drug addiction and failure. It's where casino bosses laugh privately about the idiotic losers who drunkenly drop their money at the tables and slots. The casino executive's credo, stated behind the scenes, is "Feed 'em and fuck 'em."

In 2005, Vegas residents celebrated the centennial of the May 15, 1905, auction of land owned by William A. Clark, a wealthy U.S. senator from Montana (and Clark County namesake), that started the downtown area (that is, the official anniversary—sales of the first lots several blocks to the northwest of downtown actually took place in 1904). There were more than 300 events planned for the centennial, with radio station conglomerate Clear Channel Entertainment uniting with American Express to hawk a July 4 national broadcast of a concert and, as one PR rep called it, "integrated promotional tie-ins, hospitality packages, licensing, webcasting, and advertising" over Clear Channel's stations. Among the many other tributes to the fastest-growing and most popular city in America was a self-important "American Experience" documentary on PBS.

But celebrations are about the fun stuff, which Las Vegas creates better than any other city, defined here as the Vegas metro area, including Clark County. At the dawn of what was to be its centennial year, three former members of the powerful Clark County Commission awaited trial on political corruption indictments covering up to twenty-three felony fraud and extortion charges. The state's controller from Las Vegas—who in late 2004 was the first state official to be impeached in state history for misusing her office for campaign purposes—survived to contemplate seeking a higher office. A Las Vegas city councilman, who simultaneously served as a paid consultant for a topless club and was caught on a tape seized by the FBI getting a lap dance at a competing club, decided not to seek reelection after his brother sold the family's pawnshop business for $200 million. The city's beloved mayor, Oscar Goodman, once found guilty of unethical conduct for using his office to further his son's business venture, told a Vegas fourth-grade class that his favorite activity was drinking booze. Its favorite son U.S. Senator Harry Reid got his apolitical daughter-in-law appointed to the state's elected university governing board.

In 2005, Las Vegas had the largest number of hotel rooms in the nation, about 131,500. A record 37 million visitors in 2004 helped the hotels fill eighty-nine percent of the rooms in town at an average rate (putting together the high-priced places like Mandalay Bay and cheapies like the Sahara) of just $89 a night across town. Some 8,000 new guest rooms were to be added in 2005, including 2,700 rooms from hotel mogul Steve Wynn's newest Strip megaresort, the $2.7 billion Wynn Las Vegas. Two thirds of the $10 billion that Nevada's casinos won from gamblers in 2004 came from the Las Vegas area. And in 2004, for the first time, Vegas resorts made more money from meetings and conventions than gaming. But gaming, which is taxed at 6.75 percent (by far the lowest gaming tax rate in the country), still provides about $800 million a year to the state, equal to about 25 percent of all state revenues.

The town's pervasive, international hype and publicity machine is run by the fifty-year-old Las Vegas Convention and Visitors Authority (LVCVA), a quasi-public government unto itself with a barrel of pork that expands with each new hotel room. In 2005, the LVCVA had an annual budget to promote tourism of almost $220 million, four or five times more than its nearest rivals, Orlando and Hawaii. The agency's latest vision plan for 2005 to 2010 has set a goal of luring 43 million visitors to town by 2009 and spending $400 million to improve the Las Vegas Convention Center. Its executives paint an extraordinarily rosy future for Vegas, estimating visitors will spend $186 billion in town from 2005 to 2009.

The authority has used one local PR agency for 15 years, the politically connected R&R Advertising. R&R is paid tens of millions a year to provide and place ads touting Vegas in New York, Chicago, Houston, Dallas, Phoenix, San Diego, Los Angeles, San Francisco, and elsewhere. Over the years, R&R provided flat, uninventive slogans like "America's Way to Play" and "Las Vegas: Open 24 Hours," each of which could have been written by almost anyone on a cocktail napkin and sold for a round of beers. In 2003, R&R resurrected a cliché that struck a noticeable cord with bored Americans, "What Happens Here, Stays Here." The new campaign famously included controversial TV commercials, selling Vegas as a place to get your sex and other ya-yas out, or otherwise dump on the town as you will before returning to your workaday real life.

Who Lives in Las Vegas?

While Las Vegas may never be lacking in funds to hype itself to doomsday, it consistently lacks the resources to prevent a remarkable series of social and health problems from befalling its residents. What the statistics reveal about Las Vegas absolutely boggles the mind. With more than 70 percent of the state's 2 million residents and growing each day, Las Vegas dominates Nevada, often radically skewing the results of surveys and studies comparing Nevada to other states. Nevada, which relies on gaming and sales tax money to operate, has no state income tax and other revenue enhancers that most states have, so it has less money and inclination to invest in public health measures. In 2001, the *New York Times* reported that

Nevada ranked fiftieth in spending on health and other prevention efforts. Significantly, that same year the state legislature killed a proposal to spend only $250,000 on a program for problem gamblers, on which other states with casino gaming devote millions of dollars per year. In 2004, Nevada had the lowest nurse-to-patient ratio in the country.

"But you have to understand that the growth of Las Vegas has been completely unprecedented over the last fifty years," replied John B. Walker, an environmental scientist for Nevada's Division of Environmental Protection in Carson City, in 2005. "It's adding about 50,000 residents a year. That's like adding one Carson City each year. In normal communities, you grow by births and deaths and small amounts of in- and out-migration. But you get 6,000 moving in and 2,000 moving out each month in Las Vegas. Plus, you have more than 30 million visitors a year and more than 100,000 hotel rooms and the occupancy rate is high. How do you manage your growth in that atmosphere?"

"Vegas is not a normal place," Walker said. "It's abnormal. In Florida, you have in-migration because it's the retirement area for the East Coast. In Alaska, you get in-migration because it's still the frontier and it gets unskilled workers. Those places are growing due to retirees and unskilled workers. Vegas gets both. Only Las Vegas is like that."

Some claim the state is growing so fast that people aren't counted fast enough and so the per capita rates in most studies of Nevada and Las Vegas are exaggerated. But year after year after year, the proof has been in the pudding. Nevada has consistently rated tops or near the top in the nation in rates of suicide, teen pregnancy, high school dropouts, cigarette smoking, lung cancer, and deaths due to cancer and from car accidents. Nevertheless, Las Vegas is America's most attractive city as measured by the non-stop droves of new residents. The top incentives for new arrivals: jobs and money. In 1997, the state's average income ranked twelfth in the country, at $18,795. By 2004, average income rose to $33,405. Las Vegas's unemployment rate was only 3.5 percent in November 2004 and helped the state to a record-low 3.7 percent rate. New jobs rose by 6.8 percent between February 2004 and February 2005, with construction jobs up almost 20 percent. Meanwhile, Las Vegas had the highest rate of sales of single-family homes in the country in 2004.

Las Vegans are mostly male, white, married, and from out of town. Many have problems speaking English. One stereotype of the Vegas newcomer is an unemployed man who brings his wife and kids to town, stuffed into a tattered station wagon. It's true that many who arrive and stay are undereducated and largely unskilled. The low-paying jobs many of them typically get, such as telemarketing and call center work, fail to raise enough tax revenue to pay for social programs, roads, and other infrastructures needed to service them. Typically, about half of the several thousand jobs created inside a new megaresort hotel on the Las Vegas Strip are of the unskilled type and require no education, like housekeeper and kitchen worker. But even the underachieving newcomers are able to find work thanks to the mammoth tourism industries that feed off of new residents.

City in the Desert

All of Las Vegas is framed inside the Mojave Desert that stretches west into Death Valley and southern California. Las Vegas is the driest major city in America, with only 4.3 inches of rain a year. Far more water is evaporated than received so the town relies on the massive runoff from melting snow in the

Rocky Mountains to the northeast that flows southwest into the Colorado River and Lake Mead, a body of water created by Hoover Dam in the 1930s that supplies the Las Vegas Valley with about 85 percent of its water. That's where the trouble begins for tap water drinkers in Vegas and parts of Arizona and California. Thanks to decades of seepage and neglect from a one-time rocket fuel plant in the southeastern Las Vegas Valley, the valley's water table is polluted with the toxic substance perchlorate. In significant doses, perchlorate can cause thyroid problems in humans and is dangerous to pregnant women. The concentration averages only ten parts per billion of a gallon in the lake, but the levels are higher when the water reaches Las Vegas-area homes (eighteen parts is considered high; in Las Vegas in 2003, it was measured at seventeen, and at its neighbor, the city of Henderson, nineteen). But the chemical still comes out of everyone's tap water in the Vegas valley because no solution has been found to keep it out. The United States government has drafted a safety standard of only one part per billion, but won't be ready to set policy on it until about 2006. Meanwhile, 20 million people who drink water from Lake Mead can drink Vegas valley perchlorate for breakfast, lunch, and dinner.

Nevada also has the distinction of being the nation's worst polluter due to discharges from its northern mining industry (Nevada is the top producer of gold in the country). The feds rated Nevada the nation's number-one polluter in 2000 because of the mercury emissions from mines and liquid runoff of the toxic waste cyanide. The wastewater flows from the mines and eventually into the water supply stored at Lake Mead. Meanwhile, the area's water quality officials, in order to address potential water shortages, say that they'll need to spend $2 billion on 460 miles of pipelines to send water from rural Nevada to Vegas.

Even the Las Vegas area's most popular and arguably most attractive national park—Lake Mead itself, the fourth most visited United States park—can't escape the jinx. In 2000, the *Wall Street Journal* reported the recreation area, typically infused by liquor-swilling partiers and fast-moving boats, logged more search and rescue attempts (540) and serious crimes (732) in 1999 than any of the other forty-six federal parks studied.

Social Problems

Education

Education has never been the city's or state's strong suit, not by a long shot, due to a historical unwillingness by state leaders to spend much on it. Public school teachers start out making $28,000 a year, no longer the kind of salary people can live on in town. In 2005, the county's school district was so desperate that it began recruiting for teachers in the Philippines. Another reason for the lack of focus on education is the make-up of the populace in Las Vegas itself: people holding down the town's hotel and construction positions don't need a college education to make good money. Consequently, their kids don't necessarily grow up hitting the books. The classic explanation, repeated throughout town: why would a college-age guy go to UNLV for a degree when he can make $50,000 (mostly from tips) or more a year parking cars as a valet for a Strip resort.

Whether it's the availability of tip-rich casino jobs, lack of initiative, or simply the types of low-skilled people Vegas attracts, the town routinely racks up some truly appalling figures on education attainment. A Harvard University study released in February 2004 placed Nevada forty-ninth in the percentage of residents who'd graduated from high school. Minority students fared worse. While 60 percent of Nevada's white students graduated from high school (15 percent below the United States average for whites), only 40 percent of black and Hispanic students did so (10 and 13 percent, respectively, below national averages).

Traffic

Population growth breeds traffic congestion, one of Las Vegas's most noticeable recent problems. The residential and business booms add 100 cars to the area's roads each day. Barriers are put up around ubiquitous road widening and highway reconstruction projects, and years of development-friendly planning and foot dragging on road building by local, county, and state governments have made the situation worse. A study by the Washington group The Road Information Project in 2005 gave Nevada a D+ grade for congestion and D grade for traffic safety, adding that the state would see only $7 billion of the $10 billion in federal funds required to unclog its highways. Traffic woes will cause businesses to move out of Las Vegas to less congested cities within 10 years, the group concluded.

In 2005, the state finally said it would have to buy up land and homes along U.S. Highway 95 (Nevada's most congested freeway) to widen it by four new lanes, right after the average cost of homes in Las Vegas grew by more than 50 percent to about $250,000 each. Even those plans were still on hold in early 2005 because of a lawsuit filed by the Sierra Club, charging that Nevada didn't consider how air pollution from 12,000 cars per hour on the widened highway might hurt pregnant mothers, seniors, and the hundreds of kids in the three public schools that border it.

The area's biggest effort at mass transit, the Las Vegas Monorail—a Disney-like, fixed-guideway rail line beside the Strip used mainly by tourists—has endured repeated, months-long shutdowns, and has had so few riders that the federal government refused to give the city funds needed to extend the rail to downtown Las Vegas where its stagnant "Glitter Gulch" casinos need it most.

Even the solutions to the traffic mess create new safety problems. Street widening projects, building six to eight lanes to accommodate speeding cars, make it hard and dangerous for pedestrians, who have to walk up to 140 feet to get across. In 2004, thirty-three pedestrians were killed on the streets of Las Vegas, which was ranked the eleventh deadliest city for human roadkill in a 2004 survey by the Surface Transportation Safety Project.

Gambling Problems

As for leisure activities in town, of course, there are the gambling casinos. Gambling is very popular with people who live in town. It ranked second highest on the list of favored activities among Vegas adults surveyed in 2004. The survey of local residents, released by the Las Vegas Convention & Visitors Authority, found that 21 percent said gambling was their top fun thing to do (ranking highest was going to the movies: 28 percent). In fact, 70 percent of Vegas residents said they gamble on occasion, with slot and video machines and blackjack their games of choice. Gambling is even more popular among seniors who can board busses decorated with the logos of various casinos that arrive in retirement community neighborhoods to pick them up and drop them off.

Nevada has the highest percentage of people with either problem gambling, or even worse, the compulsive variety, pathological gambling. A study commissioned by the state in 2002 found that 6.4 percent of Nevadans had the problem, which was two and a half times the national average. In 2005, the local chapter of Gamblers Anonymous reported that its Vegas group had the most meetings anywhere in the country, around a hundred a week. Meanwhile, Nevada's government has been in denial about the problem for decades, likely because it's embarrassing. Nevada was the first to permit modern, state-sanctioned casinos in 1931, but as late as 2004, it had no state funds allocated for problem gambling, while seventeen other states with gambling had been funding treatment programs for years.

Crime

Although the town has improved since it led the nation in crime in the 1980s, Las Vegas's crime rates continue to outpace the nation's averages—for all crimes. In 2005, the FBI reported that there were 5,581.9 crimes per 100,000 people in metropolitan Las Vegas (total population: 1,281,698), compared to the U.S. average of 3898.9 per 100,000—making Las Vegas's rate 43 percent higher. The rate of violent crime in metro Vegas was far worse: 743.5 crimes, or 58 percent above the American average. The area's murder rate was 11.3—double the U.S. average of 5.6. Reported rapes in Vegas were 50 percent higher (48.1 versus 31.7); robberies were off the charts at 93 percent more (272.6 versus 140.7), and assaults were 41 percent higher (411.6 against 291.1). Meanwhile, the Vegas metro area's property crime rate to 100,000 population was 4838.3—41 percent above the national average.

Drug abuse is another malady in Sin City, and not just from Hollywood celebrities and other visitors who smuggle in some pot, blow or speed for a mind-numbing weekend in Vegas. Back in the 1980s, heroin use by casino dealers in some casinos, such as Binion's Horseshoe, was rampant, with some casino dealers easing the monotony of their jobs by shooting up in elevators and bathroom stalls during breaks. The federal Substance Abuse and Mental Health Services Administration in 2002 ranked Las Vegas with older cities Chicago, New York and Washington, D.C., in the increase of drug abuse-related deaths—376 overdoses, or 38 percent more than the area recorded in 2001. Drugs such as heroin, methamphetamine and OxyContin are among the most commonly abused in Las Vegas, which experts blame on a deadly combination of the valley's "fast," 24/7 lifestyle and the isolation some newcomers feel from family and friends who might offer support.

Vegas's transient nature and growth also attracts scam artists. A study released by the Federal Trade Commission in February 2005 placed Las Vegas third behind Washington, D.C., and San Jose, California, in per capita rates of credit card and other forms of consumer fraud. The perps simply steal credit card applications from group residential mailboxes and apply for them with the recipient's name, a form of fraud that the FTC reported as the most difficult to detect. Vegas also ranked third among U.S. cities studied by the FTC in identity theft.

Nevada (again, dominated by Vegas's population) is a state that spends the least in the nation on food, clothing and medical care for its prison inmates—just $2.20 a day per prisoner—plus only 30 bucks a year each on clothing. Only 5 percent of the prison system's budget is spent on medical care compared to the U.S. average of more than 10 percent. The 11,000 prison inmates statewide in 2005 represented a 110 percent jump from 1990. And, many stay put longer. State officials admitted in 2005 that Nevada ranked forty-fifth in granting probation instead of jail time.

While the many hotels, restaurants and other businesses in Vegas offer low-paid jobs to tens of thousands of recent immigrants from Mexico, Central and South America, Vegas is among the highest in the country in illegal immigrants for its population. In Clark County, which includes all of metro Vegas, illegal aliens accounted for 6 to 10 percent of the population in the mid-2000s, compared to the national average of 3.5 percent, according to studies by the U.S. Department of Homeland Security and UNLV.

Environment

Environmental concerns are practically ignored in Las Vegas so as not to put the brakes on the development of private buildings and private land in America's fastest growing city (only about 15 percent of Nevada's land is privately owned, the rest overseen by federal agencies). Nevada's overall lack of effective state environmental protection laws is the result of wimpy state legislators unwilling to risk the wrath of gaming interests and developers who influence the state's political process and those of Las Vegas and Clark County.

That doesn't bode well for the area's wildlife, because, as reported in 2005 by the National Wildlife Federation and two other environmental groups, Clark County has the second-highest number of imperiled species of plants and animals threatened by development among the thirty-five fastest-growing and largest metro areas in the country. San Diego County is first with ninety-nine imperiled species, but Clark County has ninety-seven such species, including the Western yellow-billed cuckoo, the Mojave poppy bee, Palmer's chipmunk, Relict leopard frog, Pahrump poolfish, Nevada willowherb, and Utah sunflower.

Metro Las Vegas's local governments typically avoid following environmental restrictions on development unless they are imposed by the U.S. government, and then only begrudgingly. In one revealing example, Las Vegas developers, the area's growth-fed politicos, and the community itself didn't give a rat's ass about the fate of the desert tortoise in Clark County until Congress forced the issue on the state by adding the animals to the Endangered Species Act in the late 1980s. Instead of crushing them with their bulldozers as they did before, Vegas-area developers are trusted to pick up the creatures and transfer them to designated, undeveloped desert land; that is, when the animals aren't buried anyway in the twenty- to thirty-foot underground burrows they dig. In 2004, salivating home and commercial developers looking to expand their largess into bare federal land in the high northwestern part of the metro area were aghast when the federal Bureau of Land Management—which was to auction the public land—declared that some parcels would be exempt from development because they contained rare species of plant life.

No one's ever been elected to office in the town's 100-year history on anything approaching an environmental platform. That's too much like "the People's Republic of California," as some pretentiously claim, for these here parts. "Businesses moving to Nevada are trying to escape from that, anyway," they'll point out. But that's because they don't know or care about the area's fragile and vanishing natural habitat. While a city like Thousand Oaks, California, has strict laws protecting its decades-old oak trees, Las Vegas does not appreciate, for instance, that the routinely bulldozed Joshua trees can reach a height of thirty-five feet and live as long as 1,000 years. The creosote bushes that are uprooted almost everyday in the valley are the oldest known living plant, each taking 120 years to grow just one foot and with life spans of more than 10,000 years. The area's roundtail ground squirrels—probably the most commonly killed indigenous animal in Vegas—hibernate in shallow ground from October to January, and so are torn apart by the blades of earth movers during construction projects. The local attitude can be summed up like this: "If they ain't on one of them dang 'endangered' lists, they're, ah, fair game, so to speak."

In 2004, Larry Brown, usually one of the more conscientious members of the Las Vegas city council, made a telling statement during a televised hearing in which the council unanimously approved the site of a planned Wal-Mart supermarket. The Wal-Mart was to be built a few hundred yards from the La Madre Mountain range on a site populated by roundtail ground squirrels, white-tailed antelope squirrels, falcons, and hawks, part of an ecosystem untold thousands of years old. Just before making the motion for the Wal-Mart, Brown said that "as for the critters there, they'll just run away." Those that aren't killed do "run away" to die hungry in the trimmed, non-indigenous bushes and painted-rock landscaping of the home developments.

Air pollution, much of it from the dust kicked up from development in the valley's fragile desert, is yet another major problem. Information about the county's lack of cooperation with federal air quality standards came to light in a lawsuit filed by environmentalist Robert Hall in 2004. Hall charged the county with failing to follow federal air quality laws since 1979 by hiding behind waivers and exemptions to facilitate growth trends. As of 2005, the county has never met federal air quality standards since the passage of the 1990 Clean Air Act and yet still sought to permit development on thousands of acres of new land that would only increase air pollution from dust.

In fact, through manipulating air pollution data, the county successfully omitted reporting 97 percent of dust emissions from construction, vacant lands and unpaved roads, Hall said. County officials admitted that the county's population would expand from 1.15 million in 2001 to 1.59 million in 2006, or 28 percent, and that the federal government would sell 74,000 untapped acres in the Las Vegas Valley for development. If those acres are developed, massive amounts of dust will pollute the air even more, with the county essentially looking the other way.

"The Valley is in serious air pollution non-attainment for dust, and carbon monoxide. They will soon be in non-attainment for ozone," Hall said. "The continuing failure to conform to EPA (approved air standards) is intentional. Clark County has no incentive to comply with (federal laws) since that means slowing down Clark County's political policy of runaway growth. Runaway growth greases the gears of the current political regime."

Development in the valley, in fact, has triggered what some experts consider permanent damage to human health from the irritating clouds of light brown fugitive dust that roam overhead and sometimes obstruct views of the Strip. The desert's undisturbed ancient topsoil is able to keep the dust beneath the surface down naturally, but front-end loaders pushing it off at construction sites fling the dust high into the air, and into the lungs of residents. Builders use a piecemeal method of spraying water on construction sites, but that doesn't come close to solving the problem. It's no surprise that according to the Centers for Disease Control and Prevention, Nevada— thanks to growing and dusty Las Vegas—leads the nation in the rate of asthma—a sometimes-fatal breathing disease caused or aggravated by dust pollution—in adults. The rate was 13.4 percent in 2003, almost double the 7.2 percent tracked in 1998. More disturbingly, the University Medical Center in Las Vegas estimated in 2003 that 12 to 15 percent of children in the Las Vegas Valley suffer from asthma.

"The desert maintains its durability unless man disturbs it," said Walker, the state's environmental scientist. "It's like what happened to Los Angeles in the 1930s. When few people lived there, we had pristine air quality."

Far from pristine, Las Vegas is a city struggling to cope with a potentially overwhelming series of local troubles beyond the fabulous profits being raked in on the Strip. On a wild ride, veering this way and that, the town is creating riches for many land owners, casino execs, builders, cocktail waitresses, topless dancers, real estate agents, and former topless dancers who are now real estate agents. But eventually, the growth will have to slow, housing prices will rise, and wages will have to rise. There will be a day of reckoning, and an expensive one. For now, though, the party's still in full swing.

The Vegas Mob

2

A Hundred-Year Play in Three Acts

*L*as Vegas is one of the few large American cities with a past that can fit into the past hundred years. From a few hundred people and some canvas tents on bare land in 1905 to the only legal venue for America's most famous gangsters to join from the mid-1940s and even into the 1980s, to the tens of billions of dollars' worth of showy hotel-casinos and 1.5 million residents in 2005, the richness of that past, its legends and facts, continues to fascinate the world over.

Vegas history is hot, has been hot for years and probably always will be as long as Vegas maintains its status as American's top visitor destination and fastest-growing city. It's depicted many times every year in new popular history books and in contemporary documentaries shown on the Public Broadcasting Service and the Travel and History channels. Its history is fictionalized in reruns of big-studio production movies like *Oceans Eleven*, *The Godfather*, *Bugsy*, and *Casino*, and Home Box Office films such as *The Rat Pack* and *Sugartime*. Countless websites on the Internet are devoted to pieces of Vegas history.

Some of the books, movies, and websites exaggerate the facts, but many of the truths about Las Vegas are stranger and much more compelling than fiction. For the town's national and international visitors, the interest in its twice-told stories never seems to run out of steam.

The most absorbing aspect of Las Vegas history is its undeniable mob past. Many other American cities, small, medium and large, also had or have ties to organized crime, which was pervasive throughout most of the twentieth century. But its influence on Las Vegas is unique, so much so that the town's first century can rightfully be split into three parts. The first forty years are the "pre-mob" years from its founding in 1905, to just before Ben Siegel's crime organization made its first investment in the El Cortez hotel downtown in 1945. The next forty years, "the mob years," review the birth of Siegel's Flamingo hotel on the fledgling Strip in 1946, to the beating death of Anthony Spilotro, the Chicago Outfit's representative in Vegas, in 1986. The last twenty years represent the "post-mob" era, when gaming—once considered a vice to corporate America—has become one of the most profitable public businesses that issue shares of stock on Wall Street.

But first, before getting into that history, it is useful to describe the evolution of organized crime in America, and how, at the peak of its power and influence, it came to enter and practically create Las Vegas's gaming industry and amusing history.

Pre-History: Evolution of the American Mob

In the beginning, organized crime syndicates made their biggest killings throughout the United States thanks to Prohibition, the country's foolhardy, church-inspired experiment with outlawing booze. Prohibition lasted from 1920 until Franklin D. Roosevelt (who ran a pro-repeal campaign) became president in 1933. Only two years before, two other things had happened that would transform the tiny city of Las Vegas into a drinking and gambling oasis for hoodlums by the next decade: Nevada legalized casinos and the American La Cosa Nostra, the national crime syndicate, got its start during a convention of gang leaders in Chicago.

By 1931, underground criminal groups, comprised mainly of first-generation Italian, Jewish and (to a lesser extent) Irish immigrants, were well established in large U.S. cities. But the roots of the modern, multiethnic organized crime cells in the twentieth century, the organized crime that created modern Las Vegas and was crucial to its post-war growth, can really be traced further back in American history, to the country's founding decades.

Immigrants from England, Scotland, and Germany in the 1700s and early 1800s took advantage of the lack of Old World class constraints in America to become extraordinarily wealthy through crime and sometimes violence. There was John Jacob Astor, the dirt-poor German immigrant born in 1763, who became America's richest man from cheating Indians in fur trades, paying off politicians to excuse his illegal activities and building slum housing before he died in 1848. Cornelius Vanderbilt, born in 1794, the shipping magnate and Civil War profiteer, bribed politicians and preserved his interests in Nicaragua by hiring mercenaries to overthrow its government. James Fisk, born in 1835, bribed politicians, smuggled masses of Southern cotton to the North during the Civil War, and sold worthless Confederate bonds. Leland Stanford bribed politicians and extorted millions from cities to have his railroad built next to them. J. P. Morgan, born in 1837, bribed judges and organized a secret alliance of bankers to dominate the gold market. John D. Rockefeller, born in 1839, bribed judges and conspired with the top oil companies to form a secret cartel to fix prices for his Standard Oil Company. These infamous robber barons of the nineteenth century, whose rags to riches fortunes still dominated the American economy of the early twentieth century, laid the foundation for the new immigrant mobsters of the 1900s, who emulated them but had to resort to the vice rackets—not gold, oil, bonds, or railroads—to make their fortunes. After Prohibition, Las Vegas would become perhaps their most lucrative racket yet, a legalized one which the mobsters knew better than the government regulators how to steal from.

The American underworld that dominated Las Vegas traced its influences to southern Italy in the late 1800s. From the waves of Italian immigrants to America came affiliates of the three separate Mafia subcultures: the Sicilian Mafia, the Camorra (from around Naples), and the Calabrian Mafia from the state of Calabria. Each could be traced to the development of the rest of southern Italy, influenced by Arab culture, in response to centuries of repressive governments under their Norman, Spanish, and later northern Italian conquerors. The early term *"mafia"* meant a way of life allied to the family and strength of character. But the later term "Mafia" that emerged in the nineteenth century went way beyond that, a twisted point of view among Italy's criminals and ex-convicts that exacted violent, vigilante justice. To them, justice meant you could simply kill to get what you wanted. They adopted the historic southern Italian principles of *omerta*, a combination of keeping quiet to protect your friends, of manliness, and willingness to avenge any slight against the family. They used a dubious code of honor, preening as right and honorable "Robin Hoods" to rationalize the use of violence to make their illegal businesses run smoothly and manipulate their uneducated, sociopathic henchmen, who would follow orders right or wrong for the "family."

Before Prohibition started in January 1920, Italian-dominated organized crime included extorting money from poor Italian immigrants, run by the Black Hand group, and counterfeiting, prostitution, street crime, monopolizing small businesses and, of course, illegal gambling—the numbers (lotteries), bookmaking, and slot machines. In 1919, Congress and the states—largely at the insistence of the nation's Anglo-Saxon majority, disturbed by the numbers of new ethnic immigrants—passed the Volstead Act, which prohibited the manufacture, sale, and distribution of alcoholic drinks. Demand for liquor still flourished, so the criminals moved in and trucked imported booze mainly from Canada and England. Many mobsters of the time who'd scraped by before on shakedowns and rackets became rich on whiskey and beer. Soon, politicians, judges, police and agents of the new U.S. Prohibition Bureau were corrupted and played along with the free flow of bootlegged hooch to secret nightclubs and parties from coast to coast. Violence and murder among competing mobs also flowed. Most of the mob backers of Las Vegas casinos some twenty years later got their start either as bootleggers or their henchmen.

As Prohibition grew less popular, leaders of mobs in New York, Detroit, and other major cities met in 1931 to form an Americanized version of the Italian Mafia that would evolve three years later into La Cosa Nostra, an ethnic mix that included Jewish and Irish hoodlums but was still overseen by the Italians. The instigator of the 1931 meeting was Charles "Lucky" Luciano (born Salvatore Luciana), who called himself and his Italian and non-Italian allies the "young Americans." But first, Luciano had to purge the old-country, "Mustache Pete" Sicilian Mafia types he resented and who opposed his desire to bring Jewish and other non-Sicilian gangsters into the fold. The nation's twenty-three top ethnic Sicilian gangsters (including Luciano, who was well liked though not a Sicilian) had formed the first "national commission" to settle disputes, on December 5, 1928, in Cleveland. During a second, larger convention of gang leaders from thirty big cities convened in Atlantic City, May 13–16, 1929, the Sicilians agreed to allow only a handful of other non-Sicilians in (including a Neapolitan, Al Capone of Chicago). One agreement made during the conclave was to make Miami an open city, a designation that would be bestowed on Las Vegas about twenty years later.

Top on Luciano's hit list was Joe "The Boss" Masseria, who'd been elected *capo di tutti capi* (boss of bosses) during the 1929 meeting. Masseria had opposed Luciano's plea to add more non-Sicilians and also went against what was agreed in Atlantic City—to divide up the rackets in New York five ways, including Luciano with Frank Costello, plus Jewish gangsters Ben "Bugsy" Siegel, Meyer Lansky, Louis "Lepke" Buchalter, and Jake Shapiro. Instead, Masseria gave all of New York to the aging Mafioso, Peter Morello. Though angry, Luciano did nothing. Until one night in 1931, when he and his "young Americans" had Masseria and his successor, Salvatore Maranzano, gunned down. Luciano immediately instructed his cohorts across the country to execute older Sicilian Mafia members and about forty men were shot dead, a time dubbed "the Night of the Sicilian Vespers." After the coup, Luciano took over and eliminated the capo di tutti capi post in favor of consensus decisions by the board of the new national "Combination." Of the seven men on the Combination's board, five were from Luciano's New York, such as Costello. The others were Capone from Chicago and Frank Milano, leader of the Cleveland Syndicate that was effectively run by bootlegger Moe Dalitz (later known as "Mr. Las Vegas") with the assistance of Moe's friend, Meyer

Lansky. When he traveled to Cleveland, Luciano met with both Milano and Dalitz, who oversaw a key criminal enterprise called the Molaska Corporation that made dehydrated molasses for illegal stills across America, in partnership with Luciano, Lansky and Costello.

The modern mob was born. Lanksy and other non-Sicilians joined Luciano's rackets. In 1934, Luciano elevated Don Vitone Genovese (a Neapolitan) to the number-two spot, and added John "The Fox" Torrio (another Neapolitan), Lansky (Torrio's ally), and another Jewish hood, New York garment industry extortion racketeer Lepke Buchalter, to the board of La Cosa Nostra, or what news writers later called the National Crime Syndicate.

Luciano went into narcotics and prostitution. He granted the mob's gambling rackets in Florida and the Bahamas to Meyer Lanksy. In New York, Dutch Schultz, who was Jewish, got the policy number rackets, while bookmaking went to Frank Erickson, of Irish extraction. Abner "Longie" Zwillman took over the rackets in New Jersey. Siegel stayed in New York and ran gambling and slot machines in Philadelphia. Luciano's group later sent Siegel to Hollywood in the late 1930s to try and make a racket out of motion picture labor unions, and he did so, forming a union for movie extras. Siegel later oversaw illegal gambling in Los Angeles and cornered the West Coast's race wire—including bookies in Las Vegas in the early 1940s—that telegraphed race results to illegal bookies for a fee. Siegel, Lansky, and Dalitz would become the top organized crime figures in Las Vegas gambling in the 1940s, while Luciano, deported to Italy in 1946, watched and gave orders from afar. Lansky and Dalitz would extract tens of millions in hidden profits from Las Vegas and divvy it up to Syndicate associates throughout the 1950s and into the 1960s.

Typically, the skimming of casinos first involved hidden investments, called "points," that would get each secret investor $2,000 a month from casino money counted and separated in the counting rooms. Larger amounts of money would be distributed once a year from the end-of-year cash totals. Many of the investors would simply travel to Vegas themselves to enjoy free meals, rooms, etc., while collecting their cuts. Other times, money was skimmed by assigning the uncollected debts of high-rolling gamblers to hidden investors, or the debts of travelers from group junkets to Vegas organized by the investor. Money could be transferred out of town by the investors, couriers, and travel junketeers.

Pre-Mob Years: 1905–1945

While 2005 is considered the city's centennial year, it could also be seen as the 150th anniversary of the Vegas's civilized settlement, by a group of Mormon WASPs led by William Bringhurst from Utah in 1855. But the desolate and hot Vegas valley, and its Indians, forced Bringhurst's party back to Utah only four years later. The Bringhurst group also became the first in a line of Mormons settling into Vegas. Mormonism's roots are based more on Judaism than Christianity: Mormons trace their origins to a Jewish man said to have arrived from the Middle East by boat in Central America in the sixth century B.C. One of his sons was "dark and loathsome," and the other "white and delightsome." Mormons, mostly immigrants from England and Scandinavia, regard themselves as descended from the white guy, and have tended to view people as either of the group (and so favored) or outside it.

An important incident in the pre-history of Vegas—before it became a township in 1905—was an unsolved murder: the victim a man named Archibald Stewart, in 1884. In 1881, Stewart had arrived with his wife, Helen, to take over a bankrupt ranch. After Archibald was mysteriously shot and killed by someone on a neighboring ranch, Helen ran their 2,000-acre ranch herself for almost twenty years. By 1900, census-takers counted only nineteen people in the Las Vegas Valley. In 1902, Mrs. Stewart sold most of the land to Montana U.S. Senator William A. Clark, who ran a commercial railroad and needed a stop between Salt Lake City and Los Angeles. Stewart also sold eighty acres in 1904 to another man, James T. Williams, who started selling plots right away. In May 1905, Clark held an auction in what is now downtown Las Vegas, next to the railroad tracks. Soon, Vegas became a whistle stop and tourist trap. Rest-stopped travelers could walk over to Block 16, the town's instantly designated vice district, get an alcoholic drink, gamble (legally and illegally), or buy some time from the legal whores.

With three-digit temperatures in the summer, no air conditioning, and little going for it, there was not much to attract businesses or residents. Still, the population boomed anyway to 1,500 by 1911. Vegas opened some hotels downtown and relied mainly on parting money from the tempted visitors and mining merchants from the rail line. Its isolation encouraged freedom and lawlessness, with brothels and opium dens downtown, illegal gambling after Nevada had banned casinos in 1911 and illegal speakeasies after Prohibition started in 1920. In the years to follow, state lawmakers could see that outlawing casino gambling in Nevada wasn't working. The legalization idea came front and center in 1928, not long after the U.S. government said it would spend $175 million to build the Boulder Dam thirty miles southeast of Vegas. Hundreds came to Vegas to find work; the city grew to 7,500 people by 1930. Many dam workers staggered from their tawdry shantytowns to Block 16 and kick-started the Vegas tradition of the working man blowing his paycheck on its buffet of vices.

The state legislature added the most profitable vice of all when it legalized casinos in 1931. Legal gambling wouldn't stop at table-stakes poker anymore. New gaming emporiums like the Northern, Boulder, and Apache clubs were licensed for craps, blackjack, and slot machines. And not just in the clubs: every place from gas stations, drug stores, candy shops, trailer parks, grocery stores, and other small locations were allowed slot machines. As an added bonus, and in response to other states thinking of doing the same thing to lure visitors, the legislature reduced the amount of time to get a divorce in Nevada to only six weeks. When Prohibition was repealed in 1933, Vegas had it all—gambling, booze, prostitution, and easy marriage and divorce.

1931: Tony Cornero's The Meadows: Vegas's First Disorganized Criminal

Even though casino gaming became legal in Nevada in the early 1930s, organized crime ignored the town as too tiny (about 7,500 residents), desolate and miserably hot, save for a handful of primitive "swamp coolers" and little air conditioning except in a movie theater. Compared to the more mature cities in the East and Midwest, there wasn't much to make out of Vegas, even from the hundreds of men earning money working on the dam project just outside of town. For one thing, for guys like Luciano and Lansky, it could take eighteen hours to fly and drive there from New York to collect their cut. The older and bigger town of Reno in northern Nevada was more attractive: a representative of Chicago mob chieftan Al Capone had set his boss up in a gambling house there, the Bank Club.

The first confirmed bootlegger to operate a casino in Las Vegas was Anthony "Tony" Cornero, a one-time cab driver from San Francisco who debuted the Meadows casino (and later, hotel) with his brothers Frank and Louis in May 1931, just after the state legalized gaming. Tony entered the bootlegging racket himself along the coast of California in the early 1920s, although it remains unclear to which specific crime syndicate he owed allegiance. Cornero provided liquor from ships to San Francisco and down south to Los Angeles, but in 1926 he lost a large cache of bottles to federal agents at sea. After a few years on the lam, he found himself arrested and sentenced to two years for rumrunning. Out of prison, he joined his brothers in Vegas (who got the licenses) to operate the Meadows, which they made into the swankiest place in town by far. People dressed up to gamble at the tables and watch live entertainment in a fancy nightclub featuring traveling acts, such as the Gumm sisters with child star Judy Garland. Tourists, as few as there were, could rent the casino's thirty hotel rooms, each with running hot water. Some say it was the first true so-called Vegas resort and provided the shape of the big things to come, but it didn't last. The hotel section failed in a matter of weeks, was sold that July 1931 and promptly burned down that September. Tony and his brothers had to give up their failing casino six months later in 1932. But Tony would return to Vegas to stake new claims: the S.S. Rex casino downtown in the 1940s and the Stardust hotel on the Strip in the 1950s. Meanwhile, others took over the Meadows and ran it as a casino-nightclub well into the 1930s. By the early 1940s, the old Meadows had degenerated into a cathouse and was ordered closed in 1942 as a nuisance to U.S. Army troops training in the valley.

1939: The 91 Club and the Ex-Cop from Los Angeles

Guy McAfee was a former Los Angeles police vice captain in the late 1910s who went to the other side where the money was made. By the 1920s, he'd quit policing nightclubs to become a nightclub operator himself in L.A. In the 1930s, he knew the ins and outs of law enforcement so well, he ran an infamous illegal gambling casino, called the Clover Club, on L.A.'s raucous Westside vice capital, the Sunset Strip. Like someone out of the movies, McAfee had installed one-way mirrors and secret panels in the Clover Club that gained him time to hide the roulette wheels (converted to tabletops) to make it look like a regular club during police raids. But it didn't always work. In one raid, cops noted an estimated 300 Hollywood celebrities inside and found $15,000 in cash. The heat and the recall election of Los Angeles's shady Mayor Frank Shaw, who tolerated the city's vice centers, put McAfee out of business in 1938. In 1939, he decided to move to pro-gambling Vegas and bought the old Pair-O-Dice club on the dusty, almost deserted old Highway 91, which he would nickname the "Strip" as a joke about his former L.A. roost. He named his new place to lure motorists between California and Utah the 91 Club. He took advantage of a fortunate coincidence when Ria Gable, the wife of famous actor Clark Gable, came to town weeks after he opened in 1939. She claimed residency in order to divorce her husband after Clark took up with Carole Lombard, who would die in the plane crash outside Vegas three years later. In 1942, McAfee bought out the shares of four other Los Angeles gambling refugees in the Pioneer Club downtown, and opened the Frontier Club there in 1945. After the Las Vegas Chamber of Commerce started an official advertising campaign to hawk Vegas to visitors, McAfee created his biggest casino yet, the Golden Nugget, in 1946. In a time when downtown's Glitter Gulch defined Las Vegas, McAfee the mob-free ex-cop was the town's gambling kingpin.

1941: The Race Wire

What would really put Vegas on the map for the crime syndicate came in the early 1940s. It wasn't about casinos—that came soon enough—but Nevada's legalization of wagering on out-of-state horse races, based on results telegraphed by wire. The state legislature approved the race wire law in 1941. Its passage induced gamblers and former illegal bookmakers looking for opportunities to flock to Vegas from cities like Los Angeles. One of them was Ben Siegel, who was already charging fees to illegal bookies on the West Coast for wired race results. He jumped at the chance for a foothold in a place where it was legal. Siegel left his gambling interests in Los Angeles in the hands of mob cohort Mickey Cohen and established himself with bookies at the small downtown Vegas casinos. Fellow Lansky associate, Moe Sedway, a veteran sports bookie, entered the picture and soon controlled the books in town.

What piqued Siegel's interest in Vegas even more than the horse races was his visit to the first hotel-casino on old Highway 91, the El Rancho Vegas, a Spanish Mission-style, Western ranch tourist resort that opened on April 3, 1941, with legitimate money. The builder was Thomas Hull, a California hotelier who operated the Hollywood Roosevelt in Los Angeles and saw marketing opportunities in Vegas's growing military population, thanks to the Army's new gunnery school and the Army Air Corps lease of the county airport. The El Rancho was the town's first good hotel, 170 low-rise, air-conditioned rooms, a pool, restaurant, shops, and showroom with the El Rancho Starlets, chorus girls from California. Hull angrily rebuffed Siegel's offers to become an investor in the El Rancho. The next year, R. E. Griffith, the wealthy Texan and owner of 475 movie theaters (and, like Hull, with no ties to organized crime) opened the second Highway 91 resort, the Last Frontier. More lavish than the El Rancho, the Frontier had a bigger pool, a 600-seat showroom, cow horns on guest room headboards, and the town's first celebrity-themed room, the Carrillo Room, after the actor Leo Carrillo, who played Pancho, the Cisco Kid's sidekick, in short westerns. By the mid-1940s, everybody and his mother—people like Mae West, Frank Sinatra, and Roy Rogers—wanted to build their kind of hotel on the highway. Siegel persisted in his own idea to out-do the legit resort operators on the highway, which would become Las Vegas Boulevard.

1945: The El Cortez Hotel—Birthplace of the Las Vegas Mob

Failing to invest on the Strip, Siegel bought a percentage of the El Cortez hotel-casino downtown in 1945 with a bunch of illegal gambling operators and hoods who'd soon assume significant roles in Vegas casinos: Gus Greenbaum, Davie and Chuckie Berman, Israel "Icepick Willie" Alderman, Moe Sedway, plus Meyer Lansky (who had 10 percent) himself. While Lansky hated sweltering Las Vegas and preferred his casinos in Florida, Siegel saw tourism and population increases, rapid real estate appreciation, and casinos in the desert—and all legal. The El Cortez established a foothold for mobsters in Las Vegas that would last four decades.

The Mob Years: 1946–1986

1946: The Flamingo

Siegel's El Cortez group flipped the downtown joint to another owner within only seven months for about $166,000 more than they paid, and sank the whole $780,000 sale price into a third resort under construction on Highway 91, the Flamingo hotel and casino. It would become Vegas's most important resort: it pulled the town away from the confines of the Old West theme and toward the so-called "ultra-luxury" Strip resorts that followed. The former El Cortez guys, with other out-of-state mob cash, now owned two-thirds of the Flamingo. The Flamingo originally was the project of Los Angeles man William "Billy" Wilkerson, who'd run out of money and wartime materials to finish the place. Wilkerson was the publisher of *The Hollywood Reporter* and the man behind the Los Angeles Vendome restaurant and nightclubs Ciro's and Café Trocadero on the Sunset Strip. He was likely the one to dub the project "the Flamingo," and sought to build a big, Miami Beach-style resort with bidets in the bathrooms. Wilkerson was free of mob ties, except that he'd been a buddy of Siegel's since the 1930s and had to have known about Bugsy's connections. Didn't matter, because Siegel's investors—including Lansky, Costello and other rich gangsters—bought him out of the thing and Bugsy took over the planning, with Arizona developer Del Webb at his side. Siegel began ordering lavish, "class" changes to the Flamingo: a large swimming pool, a steam room, nine-hole golf course, handball courts, stables for forty horses, imported marble and wood, palm trees, individual sewers for every hotel bathroom. He bought steel, copper, tile, and other building materials on the black market, and some of the sellers stole his materials at night and then resold them to him after daybreak without his knowledge. The cost of the hotel soon rose to six million dollars, three million dollars more than his mob investors gave him. Siegel had invested $500,000 himself.

Siegel arranged to have the unfinished (the 105 hotel rooms weren't ready) project debut on December 26, 1946. He invited a list of Hollywood celebrities to the party for free and paid singer and comedian Jimmy Durante to headline, but planes out of Los Angeles were grounded due to heavy fog and the opening flopped. Siegel's loyal and close friend, "gangster" actor George Raft, barely made it to Vegas by himself after an arduous interstate car trip. Siegel had asked him if he could bring more of his Tinsel Town friends, but Raft told him that the newspaper publisher William Randolph Hearst had told studio chiefs it wouldn't be a good idea to send their stars to a mobbed-up casino. Still, actors Charles Colburn, George Sanders, George Jessel, and Sonny Tufts arrived by train.

The crowds were smaller than expected. Low-rolling Las Vegans, those few who had good enough clothes to meet the "coats and ties only" dress code, had little money to risk, and the out-of-town high rollers ran into hot streaks at the tables. Except, that is, for Raft, who lost the tidy sum of $65,000 on chemin-de-fer. The hotel still lost about half a million dollars to lucky gamblers and overhead, forcing Siegel to close the Flamingo down in January 1947. Desperate for cash, and with none coming from his mob friends, Siegel borrowed $100,000 from Raft and thousands more from other Hollywood contacts. He flew to meet with mob boss Charles "Lucky" Luciano personally in Havana in February and asked for more time to show a profit. Luciano coldly told him to shape up and return control of the Chicago race wire—which Siegel took over, after the murder of hoodlum James Ragen—to the Chicago Outfit. Siegel angrily refused. The frustrated Bugsy called Lansky and told him that after returning the Flamingo to profitability, he planned to get his share of the proceeds and move to Europe. Lansky traveled to Vegas himself to persuade Siegel that Combination members still angry with him about the Flamingo would not accept it, but Siegel rebuffed his old partner in crime.

He reopened the Flamingo on March 27, 1947, and this time the hotel was soon in the black, making $300,000 in May. Lansky (who'd invested a million into the Flamingo) was troubled by news that Siegel's girlfriend, Virginia Hill, had left for Europe with $600,000 skimmed from the mob's investments. Lansky figured Siegel was fixing to link up with her later. In a meeting at New York's Waldorf Astoria Hotel, gangsters who plowed money into the Flamingo agreed that Siegel and Costello (who convinced them to trust Siegel) had to be eliminated. When they met later in Havana, gang boss Luciano spared Costello but let Siegel meet his fate. He would become the first board member of Lucky's Combination to be ordered dead. In the evening of June 20, 1947, a contract killer fired bullets from a .30 caliber rifle through a window in Virginia Hill's Beverly Hills home. He hit Siegel's chest and head, blowing out one of his eyeballs. The news of Siegel's instant death was relayed to Las Vegas by phone, and only twenty minutes after the shooting, Moe Sedway and Flamingo partners Morris Rosen and Gus Greenbaum strolled into the Flamingo to announce that they had taken over for Siegel. New investors came in. The principle owners would be the El Rancho's new owners, Stanford Adler and Charles Resnick. The other investors were less than desirable, including Chicago hood and former contract killer Israel "Icepick Willie" Alderman; convicted kidnapper Davie Berman; Jack Burke and Sam Diamond, both convicted of bookmaking in California; and Albert C. Abrams, who'd been convicted of owning a brothel. Las Vegas and Nevada officials either would not or could not stop them.

Gus Greenbaum would run the Flamingo and garner strong profits (an estimated four million dollars in his first year alone) for mob and other investors into the mid-1950s, largely due to his willingness to compete with new hotels by paying top dollar to big-name entertainers. Lansky retained a hidden ownership in the Flamingo. The Flamingo's front-end owners, Morris Lansburgh and Samuel Cohen, divided with him an estimated $36 million worth of skimmed casino money from 1960 to 1967 alone. Lansburgh and Cohen were indicted on conspiracy charges in 1971, pled guilty and served only four months in jail each. The mob's interest in the Flamingo ended when (mob-free) Vegas hotel builder Kirk Kerkorian bought it in 1967.

1948: The Thunderbird

Two guys considered to be on the up and up in the 1940s, Vegas attorney Cliff Jones (who also was lieutenant governor of Nevada) and his builder partner Marion Hicks, received state licenses to construct the Thunderbird hotel, the fourth casino resort on the Strip. It opened in 1948 about a mile north of the Flamingo. The place was an immediate success and Jones and Hicks ordered an expansion in the early 1950s. Problem was, the Thunderbird was infected from the start by a hidden mob investment from Meyer Lansky, without which the T-Bird wouldn't have gotten off the ground. Hicks had run out of money, needed a loan to complete the Thunderbird and got it from the Syndicate.

Jones and Hicks weren't total idiots, they had to know. The connection came through an investor recruited by Hicks, George Sadlo, whom the state tax commission did not learn until 1955 was fronting for Jake Lansky, Meyer's brother and subsidiary. Jake made frequent flights to Las Vegas to check up on Meyer's proceeds from hidden skimming at the Flamingo. Sadlo, through Meyer Lansky, had loaned Hicks between $160,000 and $190,000 to finish the resort. Meyer worked in the background as a casino advisor to Sadlo, who relayed the advice to Hicks. As was true at the Flamingo, the Lanskys got kickbacks via skimmed cash at the Thunderbird. A story in the *Las Vegas Sun* newspaper had placed Jake right in the casino's count room. Though the extent of skimming was still unknown to regulators in the mid-1950s, the revelation that Jake Lansky was an investor was big news because Meyer Lansky was America's best-known organized criminal.

The Thunderbird case got the state moving on long-needed reforms of a gaming control system that the mob found easy to circumvent. Governor Charles Russell convinced the legislature to create the State Gaming Control Board in early 1955. That year, the board revoked the Thunderbird's license and effectively kicked Jones and Hicks out of the operation, but the decision was overturned in court. Meanwhile, the Lanskys were out of the Thunderbird for good. After several owners the Thunderbird, renamed the El Rancho in the early 1980s, died a slow death until it at last closed in 1992.

1950: The Desert Inn

In a familiar story, the builder of the Desert Inn hotel, Wilbur Clark, went through the $250,000 his three other investors (including his brother) had raised to construct the casino in 1947. Clark searched for two years for new investors while the skeleton of the unfinished project languished on Highway 91. Lacking the ability to borrow from banks—which preferred to stay of out gaming—or elsewhere, he finally turned to mob sources in 1949.

This time it was members of Cleveland's old Mayfield Road Gang (also partners with Meyer Lansky in the Molaska Corporation in the 1930s). Clark met with the head of the group, Moe Dalitz, who was a top illegal bootlegger in the 1920s and had maintained his long financial ties to mob interests, along with investments in legitimate businesses. Also on his roster were veteran organized crime associates Sam Tucker, Morris Kleinman, Thomas McGinty, Ruby Kolod and Lou Rothkopf. The interest they bought in the Desert Inn was large: 74 percent. In 1950, Clark admitted to the U.S. Senate's Kefauver Committee investigating organized crime that he did not check out his new partners "too much." Clark would serve as the smiling, lovable ambassador to Las Vegas, and a suitable front for the Dalitz group. The place was called "Wilbur Clark's Desert Inn" with Dalitz, experienced running illegal casinos in

Ohio, Florida, and Kentucky since the 1930s, the true operator on the inside. Dalitz would say they invested $1.3 million in the DI, but others estimated it at $5 million. Dalitz and crew lied about the true amount of the investment to avoid IRS problems. With some officials in Nevada opposed to the Dalitz coterie receiving state gaming licenses, an investigator for Nevada went to Cleveland and recommended them for licensing after a cursory look into their backgrounds.

Dalitz himself is said to have done what he'd learned from running casinos in other cities—pay off police and politicians to gain "juice," or the needed influence to operate. And he did, with the cash from skimming at the Desert Inn going to hidden partners Lansky and Frank Costello in New York and the Chicago mob's Sam Giancana throughout the 1950s and most of the 1960s with few problems. Dalitz and partners also invested in the Hotel Nacional in Cuba, another enclave for American mob-led casinos in the mid-1950s. Along the way, Dalitz also took over the Stardust and Royal Nevada hotels and secretly controlled the operation at the Riviera. In 1967, he sold the Desert Inn to billionaire Howard Hughes. A former FBI agent and author, the late William Roemer, Jr., who investigated mob cases in the 1960s and 1970s, made the claim (never proven) that Dalitz was killed via poison while hospitalized in Las Vegas in 1989 on the orders of aging Chicago mobster Gussie Alex, who paid a hit man (turned informant) $100,000 to do it.

1952: The Sands

Two months after Del Webb's new Sahara hotel opened (with, as far as can be known, legitimate investors), the next mobbed-up property was the Sands, which ushered in an era of high-paid entertainment as other resorts competed to give out ever-higher weekly salaries to a limited number of name performers.

The chief at the Sands was Jack Entratter, who used to work for the mob-controlled Stork Club and Copacabana nightclub in New York. He ran the entertainment and controlled 12 percent of the Sands's casino profits, including 2 percent for himself and 10 percent for hidden investors. Other major investors in the Sands were New York mafioso (and ex-convict) Vincent "Jimmy Blue Eyes" Alo and Joseph "Doc" Stacher, a man with a long list of arrests. Stacher was closely associated with Meyer Lansky and Frank Costello of New York, and many other top hoodlums of the 1930s and 1940s (he was a boyhood friend of Lansky's). Stacher, who also held investments in the Fremont and Binion's Horseshoe, got his way time after time in court in Nevada, usually through paying fines, bail, or people—in a small town in northern Nevada, he tried to bribe his way out of having to face an illegal gambling warrant in New York. Stacher would remain a behind-the-scenes driving force at the Sands until 1964, a year after a federal grand jury indicted him for tax evasion.

1955: The Riviera

It was the first high-rise hotel in Nevada when it opened on April 29, 1955, at a then-extravagant cost of ten million dollars, with pop pianist Liberace as its first performer. But the "Riv" soon ran into cash flow problems on the casino floor, and so its Florida-based owners held onto the hotel portion and sold the casino section—to mob interests, who hired their miracle casino-fixer, Gus Greenbaum to run it. Greenbaum, who successfully ran the Flamingo, had been in semi-retirement in Arizona and at first refused the job but relented when mob figures Tony Accardo and Jake "Greasy Thumb" Guzik threatened him and his family. Greenbaum was addicted to heroin, presumably due to back pain. He brought in his motley crew of gangsters, including "Icepick Willie" Alderman, Charles "Kewpie" Rich, Davie Berman, and Ben Gofstein. He watched as the casino skimming continued, but by 1958, Greenbaum had enough and quit, ignoring warnings to stay put. In December 1958, Greenbaum and his wife were brutally killed in their Phoenix home. Still under mob influence, the Riviera would be sold a number of times. At one point in the early 1960s, Moe Dalitz ran the casino operation in secret with a former casino manager of his also coordinating gaming at the Riviera.

1955: The Dunes

Another casino to open in 1955 was the Dunes, on May 23. Owners included legitimate businessmen Alfred Gottesman and Bob Rice, but a third, Joe Sullivan, of Providence, Rhode Island, was a reputed front for an investment by the Ray Patriarca crime family. The elaborate Dunes had 200 rooms, a unique, V-shaped swimming pool, and a state-of-the-art theater, but it soon fell into financial problems on the over-built Strip. The next year, it was sold to James "Jake" Gottlieb, a Chicago mob front man who once obtained a loan from the corrupt Teamsters Union boss Jimmy Hoffa's Central States, Southeast, and Southwest Areas Pension Fund. In 1958, the mob-associated Hoffa would provide Gottlieb with another four million dollars to expand the Dunes to include a golf course. In 1963, Gottlieb sold his interest in the Dunes to a firm called the Commerce Building Corporation, a shell company run by local banker E. Parry Thomas, who would use a series of asset shiftings to make a bundle on the Dunes, which owed his bank, Bank of Las Vegas, $14 million in loans. Thomas, who gained the Dunes for no money down, sold it quickly for $7.4 million to Leonard J. Campbell Enterprises.

The broker for the deal was Charles "Kewpie" Rich, a former bookmaker who fronted for Tony Giordano, boss of the St. Louis mob. Rich and his partner in crime, Sid Wyman, would remain associated with the Dunes, enriching their hidden partners for years.

The Campbell firm and another company with ties to Thomas, Continental Connector Corporation, launched a subsidiary, M & R Investments, and sold the hotel for $22.8 million in 1967 to M & R, which then sold it to Continental in 1969 for $59 million in stock. An investigation by the Securities and Exchange Commission into M & R resulted in the indictments of six partners on skimming and tax avoidance charges, although Thomas would emerge unscathed. Thomas, who as manager of the Bank of Las Vegas served as a go-between for Teamsters loans to Vegas casinos, would also help launch budding casino man Steve Wynn's career as a casino investor in the 1960s and 1970s.

By the 1980s, the Dunes was in severe decline, operated by an elderly Morris Shenker, Hoffa's former lawyer with ties to Lansky. Wynn would finally acquire the Dunes and implode it to make way for his $2 billion Bellagio hotel project.

1956: The Fremont

The Fremont hotel-casino with 155 rooms in downtown Las Vegas opened on May 18, 1956. The casino served as Meyer Lansky's "clearing house" for money skimmed from hotels like the Sands, Flamingo, and Binion's Horseshoe, in accordance with his shares in each casino, or "points." Cash pulled out of the counting rooms of those casinos was secretly delivered—some said in a hotel bakery goods truck—to the Fremont, where the money was counted to be sent to Lansky in Miami, who would then keep some money and give money out to other mob investors. FBI investigators estimated that Lansky owned forty-two points in the skim of the casinos, with each point or share requiring an investment of $52,500. Lansky's investment was about $2.2 million and his income from the Vegas skim was $1 million a year. A woman who liked to wear mink coats, named Ida Devine, the wife of a meat vendor for the Fremont, made individual deliveries of $100,000 of skimmed cash by train from Vegas to Chicago, Arkansas, and Miami. Unfortunately for federal prosecutors, the evidence of skimming against Lansky and his cohorts could not be used in court, since it came via an illegal recording by the FBI.

Running the Fremont was Eddie Levinson, whose close ties to Lansky were obvious, except perhaps to Nevada and Las Vegas government officials. Levinson ran the Havana Riviera casino in Cuba for Meyer before Lansky sent him to Vegas to do the same for the new Fremont.

The FBI's illegal bugging device at the Fremont picked up information (decades later released in declassified files) showing that Lansky had a secret interest in the hotel. "Meyer wants a breakdown," Ben Siegelbaum told Eddie Levinson, meaning who was to get what percentage of the cash from the hidden skim. Lansky's share was mentioned in the FBI tape recording and so were those of New Jersey hoods Gerry Catena and Longie Zwillman, Siegelbaum, and someone called "J.B." who was probably Vincent "Jimmy Blue Eyes" Alo. The FBI learned from another bugged recording that Catena was getting about $150,000 a month from his skimming investments in Las Vegas.

1957: The Tropicana

Owner Ben Jaffe debuted the Tropicana hotel on April 4, 1957. While he'd experienced a shortage of cash like other casino builders, he was able to raise the five million dollars he needed by selling his interest in Miami's famous Fontainebleau hotel. But just four weeks later, the Tropicana would make national headlines when someone shot and wounded New York mob lieutenant Frank Costello outside his apartment near Central Park, on May 2. Cops searching Costello, an associate of Meyer Lansky, found a paper on him listing the Trop's casino take as $651,284 as of April 27. Written on the paper were notations $30,000 to "L" and $9,000 to "H," which investigators figured meant secret payments to, respectively, Lansky and Teamsters Union leader Jimmy Hoffa. Hoffa had recently started arranging loans to Las Vegas casinos through this union's pension fund—money taken from the paychecks of his truck-driver members for their future pensions. In 1964, Hoffa was convicted of diverting a million dollars from Teamsters loans to himself and others. Meanwhile, Nevada officials learned of Costello's association with Phil Kastel, a man Jaffe wanted in at the Trop, but was then denied a license. To save himself from financial ruin, Jaffe reached out to the well-regarded local casino man J. Kell Houssels, whose team took over managing the Trop and rid it of mob influences.

Houssels sold out to Trans-Texas Airways in 1970. The Trop was doing poorly in 1971 when a Minnesota financier, Deil Gustafson, bought it. But three years later, authorities discovered that the gambling credit given by the Tropicana to a group of mob figures from Detroit, who lost money there, was left unpaid. Faced with a state investigation and possible loss of his gaming license, Gustafson agreed to sell a fifty-one percent stake to a "clean" investor, Mitzi Stauffer Briggs, the niece of the former head of the Stauffer Chemical Company. She directed the building of a new, twenty-two-story hotel tower.

In 1975, a man named Joe Agosto joined a group of new investors in the Trop, a bunch known as the Associates of the Tropicana. With no investment of his own, Agosto became chief of the Folies Bérgère showgirl show and later headed the hotel operation. Charged with being an illegal alien from Sicily, Agosto remained in America pending an appeal. Seeing nothing wrong, the Nevada Gaming Commission, which decides on recommendations by the state gaming board, permitted Agosto to remain at the Trop. Commissioners did not know Agosto was fronting for the Kansas City mob's cash fraud operation there. Skimmed proceeds at the Trop would be sent to Joseph Aiuppa in Chicago and other gangsters in Kansas City and Milwaukee.

In the late 1970s, a case the FBI called Operation Strawman shed light on what was going on at the Tropicana. A series of taps were placed on phones in Kansas City, Missouri: one intercepted calls from Agosto, who as the KC mob's representative at the Tropicana, filled in Carl "Tuffy" DeLuna about his skimming activities there in 1978 and those of the Chicago mob's chief Tony Accardo at the Stardust. Other taps were placed on DeLuna's home phone and the phone that picked up conversations by KC mob boss Nick Civella. The biggest break for the FBI came when the agency received authorization to plant a bug in the basement of a neighbor of Nick Civella's. There, on November 26, 1978, agents listened in as Nick's brother Carl Civella asked for Nick's blessing on a mob hit. Then Agosto and a Vegas cohort, Carl Thomas, entered the basement and told Nick Civella and Carl DeLuna in a six-hour conversation how skimming was done in Las Vegas. Thomas, the owner of the Slots-O-Fun and Bingo Palace in Las Vegas and a veteran skimmer since the 1950s, famously told them of the "21 holes in the bucket," or the many ways to remove money from a casino before it was counted for tax purposes.

FBI agents learned that a courier, Carl Caruso, was to be at the Kansas City airport with skimmed Vegas casino cash to drop off shares to the KC mob and Accardo's Chicago Outfit, on February 14, 1979. Agents intercepted $120,000 in cash and casino markers from Caruso and then confiscated Carl De-Luna's records of previous receipts of skimmed cash.

Nevada officials now moved to kick Trop operators Mitzi Briggs and Deil Gustafson out. In November 1979, the Nevada Gaming Commission revoked their gaming licenses. Soon afterward, the Ramada Inn hotel chain said it would buy the Tropicana.

The ensuing case against the KC mob leadership hit stride on November 5, 1981. A federal grand jury indicted eleven people on seventeen counts of fraud and conspiracy, including De-Luna, the Civella brothers, Caruso, Agosto, Thomas, Thomas's accomplices in the skim at the Tropicana (Don Shepard and Billy Clinton Caldwell), and four other KC and Chicago mob associates.

That very day, a separate grand jury in St. Paul, Minnesota, indicted four people, including Agosto and Gustafson, in a $4 million check fraud scheme at the Tropicana. Agosto got twenty years in jail, Gustafson got ten years. Nick Civella died before he was convicted, but Carl Civella, Thomas, Gustafson and nearly all of the other defendants were convicted in 1983. Agosto, who was a prosecution witness, died of a heart attack only days later.

Thereafter, Operation Strawman entered a second phase, targeting Accardo's operations for Chicago with the Argent Corporation's casinos.

1958: The Stardust

Stardust hotel creator Tony Cornero, former partner in the old Meadows casino in the early 1930s, almost realized his dream to build a Strip resort. But years before the Stardust was completed, he famously dropped over dead at the craps table at

Moe Dalitz's Desert Inn in 1955. Johnny Rosselli, the Chicago mob's rep in Vegas, notified his friends, Murray Humphreys and Jake Guzik, of the opportunity. They set up Jake "The Barber" Factor, brother of cosmetics mogul Max Factor, to take over as owner of the Stardust when it opened on July 2, 1958, with a then-record 1,000 hotel rooms. Factor injected ten million dollars in mob funds into the project to get it open. But the Chicago mob's Sam Giancana was in on the secret skimmed proceeds from the start. Other Chicago guys Johnny Drew (from the mob's casino in Reno) and Tony Accardo were in on the planning and hired Moe Dalitz's group, the United Hotels Corporation, to manage the Stardust's casino. Dalitz convinced them to run the Stardust as a "grind joint" for low-rollers so that he could keep the big gamblers to himself at the Desert Inn.

1966: Caesars Palace

When motel chain owner Jay Sarno came to Las Vegas to survey the town as a site to build a motel in the early 1960s, he quickly decided to get into the casino business. He had some grandiose ideas, but first he needed land on the Strip. So he turned to what was then nicknamed "the mob's bank," the Teamsters union pension fund, controlled by Jimmy Hoffa and his accomplice in crime, Chicago mob associate Allen Dorfman. Sarno had received a $1.8 million loan from Hoffa's union to build a motel in Atlanta in 1958. This time, in Vegas, the pension fund loaned Sarno $10.5 million, enough to lease the site of his future Caesars Palace hotel-casino, on the Strip across from the Flamingo, and start planning. When it opened in 1966, Caesars was like no other carpet joint in Vegas; it had a record $19 million price tag, imported Italian marble, statues, and an enormous front fountain. Sarno and his partner, Nathan

Jacobson, had no problem obtaining gaming licenses, despite Sarno's ties to Hoffa and Jacobson's involvement with illegal slot machines back east. Jerome Zarowitz, an illegal bookmaker who did time in prison for trying to corrupt an NFL football game, was Sarno's selection for casino manager. Later, after brothers Clifford and Stuart Perlman, owners of the Lum's fast food chain in Miami, bought Sarno out in 1969, federal investigators discovered that Caesars involved a rogue's gallery of mob cash-grabbers: Chicago bosses Tony Accardo and Sam Giancana; Vincent "Jimmy Blue Eyes" Alo and Tony Salerno of the Genovese mob clan; and Ray Patriarca, Joseph Anselmo, Jerry Angiulo, and Joseph Palermo from the New England families.

1966: The Aladdin

The Aladdin would become one of the most trouble-plagued and mobbed-up casinos on the Strip. Milton Prell, the mob-clean man behind the Sahara hotel, bought and remodeled the failed King's Crown motel into the Aladdin with three million dollars and opened it on April 1, 1966. Prell suffered a stroke and sold it a little more than a year later for $16.5 million. But the property would become a hangout and cash cow for Midwestern mobsters in the 1970s. In 1974, the Aladdin's management was accused of comping the visits of twenty organized crime guys hailing from Detroit and St. Louis. In 1977, a grand jury in Detroit investigated the Aladdin's ties to a $25 million loan from the Teamsters pension fund. That same year, the Nevada Gaming Commission looked into suspicions of hidden ownership interests in the Aladdin, including Detroit men Charles Goldfarb, Vito "Billy Jack" Giacalone, and James Tamer. Giacalone was the brother of Detroit mob enforcer Anthony Giacalone and was a top rackets producer for the Detroit and St. Louis crime families. But the investigation focused on Tamer, a convicted bank robber from Michigan who was running the hotel's performing arts center. Nevada officials learned that Tamer was overseeing Goldfarb's secret investment, taking orders from the unlicensed Goldfarb and funneling him money from the casino. They also claimed Tamer deliberately took a job with a salary below what the state regarded as a "key employee" so that he would not face a detailed background check. Tamer and two others were convicted in Detroit of conspiring to hide the secret ownership at the Aladdin, and Goldfarb and Giacalone were convicted of holding the hidden investments. In 1981, eight defendants were found not guilty of charges that they tried to obtain kickbacks from the Teamsters loan. But in 1982, a man named Lee Linton admitted to evading taxes and trying to extort money when $50 million was spent to expand the Aladdin. The property went through a series of loan defaults and bankruptcies throughout the 1980s, 1990s, and into the early 2000s.

1968: Circus Circus

Opened by Jay Sarno, again with a large tainted loan from the mobbed-up Teamsters pension fund, Circus Circus featured a carnival midway and circus acts above the casino tables. Circus Circus was where Carl Thomas—the man who would instruct the Kansas City mob how to skim from the Vegas casinos, during conversations recorded by the FBI—really learned how to skim for his hidden Chicago mob schemers. Thomas met Teamsters loan representative Allen Dorfman in the early 1960s and through him, met Kansas City boss Nick Civella. Circus Circus is also where Anthony Spilotro, of the Chicago mob, set up a small jewelry store in 1971 to serve as a front for his activities for Chicago, including loan sharking, burglaries, and other street crimes. Frank "Lefty" Rosenthal, a convicted bookmaker and member of the Chicago mob, is said to have held a small piece of the action at Circus Circus.

1972–1976: Allen Glick's Argent Corporation, the Hacienda, the Stardust, and the Fremont

A young California real estate investor named Allen Glick arrived on the Strip in 1972 and his Argent Corporation was licensed to buy the Hacienda hotel. Soon, he arranged for a loan of $62.7 million from the Teamsters pension fund to purchase the Stardust and Fremont hotels in 1974. (By the late 1970s, the billion-dollar Teamsters fund held loans amounting to a quarter of a billion dollars on Strip casino-hotels.) It didn't stop there. The Teamsters and the Chicago mob liked Glick's business acumen so much that he received loans totaling $146 million. What the Chicago mob, led by Tony Accardo and Stardust skim manager Frank Rosenthal, kept from Glick was their involvement in a massive casino cash-stealing operation right under his nose.

Following the first code-named "Strawman" investigation of the Tropicana, the FBI undertook Operation Strawman II at the Stardust. FBI and Nevada gaming control agents found an ingenious hidden skimming organization at the Stardust, involving phony fill slips and the under-weighing of coins taken from the slot machines. Glick pled ignorance of the scheme and claimed that the Chicago men had threatened to harm him and his children if he backed out of running the company.

The case took years to gel, but by the end of 1983, fifteen defendants were indicted, including some from the Tropicana case: Kansas City gangsters Nick Civella and Carl DeLuna, Milwaukee mobster Frank Balistrieri, Las Vegas boys Carl Thomas and Anthony Spilotro, and Chicago hoods Joey Aiuppa, Jackie

Cerone, and Joe Lombardo. By this time, Las Vegas casinos were considered mob-free, although the town was still obsessed with one last high-profile mobster, Spilotro, who still lived there, openly partied there and tried to operate in town for Chicago's Outfit.

1986: Death of Anthony Spilotro

In his fifteen years as Chicago mob chief in Las Vegas, starting in 1971, Anthony Spilotro (nicknamed "Tony the Ant") had shepherded the mob's interests in town, helped his Vegas mob buddy Frank "Lefty" Rosenthal and ran a brutal street crime group called the Hole in the Wall Gang, so named for its method of entering businesses during burglaries. But Tony had a series of high-profile criminal trials in Vegas, represented by mob attorney Oscar Goodman, and the years of publicity were too much for the Chicago leaders. In 1986, Tony and his brother Michael Spilotro were bludgeoned to unconsciousness and buried alive next to a cornfield in Indiana, near a hunting lodge owned by crime boss Joey Aiuppa. A farmer happened on the grave. Because their faces were broken up, dental records were used to identify the bodies.

The Chicago Outfit appointed Don "Wizard of the Odds" Angelini to replace Spilotro, but there wasn't much to exploit anymore in Vegas by then, and he couldn't match what Tony did in the 1970s. It was over. The non-entity Angelini ended up in federal prison on racketeering charges in 1993, and no one took his place in Vegas.

Post-Mob Years

1987 to 2007

The Strip entered a new phase, with new methods of parting visitors from their money, as a series of new megaresorts arrived. It began with Steve Wynn's Mirage hotel in 1989, funded in part by junk bonds provided by Wynn's friend Michael Milken, who was later convicted on felony trading charges unrelated to his business with Wynn. Other bigger, more expensive resorts grew: the Excalibur in 1990; the new, 5,000-room MGM Grand, the Luxor, and Wynn's Treasure Island in 1993; the Bellagio, Paris-Las Vegas, and Mandalay Bay in the late 1990s. Vegas was the fastest growing city in the country in the 1990s, with a $30 billion traveler and entertainment industry, and new residents fueling a billion-dollar local casino business in suburban neighborhoods off the Strip.

By 1992, Americans spent more money on gambling—in Vegas and in casinos and lotteries outside of Nevada—than on all other forms of entertainment combined. By 2005, Vegas attracted 37 million visitors, and the state's casinos took in a record $10.5 billion from gamblers. Casino companies, nearly all of them turning public to raise funds, typically traded with good returns on Wall Street. There were virtually no signs of economic decline in Vegas by its hundredth birthday. The casino industry was now legit. The vice game is now in the hands of civilians, corporate executives who struggle to convince the outside world that their immense profits come as the result of providing fun and joy to their visitors. They give them what they want. A vice where the odds are always stacked against them, with "randomized" slot machines programmed to produce losing players. In this pervasive, truly preposterous American pastime, Vegas is America's team.

3

Highway 91 Blues

BUGSY SIEGEL

Contrary to popular belief among historians, FBI Director J. Edgar Hoover did once acknowledge the existence of organized crime—when it was moving into Las Vegas in 1946. Hoover learned West Coast mob big shot Benjamin "Bugsy" Siegel had taken over the Flamingo hotel in Las Vegas that year. As a result, the FBI sent agents to Las Vegas to bug his hotel room, tap his phone, and transcribe the conversations. Hoover also planted an item with radio broadcaster Walter Winchell that would bring national attention to Bugsy and add fuel to his frustrated mob partners' decision to have him killed.

What would become a 2,421-page FBI file on Siegel from 1946 to 1947 started in Las Vegas. So, too, did the city's infamous history of hidden mob control of casinos. The Flamingo, the most respected casino of its time in America, put Vegas on the map. Siegel had the moxie to get up in front of the Las Vegas Chamber of Commerce in 1946 to pitch the Flamingo project, saying that the backers of the new Flamingo were distillers from back east. That mob money (some of it gained via "distilling" illegal booze during Prohibition) was used didn't matter much to Las Vegas. New jobs and investments mattered more, as did the bribe money Siegel bestowed on local politicians, law enforcement, and, FBI documents indicate, Nevada's powerful U.S. Senator, Pat McCarran.

Bugsy Siegel was so nicknamed for his instantaneous, violent, and some say psychotic temper that made him "go bugs." He was born in Brooklyn in 1906 to Max and Jeannie Siegel. He dropped out of school after the eighth grade and became a young street criminal. At age fifteen, he teamed with nineteen-year-old Meyer Lansky, already a veteran killer, and guarded trucks carrying illegal liquor for bootlegger (and Black Sox gambler) Arnold Rothstein. Siegel, at only sixteen, killed his first man, a would-be truck hijacker. Siegel and Lansky started the Bug and Meyer Mob, an ethnic Jewish gang that top Sicilian-American Mafia figure Charles "Lucky" Luciano would tap to join a group of torpedoes who killed "old country" Sicilian mobster Salvatore Maranzano, in 1931.

Though hot-tempered, Siegel rose in the ranks of New York organized crime as a reliable gunman and intimidator. He survived the bloody gangster purges from Prohibition in the 1920s through the 1930s. While relaxing with friends at the Hard Tack Social Club in 1932, Siegel received a severe head injury after a rival mobster lowered a bomb into a chimney and blew up the room. A year later, during a police raid, Siegel was arrested at the Hotel Franconia in New York with eight other men who amounted to a Who's Who of the Big Apple's Jewish organized crime. The dapper-dressed group included Joseph "Doc" Stacher (a Las Vegas casino investor in the 1950s) and the vicious killer Louis "Lepke" Buchalter, who, two months after the raid, formed the infamous mob hit squad, Murder, Inc., that offed hundreds of rival or uncooperative gangsters in the 1930s.

If Lepke served as chairman of Murder, Inc.'s board, Bugsy

was its CEO. Pursued by Hoover, Lepke surrendered to the FBI in 1939 after the columnist Walter Winchell—a friend of both—set up a time and place. His surrender didn't help Lepke, who got the chair at Sing Sing in 1943. By then, Siegel was well established in Los Angeles, where he'd moved in 1935, supporting, but leaving, his wife and two kids back in Brooklyn. The Luciano mob had sent Siegel west to start labor racketeering in the Hollywood film business. He took up with the Hollywood crowd and his friends would include movie performers Cary Grant, Betty Hutton, and George Raft. Siegel admired Raft and copied Raft's style of silk ties, houndstooth jackets, and embroidered shirts. He was obsessed with keeping his prematurely thinning hair straight. But his reputation as a good underground criminal rose back east when he sent them cuts from other rackets like offshore gambling ships and onshore gambling in Redondo Beach and Culver City, California.

Siegel became a licensed, legitimate casino operator in Las Vegas, despite a well-publicized national reputation as a veteran killer. In 1941, Abe "Kid Twist" Reles, an employee of Murder, Inc., became a mob canary. He testified in Los Angeles that some of the fourteen men he'd personally killed were done on Siegel's orders. Reles revealed that Murder, Inc., had murdered more than 1,000 people, and he provided specifics on eighty-five of them. Months later, Siegel went on trial in Los Angeles for the murder and kidnapping of his old friend, the mob henchman Harry "Big Greenie" Greenberg. Reles, who agreed to be a state's witness in the case and was under guard, dropped to his death from his hotel room window at Coney Island, New York. Reles's death was never solved, but the Greenberg case died with him and Siegel walked. Five years later, Siegel would remark casually to builder Del Webb, his "legit" Flamingo building partner in Las Vegas, that he himself had killed twenty people.

Siegel was handsome but slight, five feet nine inches, and less than 160 pounds, but by the mid-1940s, he was the Eastern mob's top man in the West. He, Lansky, Stacher, Longie Zwillman, and Phil Kastel were among a select group of efficient Jewish gangsters who, though not Sicilian, were accepted by mob overlord Luciano as board members of what was known as the "Combination," along with the top Sicilian hoods in the country of the day like Frank Costello, Willie Moretti and Tony Accardo. The activities pursued by Luciano's top men included illegal gambling, pimping, narcotics, extortion, and counterfeiting.

When Siegel entered the then-small-time Vegas gaming scene, he carried about three million dollars from the Combination, earned from narcotics trafficking and other illegal deeds, to finance the Flamingo. He had plenty to secretly grease the local pols for permits and licenses. One of the people who played a direct role in the licensing of the casinos in Las Vegas in the 1940s, and who recommended Siegel's company for its licenses, was corrupt Clark County Sheriff Glen Jones. Sheriff Jones actually oversaw covert drug trafficking in the Las Vegas city jail and later resigned after being caught on tape soliciting bribes in the early 1950s.

In the summer of 1946, Siegel directed the building of the Flamingo and ran a horse race wire service for West Coast bookies, with instant results telegraphed from tracks such as Bay Meadows outside San Francisco, Oaklawn Park in Hot Springs, Arkansas, Tropical Park in Florida, and Belmont in New York. Ensconced in a suite at the Last Frontier hotel in Las Vegas, Siegel, in need of still more money to build the Flamingo, increased his wire service fees so much that bookmakers in Los Angeles and Las Vegas complained they could no longer make a profit. Meanwhile, according to FBI records, Siegel traveled south early that year and paid $100,000 for a ranch in Tijuana, Mexico, for Luciano, who'd been deported to Italy. Ben's long suffering wife, Estelle, had recently divorced him, and that fall he hopped down again to Mexico, reportedly this time to marry girlfriend Virginia Hill.

With building materials scarce due to wartime shortages and restrictions, Siegel spent inflated amounts of his friends' money on copper, plumbing, and building supplies on the black market. His spending on the plumbing—in order to have water and flush toilets in every room—alone was said to be about a million dollars. To get extra cash, Siegel started shorting shares owed to his mob colleagues from the race wire and other rackets he controlled in Hollywood. But his spending, with money sent by Costello and gangsters who followed Costello's advice, would finally reach about six million dollars.

In Washington, J. Edgar Hoover took an interest in what he saw as Siegel's easy time of it getting what he wanted in Vegas. He hatched an idea on how to rattle Siegel without even using the agency's men. Hoover planted a story about the Flamingo with his loyal friend Walter Winchell, the radio broadcaster whose gossipy reports were heard by tens of millions of Americans each week. On July 14, 1946, Winchell included the Hoover-leaked missive about Siegel (without mentioning names) in his broadcast:

> According to the FBI, a prominent West Coast racketeer is endeavoring to muscle a prominent West Coast publisher out of his interest in a West Coast Hotel.

The "West Coast publisher" surely was Siegel's civilian friend William "Billy" Wilkerson, the original builder of the Flamingo whom Siegel bought out, and who was also publisher of *The Hollywood Reporter*, a movie trade magazine.

Winchell's gossip item unnerved Siegel. Not only did it

threaten the loss of local gaming, liquor, and business licenses for the Flamingo, but it also brought unwanted national attention to the project when his mob backers were concerned about his cost overruns and rumors that he was skimming from the millions they invested. Lansky went out of his way to reassure Luciano and the other hoods of the Combination upset with Bugsy, that the project would go forward.

Meanwhile, according to Siegel's FBI file, Hoover, as part of the FBI's probe dubbed the "Reactivation of the Capone Gang," sought permission from the U.S. Attorney General to tap Siegel's phone and bug his room in Las Vegas.

"In the course of the (Capone) investigation, we have ascertained that Benjamin 'Bugsy' Siegel, notorious racketeer with underworld connections on the west and east coasts and Las Vegas, Nevada, will again visit the latter city within the next few days and reside at the Last Frontier Hotel there in suite 401," Hoover wrote on July 19, 1946, asking for permission to record Siegel's private conversations. "As previously pointed out, we are desirous of following Siegel's widespread activities and therefore, are requesting authority to place a technical surveillance on his telephone at the (hotel), which will be Las Vegas 1800."

While Hoover may have been apprehensive about probing the mob later in the 1950s, FBI reports show that he aggressively pursued its members well into the 1940s, even using the misspelled term "Maffia" to describe them.

"There seems to be no doubt in the fact that (Siegel) seems to be generally respected and feared by underworld characters because he is supposed to personally have killed at least thirty people," Hoover wrote in a memo dated July 22, 1946. "Allegedly, Siegel is a pleasure smoker of opium, but he does not have the habit . . ."

"(T)he reference has been made by informant that Siegel is

instrumental in the attempt of the Chicago mob to take over the wire service currently operated by James Ragen," Hoover wrote. "Along these lines, it follows that the Maffia, operating through its New York headquarters, where Frank Costello and Joe Adonis, using Siegel as a front, have put themselves in the hotel business through Siegel and under the trade name of the Kirkeby Hotels. Also, this same mob is attempting to take over the wire service and if they are successful in doing so will extort tribute from every bookmaker in the United States. It has been pointed out that the Maffia operates through 'fronts' who are usually of Jewish or Irish extraction."

Hoover also asked for authorization to place bugs and taps in other hotels and places Siegel stayed, such as Chicago and Los Angeles. President Truman's Justice Department granted Hoover's requests on July 20, and FBI agents from the Salt Lake City office immediately installed the recording equipment in Las Vegas. Taps were placed on Siegel's two phone lines at the Last Frontier Hotel, the town's second Strip resort. Other listening devices were inserted into a pair of lines believed to be used by Meyer Lansky at the Apache Hotel downtown. FBI agents listened in from a second-floor boiler room in the Las Vegas Club downtown and got Siegel's conversations on tape.

With agents listening, Siegel first called fellow mobster Moe Sedway (whose son would became a state legislator from Las Vegas), asking him if he knew about the Winchell item. Sedway said he hadn't heard anyone talk about it yet. Then he called Winchell, who clearly knew who Siegel and his friends were and what Siegel was capable of doing. Winchell nervously squealed on Hoover as the source of the July 14 broadcast. The gossip columnist quickly sent a long letter to an unnamed hood both he and Siegel knew apologizing for the item, but making the incident all the more embarrassing for Siegel. FBI agents listened to Bugsy's inarticulate tantrum about it in his

Last Frontier suite at 7:30 P.M., July 20, directed toward his new wife, the notorious moll of many gangsters, Virginia Hill.

SIEGEL: We'll make him bring Hoover in front of me and let that cocksucker tell me where he got it from . . . You bet to Christ, I said tell that dirty son-of-a-bitch—you may say they don't give a license here and we go and spend three million dollars, every nickel we possess. He (Hoover) thinks it's Meyer and I in there. He—oh yes, I told him I said—I said—We said Jesus Christ when I started it I thought it was (*censored by FBI*) _____ just called me. Jesus Christ, I get a letter from Winchell he said, I want you to see it when you come in. Winchell apologized forty times, said I would never do a thing like that. He said all right (*censored*), you're a friend of mine but these two other fellows are dearer friends to me in there, he said and one especially is a very dear friend of mine, wouldn't do a thing in the world to hurt him, said I want you to see the letter when you get back. Jesus Christ—but I know it all instigated from him, see. He just have given it to that guy to give it to Hoover, see. He called and said I get the letter just now—You should see the front of it—right there in front of the what you call it—the Senator—that contract we signed. Yeah but Winchell's liable to cop. I'll knock his fucking eyes out—just like this—you God damned right. _____ or call me up and tell me. But now he's gone and got this God damned letter a block long from Winchell.

HILL: That means you won't get a license?

SIEGEL: What?

HILL: What kind of a license, honey?

SIEGEL: Say I came in after it and through him or something they refuse to give me a gambling license, what am I gonna do with the hotel, stick it up my ass?

HILL: Well, why don't you "get" them. Then once you get them—

SIEGEL: Well, they always revoke them—get them, never mind about that, say whatever they want. If there is no connection in this town to get these things they can put you out of business, honey. Why to you think I feel around with these politicians? What do you think I work so much time with (censored)? Give them money and this and that. Although it is legitimate business but still, you know, these bastards when you have a license (inaudible) . . .

FBI note: End. At this point a child came into the room and the above conversation terminated.

The next day, at 9:30 A.M., July 21, 1946, Siegel is overheard on the FBI's phone wiretap at the Last Frontier talking effusively to Lansky, who was in Los Angeles. Lansky is more circumspect and evasive than Siegel, possibly suspecting a phone tap and wary of Siegel's obsequiousness. Siegel, desperately seeking to reassure Lansky, later tells him about their mob friend who was to receive Winchell's written apology.

SIEGEL: Is that friend of ours still in there? The one we went up to see together?

LANSKY: No.

SIEGEL: He left?

LANSKY: Yeh.

SIEGEL: Is he coming back?

LANSKY: No.

SIEGEL: He won't be back at all?

LANSKY: No.

SIEGEL: He said he was going to stay until Monday or Tuesday.

LANSKY: Let's see, let me get this straight.

SIEGEL: No, not the fellow you went out to see, Meyer.

LANSKY: Yeh.

SIEGEL: (*censored*).

FBI note: It is believed this is (censored) of the Chicago Capone Syndicate.

LANSKY: Oh, that I don't know.

SIEGEL: I think he is, he said he would be there until Tuesday, you remember when we left him?

LANSKY: I didn't hear from him.

SIEGEL: If he's there, tell him that that's coming from (censored) and then I'll explain to you when I come in and tell him, the other fellow, nothing yet and when I come in I'll talk to him about it. He's leaving what, Tuesday?

LANSKY: I don't know.

SIEGEL: I think he's leaving Monday.

LANSKY: He said he didn't know yet.

SIEGEL: If he's not leaving till Tuesday let him tell you because I'll call you when I come in.

LANSKY: Okay.

SIEGEL: Tell him when they receive the letter it will be from (censored) not from the other guy.

LANSKY: Okay.

SIEGEL: I'll be in tomorrow night. Oh, the guy called me up. I knew I had something to tell you. Last night, he read me a letter he just got from Winchell. He (Winchell) says in the longest day he never dreamt it was him or I. He said I want you to understand that the other fellow is even a better friend than you are. I'd have never done that in a million years. The man who I thought it was is (*censored*). He said I went right back to my man that gave it to me, and then it tells him it's Mr. Hoover, you understand? And bowled the by-Jesus out of him. He says I want you to tell my mutual friend that when I come out I will explain the whole thing, you couldn't give me a million dollars to do that. He (Winchell) said I would never do that because he went on to tell him how it might have hurt me up here. But I found out that it's still him. So I'll tell you when I see you.

LANSKY: Okay.

The recorded conversation ended there. But Winchell told Hoover he never sent Siegel a letter. Did the wily Lansky perceive Siegel's verbose reassurances as a pack of lies?

While the Flamingo was under construction, Siegel had a terrible time obtaining raw materials made scarce due to the war. The U.S. government's policy was to reserve as much material as possible to build homes for American military veterans, who'd just returned to face a severe shortage of housing throughout the country. Things got worse in April 1946, when the Civilian Public Administration (CPA), which continued to oversee distribution of building materials after the war, ordered Siegel and contractor Del Webb to halt the Flamingo, citing a freeze order on commercial construction to conserve wood and metal for veterans' homes. But Siegel insisted he'd already begun the project before the March 26, 1946, freeze order, and added they'd spent more than $700,000 on it so far and had committed another half million.

Meanwhile, the FBI started to look at charging Siegel with fraud against the government. Agents learned from a source in Los Angeles that before the freeze, nothing had been done at the Flamingo site beyond "a few stakes being driven into the ground." A memo sent August 26, 1946, reported that "it was rumored that through (name censored) funds were made available to Senator (Pat) McCarran of Nevada and shortly thereafter construction was authorized."

Unimpressed with Siegel's pleas, the CPA ordered building

at the Flamingo site to cease as of August 8. The news prompted the Clark County Commission to make a scene about temporarily denying Siegel's request for gaming and liquor licenses. But Siegel's attorney got the CPA to delay its order until Siegel could travel to San Francisco to meet with the CPA commissioner and argue his case for resuming construction.

The FBI recorded a conversation in Las Vegas before the hearing in which Siegel vowed to someone, "We will not stop construction. We will go to jail first." Siegel then telephoned a man whose name was censored but was described as "a well-known gambling boss in the vicinity of San Francisco." Siegel ordered the man to "get to" the CPA commissioner. Siegel then received a call from another person, name also censored, but apparently a public official who "offered his assistance in determining the parties responsible" for holding up the Flamingo.

FBI agents in San Francisco were ordered to install a bug in Siegel's guest room at the St. Francis Hotel. It produced almost immediate results. Agents overheard Siegel say that "sixteen weeks work and two million dollars has been put into the hotel at Las Vegas," which was 75 percent completed, and now a stop order had been ordered. He further complained that "(censored) had an okay on a $1,500,000 building in the south." Siegel hinted that he may have corrupted the CPA, mentioning that he knew some of its board members and that he had "discussed opening a gambling club in Sacramento" with someone.

At the CPA hearing on August 13, 1946, Siegel brought in two lawyers, one of whom was a former regional counsel for the War Projects Board and might give him extra clout. CPA officials said that federal regulations only allowed Siegel to work on that one building and not any new ones unconnected to it. Testimony, involving Siegel, his lawyers, and his contractors from Del Webb, revealed that $1.6 million had been spent so far on the Flamingo ($400,000 less than was mentioned in the private conversation taped by the FBI). Las Vegas officials, they said, did not require them to submit any detailed building plans, so they used what they wanted. Siegel's people presented evidence based on blueprints from January 1946 that they said confirmed only one building, containing the Flamingo's casino, kitchen, and dining room, was under construction before the building freeze.

The hearings continued into the next day. In his suite at the St. Francis, the FBI bug picked up Siegel's end of a long distance call to "Baby" (Virginia Hill) in Las Vegas. Siegel complained he was being singled out. "Somebody got the setup. What's the idea of picking on us if they didn't?"

Employees of the Del Webb company agreed with Siegel to commit perjury by saying they were working off plans submitted in January instead of March, 1946. In previous private discussions, the builders said they had to use the March plan because the January one wasn't detailed enough. "It was mentioned that the Webb company is not to know anything about the March 22 plan and the most important thing is to have the Webb representative testify that he followed the plan of January 12 and no other," according to an FBI report of August 15, 1946. At one point, one of the people in Siegel's bugged room, identified as a "district manager," said he had received a letter from an unidentified man "saying that he had fixed matters with Senator (name not audible)."

Seeing no proof otherwise from the CPA's staff, the commissioner ruled in favor of the Flamingo that afternoon, but gave investigators another month to get additional evidence. Siegel took a Western Airlines flight to Los Angeles.

The quick decision was met by suspicion. When the FBI asked to see a transcript of the hearing, the CPA refused, citing confidentiality. On August 16, the FBI started an investigation into the CPA itself because, an agent reported that day, "it appears that the CPA hearing may have been a cover-up as they obviously did not present much of a case." As evidence, agents observed that prior to the hearing, a CPA investigator had bragged that the case against Siegel was "open and shut" and "he had the blueprints which showed that there were two separate buildings and they should have constructed only one." It would go even higher, all the way to Nevada's powerful political boss in Washington. Agents learned "in strict confidence that Senator Pat McCarran was in San Francisco the day of the hearing in case he was needed by the Flamingo people." None other than the head of the Investigative Division of the CPA in Los Angeles was the source of information the FBI received, according to an August 8 report, about bribery allegations involving McCarran in the Flamingo case.

The CPA would soon learn that Siegel and company had misled them. The Flamingo actually consisted of three separate, unconnected buildings: the casino, hotel, and small shopping center. But Siegel responded that they still considered them all one building and would spend $15,000 to connect them with walls and a roof. He also assured them that a high fence would be erected, FBI agents reported, "around the project so that no one will be able to observe the construction from the street."

After returning to Las Vegas, Siegel agreed to meet with FBI agents at his hotel room at the Last Frontier late in the evening of August 20. He told them that banks were refusing to lend him money because the FBI was investigating him. Agents later said he lied when he told them a friend of his had telephoned the FBI office in Los Angeles on his behalf, and heard that the investigation was about bribery and the source of Siegel's funds. They said he admitted giving a modest $500 contribution to an unnamed campaign fund but that "he was not concerned with Senator McCarran because he was already cooperative."

Behind the scenes, FBI officials figured that the government risked criticism from veterans if they heard limited supplies were being used to build a gambling casino. The August 26, 1946, FBI document mentioned an editorial in the weekly *Las Vegas Tribune* that complained, "Federal authorities were permitting the construction of the Flamingo Hotel while the veterans were homeless due to a shortage of building materials." But that did nothing to stop the project, nor did anyone else raise objections. To town fathers, the Flamingo meant new business. They ignored the dozens of U.S. veterans roaming around the streets of Las Vegas at the time, sleeping on the ground, unable to find even a hotel room.

According to another FBI memo, Siegel confided to an FBI snitch that rumors he had an unlimited supply of money were untrue, and that he was so hard up for cash he'd sold his thirty-five-room mansion at 250 Del Fern Avenue in Holmby Hills, next to Beverly Hills, to the actress Loretta Young. FBI reports also show that Siegel inquired about obtaining a construction loan from the U.S. Reconstruction Finance Corporation in August 1946, and that once Hoover found out, he forwarded a letter to the head of the RFC containing derogatory background information on Siegel and his friends. He urged that the RFC "block any such loan." As tensions over the Flamingo mounted, Virginia Hill attempted to commit suicide with an overdose of drugs in Vegas, but Siegel saved her by getting her to a doctor in time.

The FBI's chief in Los Angeles, on September 18, 1946, wrote that even though the CPA commissioner had approved the Flamingo, the FBI's goal ought to be to investigate "possible fraud in connection with the Flamingo hotel" and the overall objective remained to "stop the hotel, if possible, and secondly to trace back the money which has gone into construction of the hotel."

Hoover then redoubled the intelligence tail on Siegel, with heavy physical surveillance of his travels in Los Angeles, and lots of info on the ill-fated opening of the Flamingo in December 1946.

Siegel's gangland slaying, mainly due to his excessive spending of mob money, took place in Beverly Hills on June 20, 1947, less than a year after the bugging of the Last Frontier. The heat on him that got too much for some people started from within his guest room at the Last Frontier.

The FBI and the Los Angeles District Attorney's office investigated Siegel's death. Las Vegas police officers told the FBI they suspected Sedway ordered the hit. An informant told Vegas cops that "it was common knowledge among the gambling element in Las Vegas that Siegel had been out to 'break' Sedway, and Siegel was reported to have made the statement that he would make a 'shill' out of Sedway . . . Sedway had acted peculiarly just before Siegel was killed and since the killing has been 'nervous as a cat . . .' "

More information trickled in on why Siegel was killed. A July 1, 1947, FBI memo to Hoover from the Los Angeles office cited two reasons: that "Siegel had been losing money heavily in Las Vegas in his operation of the Flamingo Hotel and was attempting to recoup through his friend George Raft and others by attempting to gain bookmaking trade in the motion picture colony. This clashed with (censored), who had Siegel killed." The other theory revolved around a meeting "held in Las Vegas between Siegel and his associates wherein it was decided that the Trans-America Wire Service was not doing so well and arrangements were made to reorganize the same. At the meeting, it was decided that (censored) in Los Angeles would have to tell Jack Dragna, who was in the hospital at the time, that he was no longer to be connected with the wire service. The informant blamed Jack Dragna, a reported active member of the Maffia, to be responsible for the Siegel killing inasmuch as he, Dragna, was being ousted."

As to who actually did the shooting, nothing is certain. A July 1947 FBI report said that a man (whose named is censored) who was released from a prison in Derby, Kansas, shortly before Siegel's death mentioned "he had a big job to do on the West Coast and it was felt (censored) that he might have some connection to the Siegel killing."

Federal investigators also probed Lansky's possible connection to the assassination of his boyhood chum. An FBI teletype sent on July 17, 1947, quoted Lansky as denying knowing anything about Siegel's death. "Lansky stated positively that Syndicate had nothing to do with (the) killing. Lansky states that he, Frank Costello, and Joe Adonis were as surprised as anyone when they heard Siegel . . . had been killed. They received telephone calls from associates all over the country inquiring about Siegel's death but . . . were unable to answer them . . . Lansky believes the possibility that (Virginia) Hill's brother may have killed Siegel . . . because of Siegel mistreating Hill."

Lansky, of course, lied. The same teletype also speculated that while in New York on her way to Paris, "Hill may have told Adonis and Lansky about Siegel's attempts to defraud members of the Syndicate at the Flamingo hotel at Las Vegas."

Siegel's death also inspired extra chatter from gangsters that made its way to Hoover via Walter Winchell. Winchell sent Hoover a report "from two top detectives" on July 15, 1947. These detectives concluded that the "rival," syndicate-controlled horse race information wires of the mid-1940s, one controlled by Siegel on the West Coast, the other by gangster James Ragen in Chicago, were in fact "linked up secretly, their rivalry a front" to prevent the government from stopping them as illegal monopolies. What did Siegel in was Siegel himself, the report indicated.

> Now, all the big bookmakers throughout the country need these wire services and are charged a nominal rate, about seventy-five dollars a day. Bugsy, against the advice of the biggest "boys" here . . . started charging double that rate to the West Coast bookies. That is where the fight started . . . The police expect to tie up the Bugsy Siegel killing with the Ragen killing in Chicago (in 1946).

Years later, it became apparent that the final decision to kill Siegel took place during a mob commission meeting in early 1947 at the Nacional Hotel in Havana, Cuba, headed by Luciano, with top hoods such as Lansky and Frank Costello. Another visitor to the hotel, seen by undercover U.S. narcotics agents conversing with Luciano, was singer Frank Sinatra, who gave "Lucky" a gold cigarette lighter inscribed "To Charlie, From His Pal Frank." Luciano didn't care about Siegel; he wanted to reestablish himself as a casino man in Cuba (after his deportation to Italy). Mob investors, furious about losses at the Flamingo, wanted both Siegel and Costello—who'd urged them to plow money into the Flamingo—dead. Luciano saved Costello, making him pay the other mobsters back, but later told Costello about Siegel: "Him, I can't help."

Hoover, who would soon turn the FBI's attention almost exclusively to hunting down Communists, made a public comment about Bugsy Siegel:

> The circumstances surrounding Bugsy Siegel's career in crime tell the story better than words. He was an individual whose life was a constant challenge to common decency. Yet he and

his criminal scum were lionized and their favors sought after in so-called respectable social circles.

For Hoover and his FBI, it was a mixed victory. Respectable or not, Las Vegas still sought the favors Siegel's successors could provide. The notorious Siegel was out, but the mob was still in on the Flamingo, where they began a crafty and effective process of extracting unknown millions from Las Vegas for decades.

4

Mr. Las Vegas

MOE DALITZ

$\mathcal{B}$efore he died at age eighty-nine in 1989, Moe Dalitz was known as "Mr. Las Vegas," so extensive was his involvement in building it, and helping run its casinos with or for his mob colleagues. During his forty years in Las Vegas, Dalitz did much to further and foster his image, serving as mob dealmaker and peacemaker, as well as housing, hospital and golf course developer, broker and idea man who made seemingly endless donations to local politicians and charity groups. It didn't matter, not to most locals anyway, that those cash contributions likely came from casino earnings skimmed to avoid paying the taxes distributed to public agencies for public services. It also didn't matter much that Moe, as behind-the-scenes head of Cleveland's Mayfield Road Gang during and after Prohibition, had been (and still was for more than fifteen years in Vegas) connected to the Mafia. It didn't matter to the local powers that be that Moe was whisking away untold tens of millions to his hidden, connected investors in the Desert Inn, the Stardust, and other casinos. (In 1961, the FBI reported that an informant estimated that $66 million was illegally skimmed from all Las Vegas hotels in 1960 alone.)

Dalitz knew full well how to spread money in political and social circles, and to the cops. He'd learned it while operating illicit casinos in places like Miami, Cincinnati, and in Newport and Covington, Kentucky, with mob investors such as Meyer Lansky and Sam Tucker, going back to the 1930s. He was savvy about the graft side of big city politics. He had been a partner of Maurice Machke, Jr., the son of the Republican Party boss of Cleveland who was embroiled in a scandal in the late 1930s involving siphoning funds meant for streets and other public projects.

Moe was brilliant, witty, affable, and as successful in public relations as he was in operating casinos. But what Moe did best in Las Vegas, aside from making the locals happy, was to maintain the secrecy of his Vegas counting rooms throughout the 1950s—a time when organized crime all over America was at its peak in earnings and political power—and well into the 1960s. Despite the notoriety of his mob connections, Moe would die rich and happy, praised by Las Vegans who knew him or viewed him as a philanthropist.

Moe got his start in Las Vegas in 1949 by—like other mob-backers before and after—coming to the rescue of a casino developer unable to finish a project without added investment. The developer was Wilbur Clark, a former hotel bellman and card dealer from San Diego who'd previously invested in the El Rancho Vegas resort in 1944, on what would become the Strip, and sold his share in 1946 to begin building the Desert Inn.

Dalitz and his cadre of illegal casino men—including Morris Kleinman, Sam Tucker, Louis Rothkopf, Thomas McGinty and Cornelius Jones—known as "the Cleveland group," gave Clark the capital he needed to complete the 238-room Desert Inn hotel in 1950. But Moe didn't want to make the same mistake Ben Siegel made. Siegel put himself out front with the Flamingo; Moe and company wanted to be kept out of the limelight. Instead, this hotel would be called Wilbur Clark's Desert Inn (on the neon sign and everything), with the clean, white, Protestant Wilbur as the front. Clark would be identified in photos and interviews as the proprietor of the Desert Inn, while in reality he only held a minority interest and did not run the casino. It was Clark whom Edward R. Murrow of CBS interviewed on live TV in the early 1950s from inside Clark's home, the same house Senator John F. Kennedy stayed in when he was in town in 1954 and 1956. An FBI memo from 1961, in the agency's file on Dalitz, reported that Clark "is publicly acknowledged as the manager of the Desert Inn, but according to (a) reliable source, Clark has nothing to say" about the operation.

Dalitz's influence in Las Vegas began before he was even licensed by Nevada to run the DI. The elementary investigation—one that bordered on criminal neglect—that Nevada made into Moe's background in Detroit and Cleveland should have raised all kinds of suspicions. Even in 1950, the state could have used its relatively weak controls on casinos to deny Dalitz and company the privileged gaming licenses they needed. The state's gaming board sent the trusted Robbins E. Cahill and an assistant to Ohio to check into the Cleveland group. Despite a reputation as a straight arrow, Cahill, it turned out, was as gullible a Nevada hick as the wily Dalitz and crew hoped he'd be. Cahill missed loads of information on Dalitz's activities in Cleveland police files, such as Dalitz's direction of numbers and other rackets, his extensive mob associations, and his infamous Mayfield Road Gang. He mysteriously opted to interview people with good impressions of Dalitz, however they came to have had them. One was the crime news reporter for the *Cleveland Plain Dealer*, others were people involved with labor unions, the mayor's office, and the one-time head of the Cleveland office of public safety—the formerly "untouchable" Elliot Ness. Instead of a knowledgeable city police detective, Cahill asked the crime reporter about Dalitz's possible complicity in the murder of Cleveland Councilman William "Rarin' Bill" Potter in 1931. Witnesses then reported seeing Dalitz with bootlegging partner Louis Rothkopf, also suspected of killing Potter, only an hour before the murder. The reporter's reply, Cahill said: "It didn't have anything to do with (the Cleveland group), and everybody knew it. Forget that end of it." It is hard to believe that a crime reporter in Cleveland would never have mentioned Dalitz's reign as head of the Mayfield Road Gang, known in the city since Prohibition. But Cahill, his memory either bad or selective, didn't mention it. Satisfied, he let it all drop. The mob would soon gain yet another profitable foothold in Las Vegas—led by Dalitz, a longtime associate of La Cosa Nostra Syndicate leaders Lucky Luciano and Meyer Lansky—with the blessing of state officials.

"We both left (Cleveland) with the idea that the stories that had been built up around them, that the fears that had been built up around them, just didn't pan out," Cahill said later in an oral history recorded in 1977, back when Dalitz was still widely revered as a community leader. "Everywhere we went, we were told, 'Sure, they run these things (illegal gambling clubs). But they run a good, tight business. They run an ethical business. Yes, maybe they pay off people to keep an illegal operation.' This was nothing unusual to any of the people that we'd ever had that came to us from an illegal operation."

Cahill's view represented the clueless, yahoo mentality of the times adopted by Las Vegans, who just wanted the big investments that Dalitz's group would shower on them. They were willing to accept people who gained valuable casino experience managing places in states that prohibited gambling, places where gambling took place in unregulated vice districts. How else were they to learn the business, they'd ask? And as for bootlegging—everybody drinks, right?

What was Cahill thinking? An ethical illegal operation? Nothing unusual about bribing public officials to keep a criminal enterprise going? Did Cahill fail to understand the implications of licensing criminals who bribe politicians and cops to keep the casino money flowing? He did so, without regret, and with the denial that characterized Las Vegas then, and in some ways, does to this day.

"I might as well say now what I would have to say later," Cahill said in 1977. "I think the years have borne it out, that Moe Dalitz has done more for the city of Las Vegas than any single man connected with the industry. He has been a good citizen for the many years he was here, and the money that he spent in town. He was part of the local scene, participated in local activities, and never, in his operations in Nevada, did anything that was unethical."

Cahill came back to Vegas and recommended that Dalitz and the Cleveland group receive Nevada gaming licenses. Had he somehow blocked Moe Dalitz, the history of Las Vegas may have been different. Dalitz's gallery of former bootleggers turned publicly licensed casino partners included Louis Rothkopf, known for being the best liquor still man in illegal bootlegging and the prime suspect in Councilman Potter's murder; Morris Kleinman, who was arrested for tax evasion in 1933 and served three years in the federal pen in Ohio; Sam Tucker, who ran illegal hooch with Kleinman and Dalitz from Canada across Lake Erie, then worked in Dalitz's gambling rackets; and Thomas McGinty, Mayfield gang member and illegal casino manager for Dalitz since 1930. After receiving their gaming licenses from the dust-covered sagebrushers in Las Vegas, the laughter from Dalitz's bunch must have been heard all the way to Cleveland.

Dalitz did prove to be quite effective at overseeing gambling joints in Vegas, and keeping the peace among the greedy gangster sociopaths waiting for their shares of the embezzled casino cash. Along the way, Dalitz opened the Desert Inn, bought shares in the Showboat casino in 1954, took over the Stardust in 1956 after Tony Cornero's death at the Desert Inn, secretly managed the cash flow at the Riviera in the early 1960s, and in 1967, became the first casino owner to sell to Howard Hughes when he agreed to let go of the Desert Inn for an overpriced thirteen million dollars.

Born to immigrant Jewish parents in Boston on December 24, 1899, Dalitz, with his brother Louis, took over their father's laundry business in Detroit in the early 1920s. Dalitz got involved with Detroit's infamous and violent Purple Gang by helping the ethnic Jewish crime group, hired by laundry owners, "convince" laundry workers to not join labor unions.

Dalitz himself later told FBI agents in the 1970s that although he was never a member of the Purple Gang, he traded bootleg whiskey with its members during Prohibition in the 1920s. Things ran well until the Purples and a rival gang, dubbed the Little Jewish Navy, started a gang war. The Purples hired Thomas and Pete Licavoli and bloody shootouts ensued, prompting Dalitz to leave Detroit in 1926. He moved onto bootlegging in Akron, Ohio, where he met Kleinman, Tucker, and Rothkopf, the first members of the Mayfield Road Gang. He later arrived in Cleveland, "where he continued his bootlegging activities on a large scale and subsequently muscled his way into gambling, pinball, slot machine, and other rackets," FBI agents reported in a detailed memo dated February 14, 1961.

As "the leader of a powerful criminal mob," the Mayfield Road Gang (named after a street in Cleveland), Dalitz "and fourteen other known hoodlums had powerful political connections and as a result thereof controlled gambling and number rackets in the vicinity of Cleveland," the FBI report related.

"The racing news service at one time was also controlled by Dalitz and his associates . . . (T)he activities of Dalitz during the 1930s brought him into close contact with (the) Louis Buchalter-Jacob Shapiro mob in New York City; Abe ("Longie") Zwillman, hoodlum in Newark, New Jersey, the Capone mob in Chicago, and (censored) a hoodlum and racketeer in Detroit . . ."

Actually, the leader of the Mayfield gang in the 1920s was Frank Milano, an Italian-American who followed Dalitz's advice that Prohibition was winding down and it was time to get into other rackets, specifically slot machines and other illegal gambling. They ran casinos in the Cleveland area with names like the Thomas Club and the Harvard Club, from 1930 to 1941, with manager Thomas McGinty. In 1929, Milano had met and formed an alliance with Dalitz, called the East End BiPartisan Club, and their stock rose in the national mob community.

Moe used the aliases Moe Davis and William Martin in the 1920s and 1930s. In the last years of Prohibition, the Mayfield Road Gang was involved in several murders of rival Cleveland bootleggers and mobsters. Among those killed were Chuck O'Neill, Joe Porrello, Sam Tilocco, and Mayfield Road member Charles Velotta, who was shot fifty times for blabbing too much to his girlfriend. Before he killed himself, Mayfield gang member Tony Colletti told his attorney that the Mayfields even ordered him to shoot his eighteen-year-old wife to death because she witnessed the murders of Porrello and Tilocco. The body of an old Dalitz friend, Morris Komisarow, was found in Lake Erie in 1930 with the anchor of one Dalitz's boats used unsuccessfully to keep him underwater. Though suspicious, police concluded Dalitz had nothing to do with it.

Dalitz's combination of legit laundries, so-called "gyp-joint" casinos, bookmaking, real estate, and other investments with the Cleveland Syndicate would be credited by some observers as a model followed by organized criminals across the country in the 1930s. "Much of its success," wrote Hank Messick and Burt Goldblatt in *The Mobs and the Mafia*, "could be attributed to the belief of its leaders that there was, indeed, enough for everyone. Such a theory made the Cleveland bosses natural allies of Luciano and Lansky in New York, and other young men in other cities. It contributed much to the development of a system of regional alliances that became the National Syndicate."

When World War II began, Dalitz joined the U.S. Army, becoming a lieutenant while running laundries, but he kept his criminal ties open. Dalitz himself told FBI agents that while in the Army from 1942 to 1945, "he maintained a financial interest with four other partners, namely Morris Kleinman, Louis Rothkopf, aka Lou Rody, Sam Tucker, and (censored) in the operation of Suite 281, Hollenden Hotel, Cleveland, Ohio, which was considered to be the headquarters of the Cleveland gambling syndicate," according to a 1961 memo in his FBI file. "During this interview, Dalitz admitted that while serving in the U.S. Army, Morris Kleinman, during his absence, was in charge and probably had made arrangements to finance other gambling establishments in Cleveland and elsewhere . . ."

The FBI started its file on Dalitz in the late 1930s, reporting on a hunting trip he went on (probably with his hunting buddy, Mayfield gang chief Frank Milano) in Mexico, where he was identified as a "known hoodlum." Agents knew about his activities for years, but Dalitz kept his nose clean (he was indicted for selling arms to Egypt in the early 1950s, but the charges were dropped). In the late 1950s, J. Edgar Hoover's FBI was pressured by President Eisenhower to launch a comprehensive investigation of mob activities after the much-publicized meeting of seventy-five hoods in Appalachia, New York, was broken up by police in 1957. Hoover's men compiled two lists of the nation's "Top Hoodlums." Dalitz made the second-tier list. Agents said Dalitz had been observed at a "meeting of hoodlums in Las Vegas" in January 1958.

The pressure on Dalitz redoubled after John F. Kennedy became president in 1961. He and his brother, Attorney General Robert Kennedy, made fighting organized crime a top priority of the new administration. In his best-selling 1960 book, *The Enemy Within*, Robert Kennedy identified Dalitz as a "Las Vegas and Havana gambling figure" who helped prevent a laundry worker strike in 1949 (the year he invested in the Desert Inn) by sending corrupt Teamsters union man Jimmy Hoffa to extort $17,500 from laundry owners to block the strike. No one in Nevada investigated the well-connected Dalitz about the allegations in 1960, not even the state's newly formed Gaming Commission.

Dalitz would serve as the Las Vegas contact for a slew of loans for casinos and other projects furnished by the Teamsters pension fund, controlled by union chief Jimmy Hoffa and Hoffa associate Allen Dorfman, of Chicago. Hoffa, who typically received a ten percent kickback on Teamsters loans, granted Dalitz a million dollars to build Sunrise Hospital, the largest hospital in Las Vegas in the late 1950s. The fund loaned Dalitz six million dollars for the Stardust hotel in 1960 and four million dollars for the Fremont hotel in 1961. Hoffa's pension fund also lent money to Dalitz's Desert Inn and casinos owned by others in the 1960s, including the Dunes, Landmark, Four Queens, Aladdin, Circus Circus, and Caesars Palace.

The FBI's memo of February 14, 1961, is revealing in that it showed that the feds were investigating Dalitz for everything from bribery, extortion, perjury, and conspiracy to violating U.S. labor laws and the White Slavery Traffic Act. The memo also showed the difficulty the government faced in penetrating the Dalitz group for evidence admissible in court (information from secret wire taps were not) of hidden mob investors. Those investors with pieces of Dalitz's action in Vegas included Alfred "Al" Polizzi and a second hood, John King, from Miami, who were members of Dalitz's Mayfield Road Gang in Cleveland in the 1930s.

"Information furnished by (censored) concerning the Chicago Syndicate's Sam Giancana and associates; Miami's (hoodlums) 'John King' and 'Al' has removed all doubt as to whether or not undisclosed hoodlum interests have money invested in the gambling operation of the 'Cleveland group' which is headed by Morris Barney Dalitz in Las Vegas, Nevada," the memo stated.

"The Chicago Criminal Syndicate, as indicated by (censored), consisting primarily of Samuel M. Giancana, (censored), Murray Llewelyn Humphreys, and Tony Accardo, and Miami hoodlums (censored) and Alfred Polizzi, owns a large percentage of and exerts almost complete control on the operations of the Cleveland group in Las Vegas. This operation consists principally of the hotel and gambling casinos at the Desert Inn and Stardust Hotels and very likely the Riveria Hotel, an equally plush hotel in Las Vegas."

It has long been known that the mob in Las Vegas used couriers to ferret large amounts of cash in baggage carried on trains, cars, or aircraft. One such courier, the FBI stated in 1961, was George Gordon, described as "a top hoodlum of the Las Vegas office." Gordon, tied closely to Dalitz and Desert Inn partners Kleinman and Tucker in the 1950s, quit his job at the Desert Inn in 1959 and "since then has spent most of his time in travel status," the agency reported. "Gordon makes regular visits to Los Angeles, Miami, Kentucky, Chicago, and other parts of the country."

An informant told agents that the "Cleveland group's operation of Wilbur Clark's Desert Inn and the Stardust Hotel represents the most lucrative gambling operation in the State of Nevada. They know the gambling business and conduct it in a business-like and expert manner. Since their existence depends on their good behavior, informant states that they are not engaged in an illegal operation in Nevada other than taking money from the top or 'skimming from the top.'"

Even while firmly in control of the cash flowing through the Desert Inn and Stardust, the Cleveland group sought more for their mob partners by attempting to win a state license to operate the Riviera. On his license application, Dalitz stated his net worth was more than two million dollars. To its credit, Nevada's State Gaming Control Board denied the request in 1960, citing the possibility the group would have a monopoly on Las Vegas casinos (little did they know that, with the mob in casinos all over town, it already existed). The Dalitz group decided to run the Riviera anyway, in secret. Dalitz got the Riviera to hire his former Stardust casino manager, Johnny Drew, to oversee the Riv's cash flow, and the hidden skimming.

During this time, Dalitz owned a 3,000-head cattle ranch in Garlock, Utah, a few hours northeast of Las Vegas. He built an airstrip there, bought a small airplane, and hired a pilot who could fly to and from town. He kept a yacht, "The Howdy Partner," in Miami.

Determined to find evidence to charge Dalitz, the FBI placed a bugging device in the executive office of the Desert Inn, on March 22, 1962, under a conference table where Dalitz and his cohorts met. Conversations were recorded and sent to Washington. Taps were placed on the work and home phones of several Strip executives from other hotels. The FBI also convinced a Dalitz insider to serve as a "live" informant (the FBI censored the informant's name from its records). The bug in the room recorded conversations, none with much to use in a criminal case, until it was deactivated on August 15, 1963.

By the mid-1960s, Dalitz began to lose interest in Las Vegas. He owned two yachts and a home in Acapulco, Mexico. He decided to branch out with some investors to build a large golf resort and health spa, La Costa, north of San Diego. When *Penthouse* magazine wrote a story describing him and his investors in La Costa as organized crime, they sued. Dalitz had to testify at trial about his rumrunning days but denied he was connected. The trial took place years before the FBI released Dalitz's file detailing his mob past. *Penthouse* got off with a clarification.

But back home, Dalitz enjoyed praise and award after award from community organizations in Las Vegas in the 1970s and 1980s. He was considered the town's elder statesman and even the state looked the other way to let him participate in a small casino, the Sundance in downtown Las Vegas, in the 1980s. When he died in 1989, newspaper obits stressed his positive influences on the town. And Dalitz did make positive contributions in developing Las Vegas, beyond the casino business. In hindsight, despite his extensive mobbed-up background, it might be said that it wasn't a mistake to grant him a casino license for the Desert Inn in the first place, as he played such a pivotal role in the development of Las Vegas and the Strip. But it's just as possible that "Mr. Las Vegas" did even more to enrich his organized criminal cronies throughout the United States. His skimming denied Nevada and Las Vegas millions in tax funds, money the people could have made decisions on how to spend, what land to buy, or hospital or college building to build—not Moe.

10 Feet From Hell: Las Vegas, the largest U.S. city founded in the twentieth century, is the driest city of its size in America, with only 26 rainy days a year, high temperatures averaging 105 degrees F (40 C) from May to September and several days of 115 F (46 C).

An old Vegas refrain is: "Yeah, you lost, but did you have fun?" Not these depressed suckers, eyeing a roulette wheel, around 1960.

Chimp TV star J. Fred Muggs tries out a Vegas slot machine in the 1950s. Money lost by humans in slot machines today accounts for about 70 percent of all gambling revenue in Nevada.

Before she was committed, actress Clara Bow, seated left, smiles next to cowboy actor-husband Rex Bell, and unidentified local shotgun toter, at her refuge Rancho Clarita outside Vegas, circa 1940.

The El Cortez hotel, in the 1950s, where it really all began for the Las Vegas mob. Ben "Bugsy" Siegel and his Syndicate investor/friends bought the downtown Vegas casino in 1945, flipped it in 1946 and bought the Flamingo, the Strip's first big hit.

Wilbur Clark, holding a beer in about 1950, was the amiable WASP front at the Desert Inn hotel for Moe Dalitz's former liquor bootleggers, the Mayfield Road Gang of Cleveland.

Wilbur, with then-Senator John F. Kennedy, mid-1950s. Kennedy stayed at Clark's so-called "ultra-modern" home on the Desert Inn's golf course, during campaign/pleasure trips to Vegas in 1954 and 1956.

JFK Swam Here: Clark's indoor swimming pool featured a large mural with a decadent Roman scene, 1950s.

Clark stands next to a collage of photos of the many unsuspecting dignitaries he posed with while fronting for the mob at the Desert Inn. The subjects included Harry Truman, Winston Churchill, Lyndon B. Johnson, Adlai Stevenson, Eleanor Roosevelt, and, oh yes, Ed Sullivan.

Nancy and Ronald Reagan, at Lake Mead in 1954, when Ronnie M.C.-ed a chimpanzee act at the Last Frontier hotel. One night, the chimp went crazy on stage. The future president viewed his Vegas act as the low point of his career.

Louis Armstrong, aka "The Grinder" who fathered his child while at the Sands Hotel, waxes with some of the chorus girls from the Moulin Rouge, Vegas's short-lived integrated casino, in 1955.

The Flamingo's mobbed-up hotel partners Ben Goffstein, left, Moe Sedway, center, and Gus Greenbaum, right, about 1950. Greenbaum, who later managed the Riviera hotel, was one of the most effective casino men the mob ever had. In 1958, he and his wife were murdered in Phoenix after he refused to continue running the Riviera.

At the then-segregated El Rancho Vegas hotel, late-1950s, Eleanor Roosevelt stands by hotel man Beldon Katelman, center, and black singer Pearl Bailey, who wouldn't be allowed there if it weren't for Eleanor.

The El Rancho Vegas, with its trademark tower and windmill, in the late 1950s, not long before the still-unsolved fire that destroyed it in 1960.

Aftermath of the El Rancho Vegas fire, June 17, 1960. Some say hotel owner Katelman kicked out gangster Johnny Rosselli a few weeks before, prompting a mob-ordered arson. Katelman never rebuilt it, and the land has remained vacant for 45 years.

Actress Lauren Bacall (seated left) wets her lips at a chubby Judy Garland (seated center), at the Sands hotel's Copa Room, while hotel freebies chief Jack Entratter stands over them, late 1950s.

Frank Sinatra, looking silly in a gag space helmet, mid-1950s, doing his part to promote the Sands, of which he owned a piece of the profits from 1952 to 1963. Jack Entratter wears a cowboy hat at right.

A turbaned Sinatra is offered a glass of milk from one of the harem girls in this painful public relations effort for the Dunes hotel opening in 1955. Frank also got his picture taken while riding an elephant.

Excess Celebrities

5

Rancho Sanitarium

CLARA BOW

$\mathcal{L}$as Vegas's first celebrity resident was Clara Bow, the Betty Boop-voiced film actress who exemplified the sexually liberated flapper of the 1920s. She was also the first local celebrity to overdose on Nembutal. Her self-imposed exile at a ranch outside Las Vegas came after she'd ended a film career in which her raw talent made her the biggest box office draw in America during the silent film era of the 1920s. She was dubbed "The It Girl" from the breakout silent film, "It." She'd had affairs with film director Victor Fleming and actor Gary Cooper. Then, her one-time best friend tried to extort money from her over some stolen love letters. She and her funny Brooklyn accent didn't come across in the new "talkie" films. In 1931, after a gossip rag published a lie-filled story charging her with everything from lesbianism to bestiality, Bow exited the Hollywood scene at age twenty-six. She quit films, bought a 300,000-acre ranch in southern Nevada and went to Las Vegas to marry cowboy actor Rex Bell, who'd just signed a deal to star in ten cheap westerns for $500 a pop.

Bow's Vegas marriage garnered worldwide attention. It also

attracted what was said to be the first transatlantic phone call ever to Vegas, from a news reporter in London. The story got her a big new contract offer and she went back to Hollywood to make a couple more movies. But she grew tired of it again and returned to her self-named southern Nevada ranch, called Rancho Clarita, to start a family with Rex. She had two boys between 1934 and 1938, but all wasn't well. Clara suffered from mental problems and insomnia, and was taking handfuls of barbiturates to fall asleep.

In the late 1930s, while Clara lived on the ranch, another celebrity story added attention to Las Vegas. The economic bonanza the town enjoyed from the federal Hoover Dam project—fueled by what dam workers spent boozing, gambling, and whoring—had petered out. In 1939, the town received a needed lift thanks to two things: the state's liberal divorce law (six weeks and out) and Clark Gable's wife coming to town to end their marriage. Their celebrity put Vegas on the national map. The news coverage given to the Gable divorce would make the town a comfortable divorce Mecca—and closer to L.A. than its divorce-factory rival Reno—for wealthy Californians.

The Gable story made the front page of newspapers nationwide. Maria (Ria) Langham Gable came to Vegas on January 20, 1939, and set the clock ticking on her residency at 700 South Seventh Street downtown. The photo of her on the front page of the *Las Vegas Evening Review-Journal*, smiling beside Mr. Gable, showed why Clark was leaving her, aside from taking up with the beautiful actress Carole Lombard. Ria was an unpreserved forty-eight years of age, ten years older than her husband, and looked old enough to be his mother. The news coincided with a story about the singer-actor Nelson Eddy's whirlwind marriage in Vegas that same day and his immediate return to Los Angeles. "Our honeymoon was a twenty-minute look at (Hoover) Dam," Eddy gushed. "It is a very lovely dam."

Clark Gable, one of the top movie idols of the 1930s, was filming *Gone With the Wind* in California, and had been linked with the blonde Lombard in Hollywood for a couple of years. Ria charged that he deserted their home back in 1935 when he said he wanted "more freedom." She spruced up for the media in a black and pink wool suit and a tall black pagoda straw hat, and got her divorce during a five-minute hearing on March 7, 1939. Local businessmen were ready to exploit the mass press interest. Guy McAfee, the crafty ex-police captain from Los Angeles, exploited coverage of the Gable divorce to publicize his new 91 Club casino on Highway 91, a place he jokingly called "the Strip." Meanwhile, four other local casinos expanded and the Boulderado Dude Ranch opened outside town, catering to female divorce filers.

But 1939 was not a happy year for the Clara Bow-Bells. Clara complained about Rex's now-frequent business trips to town. She found herself alone at the ranch with her convicted bootlegger father, Robert, who physically abused her children, and who had raped her when she was sixteen. One day, when Rex returned from an overnight stay in his car, she grabbed a rifle and flattened his tires with gunshots. She yelled and screamed at him frequently. Rex sent her to stay several months at a sanitarium in Los Angeles.

By 1942, their ranch totaled 600,000 acres. One evening, Clara and her boys saw the burning wreckage of Carole Lombard's plane after it had crashed into a mountain not far from the ranch, with no survivors. The crash would prompt Gable, who didn't show for his Vegas divorce, to rush to town to see if Carole had somehow lived, but instead had to claim her body.

Clara hated Rex's involvement in Republican Party politics

in Nevada and his decision to run for the House of Representatives in 1944, on a states-rights, anti-New Deal platform, mixed with his folksy cowboy way. Clara's family didn't know how upset she was about the prospect of being a politician's wife and, worse, living in Washington. One afternoon in the fall of 1944, her two boys found her unconscious next to an empty bottle of sleeping pills and a suicide note. She woke up eventually anyway in a hospital; after years of abusing drugs like Nembutal, her body had become tolerant of an amount that would have killed someone else. But the publicity embarrassed Rex, and stopped what little momentum he had achieved while campaigning in and around Las Vegas in another pro-Roosevelt Democrat year. The 41-year-old Rex lost the House race big, to former Nevada U.S. Senator Berkeley Bunker, 63 percent to 37 percent.

Rex then moved them all to downtown Las Vegas, to a house at 1816 Goldring Avenue. He kept Clara's violent father in a separate apartment nearby. Robert Bow, seventy-two years old, would typically wander over, dressed in a bathrobe. Once, Clara gave dad and son Rex "Tony" Bell, Jr., some boxing gloves to put an end to their disputes. The twelve-year-old Rex Jr. promptly floored grandpa.

Clara, once perhaps the most famous woman in America in the 1920s, had become less than a trivia subject by the late 1940s. She appeared as the mystery guest on the NBC radio show, "Truth or Consequences," a show where contestants are given clues about the guest, for almost two months before anyone guessed who she was. Still an insomniac, she now took to drink. When Rex sent her to a mental hospital in Connecticut, doctors determined she suffered from schizophrenia, brought on by her sick mother's attempt to kill her and her brutal father's sexual abuse.

Clara wanted to return to Vegas, but Rex decided she

shouldn't, and put the ranch up for sale. Separated from her now, Rex, still a Republican, went on to political success in Democrat-leaning Nevada, winning election as lieutenant governor of Nevada in 1954 and 1958. Clara lived by herself in Los Angeles. In the late 1950s, her dad quit his job as a shill—trying to induce tourists to wager at the Thunderbird Hotel in Vegas—and moved to be near her in L.A., but he soon died. Rex, although dedicated to staying married to Clara, took up with a much younger woman. He got what he wanted in 1962—his party's nomination for governor of Nevada—and was favored to win in November. But right after speaking at a 4th of July picnic, he died of a heart attack at age 58 inside his girlfriend's Vegas home. Rex's will left property to his girlfriend, but left out Clara completely.

In 1965, while watching a movie on TV directed by Victor Fleming and starring Gary Cooper, Clara died of a sudden heart attack in Los Angeles, at age 60. Her son Rex Jr. later became District Attorney of Clark County in Las Vegas.

6

Norma Jeane's Perjury

MARILYN MONROE

On a hot spring day in 1946, a brown-haired young woman named Norma Jeane Dougherty stepped off the train in downtown Las Vegas and was greeted by a much older lady, Minnie Willett, the aunt of Norma Jeane's foster mother in Los Angeles. Aunt Minnie lived in a clapboard, 1920s-vintage home at 604½ South Third Street and Bonneville Avenue. Norma Jeane immediately complained that her mouth was sore so the two went to Las Vegas General Hospital, where a doctor treated the teenager for a case of trench mouth, a bacterial infection that produces crater-like, stinging ulcers on the gums. The condition can be caused by poor oral hygiene, bad nutrition, or emotional stress. The remedy for it back then, before the widespread use of antibiotics, was an agonizing rinse of hydrogen peroxide over the sores.

Norma Jeane's painful trip to Las Vegas would put her on the road to stardom and tragedy. That spring, she sought to end her three-year marriage to merchant marine Jim Dougherty with a quickie Nevada divorce. Jim, who thought her modeling cost more in clothes and make-up than it brought in, rejected her career choice and couldn't be convinced otherwise. To her, there was no other choice. It was easy; all she had to do was live with Minnie in Las Vegas for the legally required six weeks and file the papers.

She sought a Las Vegas divorce to fulfill an overriding desire to become an actress. While at home in Hollywood, California, she tried and failed for months to get a screen test with Twentieth Century Fox. Norma Jeane's modeling agent, Emmeline Snively, had insisted that Hollywood studios avoided married young actresses, who might choose to become pregnant while under contract. She'd also attract more publicity if she were single. With Jim overseas in Asia, there was little he could do to stop the divorce action he knew nothing about.

Going to Vegas was actually the idea of Grace McKee, Norma Jeane's foster mom who raised her in Hollywood. Las Vegas was already known as a divorce haven. Other stars and starlets had done it there. Clark Gable's Vegas divorce carried special appeal to Norma Jeane, who confided to friends she fantasized that Gable was her real father, even after co-starring with him in the film *The Misfits* in 1960.

Though only nineteen, she already had almost two year's experience as a magazine model, with breakout success in 1946. Her face and body had appeared on the covers of more than thirty national magazines, mainly of the cheesecake variety directed toward men, such as *Peek*, *Laff*, *See*, *Titter*, *Sir*, *U.S. Camera*, *Pageant*, and *Swank*. She'd received international attention for a daring, leggy promo shot, wearing nothing but four copies of magazines with her pictures on the covers (one over each breast). Norma Jeane was a certified head-turner, particularly to the tens of thousands of horny U.S. servicemen who'd recently returned home, still drawn to the cheesecake shots made famous during the war. According to the memoirs of a boyfriend, she'd already conducted many brief affairs, with more to come in the months before her divorce trial. She had sexual experience far beyond most women her age in the sexually repressed America of the mid-1940s. Cavorting though the Hollywood bar scene since her late teens, Norma Jeane had indulged in romps with men her age and much older while her sailor husband worked overseas in 1944. She had sex appeal, and she used it to advance her career in modeling and movies.

Jim Dougherty had been the unsuspecting, cuckolded husband for quite some time. Her search for modeling work and contacts in the movie industry began two years after their 1942 marriage, while Jim was thousands of miles away. Ted Jordan, the one-time bit-part film actor, claimed he met Norma Jeane at a poolside photo shoot at a private club in Los Angeles, where he worked as a lifeguard. She told Jordan that she was separated from Dougherty. She seemed unsure when Jordan asked her out until he revealed that Dixieland jazz bandleader Ted Lewis was his uncle. She gleefully agreed to the date and insisted on meeting Lewis, even asking a surprised Jordan who Lewis's agent was. While deciding where to meet, Norma Jeane rattled off the names of several bars she'd been to. "(I)n my smitten state, I was not paying too close attention and thus did not wonder how a seventeen-year-old [she was actually eighteen] model knew the ins and outs of Hollywood nightlife."

Norma Jeane years later told Lee Strasberg, her acting instructor in New York, that she became a call girl around this time. In his 1989 memoir, Jordan claimed she told him prior to her divorce that "you know I've been promiscuous . . . you know that I don't have much money. You can't make it without money, you know that. You know what acting lessons cost, what modeling lessons run. And you know I have to pay my Aunt Grace's room and board."

She also admitted to a friend later in life that she had endured twelve abortions, starting back in mid-1940s Hollywood.

Jordan claimed he accompanied her to Tijuana in 1945 so she could abort their child. In early 1946, he introduced her to Ted Lewis, the writer Damon Runyon and radio gossip announcer Walter Winchell. She told Jordan she had affairs with all three to benefit from their contacts in Hollywood. That year, Jordan said she also confessed to accepting an invitation from Ben "Bugsy" Siegel to fly with him for a tryst in Sin City. She had met Siegel at a party he threw at his home in Beverly Hills that year.

"Siegel is a good man to know in this town, and I fucked him," Jordan recounted her as saying.

Another confession, via Jordan: she had carried on a lesbian affair in the mid-1940s with beautiful blonde dancer—and later a Las Vegas staple in the 1950s—Lili St. Cyr.

"As Norma Jeane had vowed to me, whoever she had to fuck, she was prepared to do it," Jordan said.

She had married Dougherty when she was sixteen, an arrangement made by Aunt Grace herself, who knew Jim's father. Norma Jeane's modeling career kicked off by sheer chance late in 1944, when a photographer on assignment for a military magazine, *Yank*, ran into her as she worked at a Los Angeles munitions factory, and practically hired her on a freelance basis on the spot. Weeks later, in early 1945, some of his photos of her made it to a top Hollywood modeling company, the Blue Book Agency. Blue Book got her pinup-girl cover shots into magazines and enrolled her in training for photo and fashion modeling. She was five feet five, 118 pounds, and a size twelve with measurements of 36-24-34.

Jim came back on leave in 1945 and grew tired of her frequent modeling appointments. It's your career or me, he said. Norma Jeane's new friends and lovers urged her to try to become a movie actress. Foster mother Grace encouraged her, too, telling her she resembled the 1930s film siren Jean Harlow.

She decided to divorce Jim in early 1946, after he had left on another oversees trip with the Merchant Marines.

She moved into Aunt Minnie's Vegas home on May 14, 1946. While in town for her six weeks residency, she was forced to make yet another trip to the same Las Vegas hospital, this time for a case of the measles.

Divorce filings in Las Vegas were breaking records each year since the state's divorce law was liberalized in 1931. Post-war growing pains in Las Vegas were excruciating. The city approved requests for hundreds of new slot machines in casinos, ice cream shops, grocery stores, gas stations, and motels, but growth was hampered by a severe, national shortage of construction materials. Crime, particularly robberies, juvenile delinquency and drunken driving, was growing, too. When Norma Jeane lived in Las Vegas, about 300 recent war veterans, in town waiting for divorces, roamed the streets looking for jobs. With new housing in very short supply, even permanent residents jammed local hotels, motels, and motor courts.

On Sunday afternoon, May 26, Norma Jeane walked down Third Street to Fremont Street—then the business and gambling center of Las Vegas—to watch Helldorado, an Old West-themed parade. The then-annual parade drew national attention that year, as Hollywood and the newspapers and newsreels took notice of the budding gambling capital. Gossip columnists Luella Parsons, of the Hearst newspaper chain, and Hedda Hopper, of the *Los Angeles Times*, covered it. Frank Sinatra, then a youthful, rail-thin pop singer, enhanced publicity for the parade by agreeing to be Grand Marshall, but he breezed out of town for Chicago only days before the parade without an explanation.

Norma Jeane joined thousands who lined Fremont Street to watch. The spectacle included parade floats, mounted police, covered wagons, horse buggies, people in Old Western costumes, a "Kangaroo Kourt" that judged a beard contest, and marching Indians "in all their regalia," as parade planners put it.

Leading the parade on that day, on his famous trained horse Trigger, was Roy Rogers, the singing "King of the Cowboys" and hugely popular B-movie star. Rogers was in town filming *Heldorado* for Republic Pictures (the fifty-seven-minute film was released in 1946 with the "Hell" part of the parade's name misspelled to avoid censorship). Virtually every American knew about Roy. He was the biggest-grossing cowboy star in the United States. From the early 1940s and into the mid-1950s, he filmed an average of six "horse opera" movies that together sold 80 million tickets each year.

The plot of *Heldorado* the movie turned out to be quite a prescient one. Filmed seven months before Ben Siegel and the East Coast mobster backers opened the Flamingo—the first mob-controlled Strip casino—in December 1946, *Heldorado* cast Rogers, as one synopsis put it, "as a ranger (who) helps Las Vegas authorities track down racketeers who are passing untaxed earnings."

During the parade, Rogers, a veteran of many such public events, was accompanied by his co-star (and future wife) Dale Evans, chosen as Helldorado parade queen, and Gabby Hayes, Roy's toothless movie sidekick. Part of Republic's filming of the movie included parade floats displaying Helldorado's "bathing beauties" as they drifted down the crowded boulevard.

But one budding beauty not on a float—Norma Jeane, standing in the crowd—caught Rogers's eye as he rode Trigger on the parade route. He stopped next to her, helped her onto the saddle, and took her for a brief ride on Trigger as the crowd watched. Rogers let her down off the horse and invited her to have dinner with his movie crew. She accepted and ate with them after the parade at a restaurant inside the Last Frontier

Hotel (now the New Frontier) on Highway 91 (later the Strip), where part of the film was shot. Then she walked across the street with the crew to watch the rodeo shown in the movie.

Norma Jeane's case of the measles would keep her indoors and no doubt made her life with her foster mom's sister a bore compared to her rising prospects in Hollywood. After recovering, she passed the time sunbathing outside Minnie's home (at the corner of Third and Bonneville streets). Finally, with her minimum residency completed and appointments to keep in Los Angeles, she was ready to go to court, get it over with, and move back to California. She was living in Las Vegas when she turned twenty years old on June 1, as the 100-plus-degree summer weather in Las Vegas kicked in.

On July 5, Norma Jeane Dougherty vs. James Edward Dougherty was filed in Clark County's Eighth Judicial Court. The divorce papers were signed by Norma Jeane and her lawyer C. Norman Cornwall, who doubled as Las Vegas's city attorney. The suit charged Dougherty with "extreme cruelty, (mental in nature) all without cause or provocation on the plaintiff; and that plaintiff's health is and was thereby and therefrom impaired." Her sweeping penmanship on the one-page summons for her husband to appear—the tail of the capital "N" on Norma and the "D" in Dougherty extend into the typed copy of the summons—is expressive and inspired.

The summons was mailed to Dougherty, care of the San Francisco company that owned his ship, the Joplin Victory. Dougherty, served with the papers while overseas, desperately tried to change her mind. He made expensive long distance calls to her that lasted for hours at Aunt Minnie's, to no avail. Finally, he gave up. Back in Los Angeles on August 3, Jim signed a court document waving his appearance at the divorce trial.

Now she could boast to Hollywood that she'd filed for divorce, and it worked. She entered the office of Twentieth Century Fox without an appointment on July 16, 1946. Impressed with her, a studio assistant got her a screen test at Fox. She was asked to cavort before the camera in a gown and heels, with a cigarette holder. The awestruck man shooting the footage said years later that she "had something I hadn't seen since silent pictures. She got sex on a piece of film like Jean Harlow." Fox chief Darryl Zanuck saw the test, and signed her to her first movie deal as a contract player for $75 a week on August 26. Soon, Norma Jeane and Ben Lyon, her casting agent at Fox, came up with her Marilyn Monroe stage name, after actress Marilyn Miller and Norma Jeane's mother's maiden name.

While her divorce trial in Las Vegas loomed, her star was born. But would she have to lie to the court in Vegas to get there?

On September 13, 1946, at 2 P.M., Norma Jeane took the witness stand in a Vegas district courtroom. Under oath, she swore she had been living at the Third Street home from May 14 to July 5, that she had always intended to make it her permanent place of residence and still did.

She undoubtedly committed perjury, since her true intention was to return to Hollywood. After all, she was already under contract with Fox in Los Angeles and was taking modeling assignments there. Ambition had taken over months before. Lying under oath in Las Vegas didn't faze her a bit, or at least no more than the thousands of other divorcees who'd sworn allegiance to Vegas and promptly skipped town.

In court, her attorney established that Norma Jeane had lived in Las Vegas from May 14 to July 5, the requisite six weeks. She answered "yes" when Cornwall asked her: "And when you came to Nevada May 14, 1946, was it your intention to make this your home and permanent place of residence?"

"Has it been your intention ever since then?" Cornwall asked.

"Yes," she answered.

"Is it your present intention?"

"It is."

"You intend to remain here permanently or for at least an indefinite period of time?"

"Yes."

"You have no other residence or domicile since you first came here on May 14?"

"That's right."

"Have you read the complaint which is on file in this action?"

"Yes, I have."

"And are all the allegations therein contained true?"

"Yes."

"You have alleged that your husband treated you with extreme cruelty without just cause or provocation on your part. Will you tell the court some of the acts upon which you base this cruelty charge?"

According to the court transcript, the aspiring actress explained why she charged Jim with cruelty: "Well, in the first place my husband didn't support me and he objected to my working, criticized me for it, and he also had a bad temper and would fly into rages, and he left me on three different occasions and he criticized me and embarrassed me in front of my friends, and he didn't try to make a home for me."

"Did that conduct on his part continue over a considerable period of time?" Cornwall asked.

"Yes, it did."

"And did it grow better or worse?"

"Worse."

"What effect did it have on your health?"

"It upset me and made me nervous."

"So much so you cannot live with him under the conditions
and enjoy good health?"
"Yes."
"Is reconciliation possible?"
"No."

Aunt Minnie then took the stand and swore that Norma
Jeane had indeed lived with her from May 14 to July 10, "and
then I saw her occasionally since."

The judge in the case, A.S. Henderson, got right to the bottom line. He turned to Minnie and asked, "You know Mrs. Willett, that Mrs. Dougherty has been in the County of Clark, State
of Nevada for six weeks prior to July 5, of this year?"

"Honestly," she answered.
"You saw her in Clark County, Nevada, every day?" the judge
inquired.
"I did."
The judge responded immediately: "A decree of divorce is
granted."

Jim signed the final papers in front of Norma Jeane back in
Los Angeles a couple of months later. He would describe her
as very happy at the time, but not about their split. It was about
her new name, which Jim said he liked.

Norma Jeane visited Las Vegas occasionally over the years.
Not long before her death in 1962, she sat at the same table as
her "enemy" Liz Taylor (who hated Monroe, whom she referred
to as "that whore") to watch Dean Martin perform on his birthday at the Sands.

But she might have made it on the Strip stage herself. She
received a number of offers to appear in a Vegas act over the
years, including one in 1955 that came close but never materi-
alized. Only days before her death on August 4, 1962, Marilyn

was reportedly considering a deal to star in a live stage show, with Sinatra and Elvis, in Las Vegas.

Today, Marilyn's memory is revered more in Las Vegas than in any other city. The town offers dozens of Monroe impersonators, available for hire at straight and gay wedding chapels, company meetings, and parties. The Imperial Palace hotel has used a Marilyn look-alike in a show called "Legends in Concert" for years (the impersonator also deals blackjack in the casino). The real Marilyn's 1955 Lincoln Capri convertible is part of the hotel's permanent auto collection.

Madame Tussaud's Celebrity Encounter, a collection of life-sized wax figures at The Venetian hotel, includes a replica of Marilyn in a backless cocktail dress and hoisting a champagne glass, as if to toast the town. Next to her wax statue is the seated, smiling figure of Ben Siegel, who seems to be giving her a sly once-over.

7

The Sahara's Freak Show

CHRISTINE JORGENSEN

It was spring 1953 and the Sahara hotel, less than a year old, was riding a wave of popularity with curious American tourists making their first trips to Las Vegas. The Sands had opened two months after the Sahara in late 1952 and competition for performers—the biggest draw for the gamblin' fools— was fierce. So much so that Sahara chief Milton Prell consulted the headlines for his next gimmick and chose Christine Jorgensen, the Bronx native and former G.I. whose revolutionary sex change surgery in Denmark from man to woman caused an avalanche of publicity, starting in December 1952. The tall, blonde, and long-legged Jorgensen, with no income, sought to exploit her sex operation with a nightclub career. She'd been approached by burlesque stages and carnival freak shows, and—cut out of the same cloth—Vegas beckoned, too. But Jorgensen confided to her new agent in Los Angeles that "I can't sing, I can't dance, and I can't give out snappy chatter." Nightclubs even turned her off, for of all things, moral reasons. "Although I'd been in a nightclub only once or twice in my whole life," she said in her 1967 autobiography, "I had an exaggerated idea of their low moral tone. There's no doubt that at the time, I was something of a self-righteous prude."

Prude or not, her Hollywood agent lined up a gig for her at the Orpheum Theater in Los Angeles, and a pre-show, warm-up stint at a club in Waterbury, Connecticut. She cut her 120-minute autobiographical film to just twenty minutes to supplement a pathetic song and dance act. Prell booked her sight un-seen and soon wished he hadn't. To say that Jorgensen was developing as a performer was putting it mildly. Weeks before her scheduled Vegas rendezvous, Jorgensen's so-called "act," featuring her voice-over for the edited film about her he-she switch, proved a disaster in Los Angeles. Prell sent some staff-ers to view the Los Angeles show and were distressed to see Miss Jorgensen lay an egg. Now it was Prell's turn to be self-righteous. Desperate for an excuse to cancel her Sahara con-tract, he made an incredibly lame public pronouncement—she, or he, didn't inform the hotel that she was really a he—that had the obvious, dual advantage of attracting national attention to the Sahara. Bill Miller, who booked the hotel's shows, sent (and leaked) Jorgensen a "Dear Sir" letter, stating: "Before I let Christine Jorgensen mingle with women, I want proof that she's a she! I'm not going to pull a farce on my customers. I won't give them a man dressed in women's clothing. I bought a 'she.' If the party can prove she's a woman, I'm willing to pay her $25,000 for two weeks."

Her agent filed suit. But there's no telling what would have happened if Christine had been forced to bare all for the Sa-hara—her operation in Copenhagen only involved removing her penis and testicles, plus hormone shots (her vagina-con-struction surgery took place in the late 1950s). But anyway, she rehearsed her singing and dancing with an instructor and ordered a series of expensive gowns. Her efforts paid off, against all odds. Her sold-out debut in Pittsburgh in August

1953 drew rave reviews ("The gowns made the predominantly femme audience drool, but all in all, look for Christine to be more than a once-around sensation. The girl has an act," wrote *Variety*). Prell and company at the Sahara took notice of her ticket sales, and her performance at the mob-owned Tropicana hotel in Havana, Cuba, and agreed to bring her to Vegas. Miller himself greeted her at the airport that November.

On stage, she wooed the mostly straight-laced, middle class audiences during her two-week stay, prompting Prell to declare her show a hit. While becoming, she said, "addicted to slot machines" in the casino, Jorgensen was hit by another Sahara publicity release seeking to capitalize on her. Publicists traced a large bouquet of yellow roses sent to Christine in Vegas to a Pat Flanigan, a male friend of hers in Washington, D.C., and then planted a story that Christine and Pat were engaged. They both denied it, "but the damage had been done," she lamented in her book, probably because it painted Pat as a "homo" in the repressed 1950s. "Pat felt repercussions at once, and lost several jobs because his name had been linked with my name." Thanks to the Sahara, the media "were no doubt responsible for the misconception that I was, or still am, married—a false impression that prevails to this day." Jorgensen died of cancer in California in 1989 at age sixty-three.

8

Mrs. Bates's Closet

VERA KRUPP

She'd finally married a millionaire, and would never again have to stoop to the indignities of earning a living, like working in a department store. But Vera Krupp was restless in her husband's isolated family home in Essen, West Germany, in the mid-1950s. It was where her sensitive hubby, Alfried Krupp, once the arms builder for Adolf Hitler's formidable war machine, lived while trying to reorganize his German family's famous businesses. Vera finally left, denouncing Essen as "a hideous, provincial, joyless city," and fled into the arms of the president of a construction company she owned. Exposed in her affair by the man's wife, in 1956 Vera returned to a place that had served her well as a refuge from the responsibilities of her four marriages and her chronic boredom—Las Vegas.

That refuge today is a Nevada state park, the Spring Mountain Ranch, about fifteen miles west of Las Vegas. Guides inside the 1948 ranch house talk almost wistfully of its wealthy former owner, the late German aristocrat and former actress Frau Krupp. The place is sort of part museum, part shrine—to denial.

The guides show the curious her closet, now covered by a glass window, displaying some of her expensive, small-sized, dresses, shoes, and furs. She was once an actress in the German theater, they'll explain. And despite her great wealth, she loved the simple life on the ranch. She was also wily and clever about guarding her privacy. The closet door leads to a secret corridor and a secret back bedroom and bath. And, yes, she once owned the fabulous 33.6-carat Krupp diamond that would later grace Liz Taylor.

It's far less likely the curators of the ranch house will say much about the controversies that followed Frau Krupp throughout her free-spirited adult life as one of history's most infamous and unabashed gold-diggers.

Vera Hossenfeldt, the daughter of an insurance man in Germany, was an unsuccessful actress who had already been through three marriages by the early 1950s. She left her first husband, a German baron, in 1938 and immigrated to Hollywood to marry a would-be movie producer. But in the 1940s, with World War II and all, Hollywood was cool about casting Germans in American film roles, and both she and her husband failed to make it in the movies. While in Southern California, where she became a U.S. citizen, she—likely with considerable disappointment—worked in a department store on Wilshire Boulevard and then as a receptionist for a naturalized German-American doctor, for whom she dumped her second husband to get hitched again.

During the 1940s, Vera came to know the growing burg of Las Vegas very well. It's where she divorced her last two husbands, including the doctor. She left for her native Germany, after forwarding her alimony checks from her third marriage, a few years after the war.

She would marry Alfried in 1952. The infamous Herr Krupp had run the age-old Krupp family military weapons company that built the Panzer tanks and other major accessories of Hitler's military. Alfried had joined Hitler's fledging SS security forces in 1931 and was a top financier of Hitler's election campaign for chancellor in 1932. During WWII, Alfried ran the outsourced Krupp company that oversaw 100,000 concentration camp slave laborers, who were subject to torture and persecution in miserable conditions, making armaments for Germany. The company also managed Bushmannshof, a concentration camp for the infants and children under two years old of the forced laborers.

Alfried was convicted of war crimes during the post-war trials of German VIPs at Nuremberg in 1948 and sentenced to 12 years in prison, but he negotiated himself out of jail in 1951. Vera, his prison pen pal, saw him as a good catch. She soon married him in the scenic German mountain village of Berchtesgaden—Hitler's favorite place. Her official name thus became Frau Vera Hossenfeldt von Langer Wisbar Knauer Krupp von Bohlen und Halbach.

William Manchester, in his 1968 book on her husband's family, *The Arms of Krupp*, described Vera as "a sophisticated, aggressive, kittenish blonde, beautiful, petite, with a heart-shaped face, a stunning figure, a yearning for adventure and no conspicuous inhibitions; she was one of the charter members of the jet set. (Alfried) Krupp was defenseless against such a woman. She could devour him. She did."

As for Alfried, he was in love with his pretty new wife. "The only time I saw him smile after the war was when he was with Frau Vera," one Krupp servant stated in Manchester's book.

She drove her Porsche to high-class shops and beauty parlors away from Herr Krupp's German castle in the mountains. Poor Vera was before long fed up with Krupp's for-rich-men-only pursuits such as hunting and sailing, his inattention and obsessive devotion to his revived family company. She took off by herself on Alfried's dime to spend vacations to Monte Carlo and the Lido beach in Venice. Frau Krupp missed the Yank nightlife out west. She once exclaimed to a witness, "Oh, how I miss Las Vegas, Los Angeles, my golden California sunshine!"

Alfried soon realized how different he and his wife were. He was committed to his family's 150-year-old munitions business. Alfried's millions mattered far less to him. While many German women of the time were homebodies, the Americanized, independent Vera was not. Unlike her female contemporaries in Germany, she tried to inject herself into her husband's business decisions. She could not understand why "a man could drive himself day after day when he could write a check for a hundred million dollars," according to Manchester. She asked why he never read books, or took her to concerts, or held lavish parties with society people. His answer: "A man like me, living a life like mine, has very little free time."

Vera was wily and strong-willed, probing about her husband's net worth. She learned he had about $250 million socked away in banks in six countries. She quickly left her fourth husband behind for more jet-setting in America.

"Gossip columnists reported her surfacing in New York café society, emerging from Las Vegas gambling casinos, bathing in the California sun," Manchester wrote. "Alfried's wife had become a swinger before the word was known. She preferred to dine with actors, mobsters, and rich European expatriates."

She voyaged back to the United States and headed for Vegas. Now settled in her web, the devious Vera was ready to dump the unsuspecting Alfried and file for her third Nevada divorce. Boy, would she make him pay for his foolish choice of a spouse! In October 1956, Vera's Vegas suit listed much of Alfried's extensive financial holdings, asked for a check for $5 million immediately, plus $250,000 in alimony per year, which she thought was more than fair.

Besides, Vera had her lawyer write in her Vegas divorce papers, Alfried was a failure as a doting rich husband; he made her kowtow to his mother's rigid house rules in the castle of Krupp and even insisted that she abandon her U.S. citizenship. "I prize my freedom in the United States more than all his gold!" she related in an interview with a German journalist. The German press called the settlement offer "her price for freedom and silence."

To sweeten the pot, so to speak, she ignominiously accused Alfried of depriving her of sex. "The defendant did, willfully and without cause, withdraw from the marriage bed and has persistently refused to have matrimonial intercourse with the plaintiff," her filing read. But as author Manchester pointed out, she couldn't have counted on having sex from a man living in Europe while she lived in the United States, where Alfried as a convicted war criminal could not even visit. There was worldwide publicity. The stoic, but inwardly suffering Alfried settled privately.

It was her Alfried who suggested through intermediaries she settle down in a place he'd heard about, the isolated, 520-acre Bar Nothing Ranch in Red Rock Canyon outside her beloved Las Vegas. Herr Krupp bought it for her from former "Lum & Abner" NBC radio comedian Chet Lauck for more than a million bucks. It was Vera who would rename it Spring Mountain Ranch and remodel and modernize its quaint ranch house.

Vera got busy with her money. She received a Nevada gaming license and acquired a 17-percent share of the Last Frontier hotel, one of the few casinos without mob ties on the Strip. But she couldn't get along with the managers of the money-losing Vegas hotel and she sold out less than a year later.

As rich as she was, she didn't consider what a sitting duck she was in her secluded hideaway. In 1959, after word got out that the $250,000 Krupp diamond was at the ranch, three thieves tied up Vera and her employees and ripped it off. The ring-mounted rock later turned up in New Jersey, seven men were eventually convicted, and she got it back.

By early 1967, Vera, who now owned a hefty collection of expensive Russian art, had grown weary of the ranch. She tried to sell it as a park to the state for $1.1 million, but the multi-millionaire Howard Hughes, still in his buy-up Vegas mood, paid for it in June that year after taking a tour. The ranch finally did become a state park in 1974.

The former Frau Krupp didn't enjoy her new cash for very long. She moved to West Los Angeles, but died on October 16, 1967, only eleven weeks after Herr Krupp's death. In May 1968, actor Richard Burton bought the gaudy Krupp diamond for $305,000 for his wife Liz at Sotheby's auction house in New York (it was not nearly as gaudy as the sixty-nine-carat rock Liz later demanded, which cost poor Richard $1.1 million). Of the diamond's Krupp family origins, Liz was quoted as saying: "It's fitting . . . that a nice Jewish girl like me has ended up with the Baron's rock."

But today, Vera Krupp's dubiously revered ghost—and Mrs. Bates-like closet of clothes out of the movie "Psycho"—lives on in her former oasis.

9

Striking Oil

LOUIS ARMSTRONG

When famed jazz trumpeter Louis Armstrong arrived at the airport off the Las Vegas Strip on August 1, 1955, a baggage man placed Armstrong's portable typewriter precariously on top of a pile of luggage in a truck headed to the new Moulin Rouge, Vegas's first integrated hotel-casino that opened only five weeks earlier. Armstrong, a prolific writer, used it to type letters he sent to friends. But the typewriter fell to the ground with a crash and broke. So when he got to his room at the Moulin, he had to use pen and paper to write a long, inspired letter to his business manager, Joe Glaser. Armstrong, then fifty-four, was happy about his toddler daughter, and something else: "All the money couldn't make me happier than I am now—this minute. Why? Because I've just came from the bathroom taking A Good 'Sh-t' And what's better than A Good Sh-t?—Hm?"

The main purpose of his letter was to express his confidence in Glaser and discuss business, and other private things, before Armstrong's wife Lucille was to arrive by plane that night. One thing he wanted to get across was "it's so grand to be with a woman, so why fight it . . . that's why I have several Chicks that I enjoy whaling with the same I do with Lucille. And She's, Always the Choicest Ass of them All."

He described just how good the sex he had with his wife was in Las Vegas two years before—when his daughter was conceived—after some lesser sessions on tour. His inspiration in bed in 1953 followed his celebrated pairing with Metropolitan Opera singer Robert Merrill at the Sands.

"When two people are in a room by themselves, Kissing will lead to fucking every time. P.S. of course Sweets + I didn't Swing but once in Montreal. Sort of a 'Warm-Up.' Once in Toronto—Minneapolis, etc.—But where we really *Whaled* and that Cute little baby girl was made—was in Las Vegas—during the time when we were appearing at the *Sands Hotel*—And Robert Merrill and I did that fine finale together. Every night, we *Whaled*. I mean, I really *Grind* in that Cunt. I Could feel it Just as good when I *Struck Oil*—And planted that cute little Baby . . . You see, I don't live to do Anything wrong. It's so much easier, and more wonderful to do things Right."

10

Get Happy Pills, Please

JUDY GARLAND

On New Year's Eve, 1957, the famous but declining film star Judy Garland got ready to take the stage in the Flamingo hotel showroom.

Two years before, wearing a hat and short skirt that showed off her trim legs, she'd sung—while drunk as hell—to good reviews at the New Frontier hotel. But she had to perform another night there just to recoup the money her husband and manager, Sid Luft, had gambled away on the Frontier's casino tables (customers could hear her backstage shrieks at Sid about his losses). In May 1957, on stage during another stint at the Flamingo, she introduced her nine-year-old daughter, Liza.

By December, exhausted after five weeks of shows in London and a command performance before Queen Elizabeth II of England, Judy tried to get out of her contract for another series of Vegas shows, but the Flamingo refused. The pay was lucrative, and Sid produced the gig, but in Vegas there would be no celebrity galas like she'd have with Donna Reed and Petula Clark, and no stage full of bouquets that greeted her in England. The cultural downshift was considerable. When she arrived on the Strip, Garland was weary and alarmingly fat, due to a liver condition from drug and alcohol abuse that made her retain huge amounts of fluid. After opening night on December 26, she lost her voice and cancelled several performances. She would not be forgiven.

Minutes into her New Year's Eve's act, some drunken rowdies in the crowd turned mean and started jeering. Their once-diminutive Dorothy had become bloated and obese, double her former size. Though only thirty-five years old, she looked more like fifty-something. The taunts continued in breaks between songs, despite pleas by her and her fans. Some threw paper hats at her on stage and yelled for her to party with them. When she again tried to get the crowd to stop, an angry goomba up front yelled, "shut up!" and then shouted, "Get outta here! You're too fat, and we don't wanna hear you anyway!" The final straw came when a pair of sauced women leaped on stage and did a hula dance. The humor was lost on Judy. She not only walked off stage, she skipped town with additional performances remaining in her contract. The Flamingo later sued her over it, but lost in court.

A couple of years earlier, Garland had become one of the first members of Humphrey Bogart's original Rat Pack, a group created purely by old-fashioned Hollywood-hype publicity. What began only as a momentary diversion during a 1955 dinner party in Holmby Hills above Beverly Hills—during which Lauren Bacall made her infamous remark, "I see the rat pack is all here"—would by 1960 turn into the single most successful publicity gimmick ever for Las Vegas.

Garland, her husband Luft, Frank Sinatra, Bogart, and others had fun with Bacall's "rat pack" remark that night (at the time, clashes involving Los Angeles police and a violent youth gang the newspapers called "the rat pack" made national headlines). Bogart's partiers appointed gag "officers" of a "board," and that might have been that, if the *New York Herald-Tribune* hadn't splashed: "The Holmby Hills Rat Pack held its first annual meeting last night at Romanoff's restaurant in Beverly Hills and elected officers for the coming year," wrote gossip reporter Joe Hyams. "Named to executive positions were: Frank Sinatra, pack master; Judy Garland, first vice president; Lauren Bacall, den mother; Sid Luft, cage master; Humphrey Bogart, rat in charge of public relations . . ."

It's hard to picture the frail, bipolar Garland as a cool Rat Packer with Frank, Dean, Sammy, Peter Lawford and maybe Joey Bishop. But Garland made it to Las Vegas long before any of them, or practically any other noted American performer. She sang and danced at the Meadows—opened in 1931, the first modern nightclub and casino in Las Vegas—in the early 1930s at the tender age of ten. Her name then was Francis Gumm, the youngest of the three Gumm Sisters, a traveling vaudeville act (later renamed the Garland Sisters) managed by her bisexual father, Frank. Studio employees introduced Judy to amphetamines and barbiturates—uppers and downers, available then without a prescription—to cope with the pressure when she was a sixteen-year-old film actor with MGM in Hollywood in the late 1930s. She used them and landed the role of her life, as Dorothy in *The Wizard of Oz*, in 1938. But by age twenty, Garland was a confirmed pill addict, and it would take its toll.

Preparing for a return engagement in Vegas in 1962, perpetually in financial difficulty (her former manager, David Begelman, had recently embezzled hundreds of thousands from her), Garland was determined not to suffer through what happened at the Flamingo in 1957. She had slimmed down after treatment for her liver ailment (and the removal of more than two gallons of fluid from her body) and visits to a celebrity weight control ranch north of Los Angeles. Days before her arrival, a daily diet of only two cups of unsweetened tea landed her in the hospital with kidney trouble. She had just finished her final movie, *I Could Go On Singing*, a box office failure that ended her twenty-five-year film career. Her six-week engagement at the Sahara that year served two purposes—a badly needed paycheck, and qualifying for residency to obtain a Nevada divorce from husband Sid. Performing at night, Garland stayed in all day, sedated in her hotel bed. To get her off the downers before her performances, the Sahara had to bring in a local doctor to give her an injection that neutralized the drug (as was used for singers Eddie Fisher and Betty Hutton). To meet her physical requirements (chronic insomnia), and keep gamblers up late, the Sahara scheduled her shows at 2:30 A.M. Meanwhile, Judy's manager fended off calls from local reporters, who gossiped about her premature aging. One former Las Vegas journalist said years later, without sympathy: "If you know what a hag looks like, she was a *hag*."

Judy was on tour in the Far East in 1964 while Sue, her eldest Gumm sister, lived alone in Las Vegas, depressed and, like her youngest sister, pill-addicted. Judy offered little help during Sue's desperate phone calls from Vegas. Sue's husband, Jack Cathcart, musical director for the Riviera (and Judy's conductor in Vegas), had just divorced her to marry a younger woman. Sue survived several overdoses but she finally died that year from too many Nembutals. As Virginia, the middle Gumm sister, later observed about Sue's life: "Living in Las Vegas, that's not a particularly tranquil atmosphere; the gambling, the girls, the temptations. When Jack and Sue obtained a divorce— that was the end for her. She went the sleeping pill route." So would Judy. She married homosexual actor Mark Herron in Vegas (in the Little Chapel of the West, a fifteen-minute, get-hitched shack at the Frontier hotel) in 1965. Judy said they never had sex during the five-month marriage, although Mark would later have a gay affair with—ironically—Liza's husband Peter Allen, only months after Allen had married Liza in 1967. Still in financial trouble, Garland performed despite pleas from her doctor to retire. Her last Vegas performance was a week of midnight shows at Caesars Palace in late 1967. One performance was described by the normally fawning *Variety* as "unsettling . . . sometimes awkward and disturbing . . ." In 1969, at age forty-seven, while locked in the bathroom of a hotel in London, Judy died from an accidental overdose of barbiturates while battling strep throat.

11

Sagging Career

JAYNE MANSFIELD

*I*f Las Vegas is known as the elephant's graveyard of washed-up entertainers, Jayne Mansfield proved to be a fine specimen. Her acting career skyrocketed on Broadway with her squeaky, bosomy turn in *Will Success Spoil Rock Hunter?* for 450 performances from 1955 to 1956, followed the next year by the successful movie of the same name, with actor Tony Randall. Shamelessly exploiting herself in tight dresses and barely covered, huge breasts (her full measurements: 40-21-35), she would be regarded as the world's most photographed Hollywood celebrity. Her notoriety landed her a six-week stint in Vegas in 1958 at the Tropicana. For $20,000 a week, backed by her new husband, former Mr. Universe, Mickey Hargitay, and a chorus of leering men, Mansfield cavorted on stage in a "net dress" with sequins designed to cover her nipples and pubic hair but that were revealed anyway whenever she moved. By 1959, her movie career was sinking. Mansfield made second-rate films and paid appearances at White Front discount department stores. It was time to return to Vegas, where her biggest paychecks now awaited, while she served as casino bait. In

1960, she made $25,000 a week for something labeled "House of Love," at the middle-class Dunes Hotel. With nipple sequins on her chest, she chased after Mickey, dressed in pajamas (for a measly $1,000 a week), who'd sit on a heart-shaped bed reading Sigmund Freud. Her bra strap was designed to fall on opening night. But the show made her self-conscious; she lied about he age to the press (twenty-five instead of twenty-eight), and started to drink heavily. She told her publicist she feared her sex-symbol shtick was wearing thin, even in Vegas, and her career along with it. "She made a lot of pictures that weren't successful so she got to thinking she wasn't going to make it on talent," the publicist told a biographer, Martha Saxton. "She tried to go the other way. Agents lost respect for her. They forgot she had talent because of the schlocky things she'd do. People forgot she was good."

Mansfield's career blipped up after she divorced Hargitay in 1964 and married low-budget movie director Matt Cimber. Cimber steered her into a hit play in New York that paid $11,000 a week, but he turned down the part offered her on TV's *Gilligan's Island* which later went to Tina Louise. By 1965, Jayne headed down again; her latest film, *Single Room Furnished*, directed by Matt, made it to only a handful of drive-ins. She returned to Vegas again. Cimber directed her in *The Las Vegas Hillbillies* (1966), an awful, micro-budget movie in which Jayne aids a pair of Appalachian hicks opening a country music bar in Las Vegas. Divorced from Matt, in the hole to the IRS for $50,000, Jayne took her sagging act to the staid Fremont Hotel in seedy downtown Vegas for four weeks and a lot less money than her Strip shows. While in her suite at the Fremont, her divorce attorney, Sam Brody, visited her, fell in love and left his wife and kids and law practice, all for Jayne. Her agent Sam Cowan entered the suite and saw dolls, teddy bears, and other presents from Brody. Brody's devotion would take him on a car trip to New Orleans with Jayne on June 29, 1967, when both were killed after their car drove under a truck in a blinding night fog. The Fremont Hotel later sent a bill to her estate for $7,074 in unpaid costume expenses.

12

Meet Me in Las Vegas

JFK

In the late evening of Sunday, February 7, 1960, five weeks after he announced he was running for the Democratic nomination for President, the forty-two-year-old Massachusetts Senator John Kennedy sat in the narrow Copa Lounge, overlooking the casino at the Sands hotel, with his younger brother Teddy, both guests of Frank Sinatra. JFK had just been campaigning— without his wife—in Indiana, West Virginia, North Dakota, and New Mexico. It was time to have a little fun at the Sands, the coolest spot in town. That weekend, the cameras were rolling on two feature films at the Sands—*Ocean's 11*, starring Frank and "The Clan," and *Pepe*, with Mexican actor Mario Morenas Cantinflas, Dan Dailey, and Cesar Romero. Photographers from *Life* magazine, in town to see if Sinatra would let them shoot the *Ocean's* set (he wouldn't), ignored Kennedy.

The trip would be the first of two visits Kennedy made to Las Vegas in the early 1960s. The Sands visit triggered a foolish, two-year affair with a Sinatra party girl that would threaten to wreck his career, and even put national security at risk in the months leading to the Cuban Missile Crisis. The other trip took place only seven weeks before his assassination on November 22, 1963, a brief stop during which he rode in the same open limousine that would take him through Dealey Plaza in Dallas.

Kennedy reached Nevada just as the campaign for the 1960 Democratic Presidential nomination was heating up. The front-runners included Kennedy and Senators Lyndon Johnson of Texas and Hubert Humphrey of Minnesota. Nevada had no party primary in 1960; Democrats there elected delegates to the national convention at a state convention. Kennedy was in Las Vegas to meet with local Democratic party leaders and line up support at Nevada's convention—to be held in April in Vegas—and send delegates to the national convention in July in Los Angeles. He faced an uphill battle; both of Nevada's Democratic U.S. Senators, Alan Bible and Howard Cannon, were Johnson supporters.

Hours before Kennedy landed in Las Vegas, Senator Barry Goldwater, an Arizona Republican, told radio reporters that if Johnson ran with Kennedy as his vice-presidential running mate, they would be the hardest for Republicans to beat in 1960, because, Goldwater believed, Johnson was the only Democrat who could carry the South. Also that day, Kennedy had stood before a crowd of 4,000 people in Albuquerque, New Mexico, and criticized Johnson for not entering any of the Democratic primaries, which only recently had become a popular method of selecting convention delegates.

Kennedy, who had already ruled out a bid for vice president, had qualified to be on the primary ballots in seven states. Johnson chose to avoid the primaries and appeal directly for delegates from individual states. While selling himself to Western voters, Kennedy had informed the New Mexicans that the population of the West would grow an estimated four times faster than the rest of the United States and so would "need twice as much water" to sustain itself.

Hidden mob ownership in Strip and downtown casinos—including members of Mafia families in Chicago, Cleveland, New York, Miami, and Boston—was at its height at the time of Kennedy's 1960 trip. The town was an infamous den of vice, where sex could be delivered by "house" girls run by pit bosses in the casinos and by "freelance" girls and boys in unlicensed, so-called "massage parlors."

The same day that JFK arrived, Las Vegas police had arrested two notorious Los Angeles-based mobsters, John "The Bat" Battaglia and Louis Tom Dragna, on vagrancy charges as they sat in a hotel cocktail lounge on the Strip. Dragna, an ex-con, had been free on $25,000 bail while on trial in Los Angeles on charges of fixing boxing matches for welterweight fighter Don Jordan with co-defendants Frankie Carbo, Frank "Blinky" Palermo, and Joseph Sica, and ousted former National Boxing Association president Truman Gibson. Police also saw Battaglia as a suspect in a scheme to bilk money from a Texas man who gambled in Las Vegas hotels.

Sheriff W. E. "Butch" Leypoldt, upon hearing that Battaglia and Dragna were in town, ordered deputies to arrest them for vagrancy, telling the news media later that his department would do its best to break up meetings of underworld figures in town. Vegas attorney Harry Claiborne, who specialized in defending local hoodlums, got both men out on $500 bail. After he was released, Battaglia was arrested again that day for driving forty miles per hour in a school zone.

Battaglia and Dragna beat their vagrancy raps the following day, Monday, February 8, after District Attorney George Foley concluded there wasn't enough evidence and dropped charges. Later that day, while JFK was staying at the Sands, Foley and Sheriff Leypoldt approached Clark County commissioners with a proposal to strengthen the vagrancy law to crack down on prostitutes and Mafia hoods.

Foley labeled the county's vagrancy law "a farce," leaving law enforcement "powerless to keep the big hoodlums out of here." The district attorney and police also requested a new law to make it illegal for a woman to proposition a man for sex for money. House whores then included married women and even schoolteachers working weekdays in Los Angeles and plying their trade on Fridays and Saturdays in Las Vegas for hotel guests. About twenty-five of these "weekenders" might work inside a single Strip casino on a given night, but arrests were few and hard to make stick in court.

"The problem today is the woman who is solicited by pit bosses, hosts, bellhops and other persons where it is almost impossible to catch them," complained Foley. "These people are laughing at the law . . . You're going to have a hard time getting a seat at a bar if we don't control it some way."

Las Vegas-area Democratic leaders announced they'd hold a reception for Senator Kennedy, at the newly completed Las Vegas Convention Center set for 5 P.M. that Monday.

Kennedy might have had a lot on his mind while in Vegas, but on that Sunday night, there was no press to be seen and he was able to focus on the pursuit of pleasure with Frank, Teddy, and friends at the Sands.

It was there in the Sands lounge that JFK brother-in-law and Sinatra "Clan" member Peter Lawford introduced Jack to Frank's friend and former bedmate, Judith Campbell (later Judith Campbell Exner). She was a bright, pretty, twenty-five-year-old raven-haired, blue-eyed divorcée and celebrity sexual adventurer. Unemployed and a frequenter of Las Vegas, Campbell supported herself with money from her wealthy dad, a Los Angeles architect, and alimony from a failed marriage. Frank made sure she was comped during her trips to Las Vegas.

It was a fateful meeting. The Kennedy-Campbell affair would last over the next two years, until FBI Director J. Edgar

Hoover learned through wiretapped telephone conversations that Campbell was a close friend of two of the most notorious celebrity mobsters of the time, Johnny Rosselli of Los Angeles and Sam Giancana of Chicago. Giancana and other Mafia leaders had appointed the ex-con Rosselli to oversee the mob's clandestine casino investments, and multimillion-dollar skimming of casino proceeds, in Las Vegas in 1957. Rosselli, in whose West Hollywood apartment Campbell would live in 1963, was a regular visitor to Las Vegas, and frequently sunned himself poolside at the Desert Inn, a block north of the Sands.

From late 1960 to 1961, Rosselli and Giancana had worked with the CIA on a secret plan to hire an assassin to kill Cuban President Fidel Castro, hopefully before the CIA's planned Bay of Pigs invasion of Cuba in April 1961. By late summer 1960, unable to neutralize Castro on their own, CIA officials decided to hire mobsters. The mobsters knew Cuba from the casinos they ran in Havana that Castro closed in 1959. The agency turned to a U.S. spy (and later a key aide in Las Vegas to Howard Hughes) named Bob Maheu, who met and hired Rosselli. Rosselli subsequently brought his associate Giancana and Cuban-born Miami gangster Santo Trafficante, Jr., in on the planning to do away with Castro. The incredible scheme Rosselli and Giancana hatched in October 1960 involved a female assassin who would get close to Castro, drop a slow-acting poison pill in his drink, and leave.

Campbell, formerly Judith Inmoor, was a native of New York City but was raised in a twenty-four-room house in Pacific Palisades, an exclusive, seaside neighborhood next to Santa Monica, California. Film comedians Bob Hope and Bert Lahr were family friends. In 1950, at age sixteen, she dated budding actor Robert Wagner. One night, Wagner introduced her to her future husband, a struggling movie actor named William L. Campbell, who would act opposite John Wayne in

Operation Pacific in 1951 and Humphrey Bogart in *Battle Circus* in 1953 (he is best known as the spoiled alien Trelane in a 1967 episode of TV's *Star Trek*, called "The Squire of Gothos").

When Judith turned eighteen in 1952, she married the twenty-six-year-old "Billy" Campbell and moved to the Hollywood Hills, but it proved a bad pairing. In her 1977 ghostwritten book, *My Story*, Judith ripped her spouse apart, describing him as "an extremely weak man" and "dull, selfish." She rebelled, went off on a trip to Vegas with her sister, and broke wall mirrors during tantrums.

By the late 1950s, the marriage was spiraling down. Judith claimed that after she confronted Billy about another woman, he hit her. Judith then had an affair of her own, filed for divorce in 1958, and got one in 1959, along with the monthly alimony. She shacked up with a new boyfriend for a few months before meeting Sinatra at a Los Angeles restaurant. The Chairman promptly invited her to Hawaii and she dropped everything to fly over at his expense. On November 7, 1959, she met Lawford, Lawford's wife, Pat (JFK's sister), and other Sinatra pals there. The Rat Pack, also known as "The Clan," then included Sinatra, Dean Martin, Sammy Davis Jr., the comic Joey Bishop, songwriter Jimmy Van Heusen, and Lawford. Frank was working with Van Heusen on music for *Ocean's 11*, Frank's Strip casino robbery movie to be filmed in Las Vegas in a couple of months in early 1960. Campbell was the Chairman's kept woman for the week.

They had sex three times that first night and morning in Frank's Hawaiian hotel suite. When she returned to Los Angeles, she had dinner with her unsuspecting boyfriend and his mother, and no doubt carefully selected the details of her trip.

All through December, Campbell continued her affair with Sinatra at his Palm Springs home, a couple of hours southeast of Los Angeles. There, Frank first told her about his friend Jack Kennedy who was running for president. Both playboys, Frank and JFK, who also met through Lawford, had clicked. Frank made Jack an honorary member of the pack, and nicknamed it "the Jack Pack."

Campbell's sexual relationship with Frank ended one night in December 1959 in Palm Springs, when he entered their boudoir with a naked black woman, who went down on him in their bed before leaving. Judith, in tears, ran from the bed to the bathroom, and the easy times were over despite Frank's attempts to make things right. That didn't stop Judith from accepting his invitations for free stays in Vegas to watch Frank's "Clan" shows at the Sands. Each time, when Frank would come on to her, she'd spurn his advances, pout like a princess, and come back again.

Sinatra had made the Sands the town's most popular casino. He'd opened the Copa Room himself when the Sands debuted in 1952, when its interest holders included a list of organized crime associates led by Joseph "Doc" Stacher of the New Jersey mob, who still ran the hotel into the early 1960s. Frank, who owned a 9 percent interest in the Sands casino in 1960, was earning as much as $100,000 a week as a performer there.

Campbell was maintaining this "hands-off me Frank" pretense during one such free Vegas trip when she met JFK. By then, Frank and company were about halfway through filming *Ocean's 11* at five hotels on the Strip. The shooting days would end in the late afternoon, after which Frank, Martin, Davis, Bishop and Lawford would relax in the Sands steam room and later perform two or three shows a night. At the time, showroom fashion among spectators was on the formal side; men in suits and women in mink and sable wraps, even on hot nights, were common in those days.

The Clan's shows on this run were booked from January 20

to February 16. Frank had dubbed the grouping "The Summit" after the recent Summit Conference held by the United States, France, and the Soviet Union. Frank's version drew almost as much press attention, as stories about the Clan's Summit in Vegas made headlines in newspapers from Latin America to Europe.

"The Sands was the hub and you could hardly push your way through the lobby and casino," Sammy Davis wrote about those few weeks in his autobiography. "Hundreds of people crowded the entrance to the Copa Room."

Campbell would state that when she met Senator Kennedy in the Sands lounge, he "looked so handsome in his pinstriped suit. Those strong white teeth and smiling Irish eyes." She was invited to dine that night at the Sands small Garden Room restaurant with the Kennedy brothers, Lawford, and Gloria Cahn (wife of Sinatra songwriter Sammy Cahn, whose song-writing credits included the movie *Meet Me in Las Vegas*). Campbell and Mrs. Cahn indulged in a barely concealed catfight while vying for consideration from the male VIPs. Mrs. Cahn, Campbell said, "butted right in with some inane political comment" every time Jack or Teddy tried to talk to Campbell. "Anything to keep the attention away from me and on herself," Campbell hissed. Lawford, she claimed, "expounded on interminable lengths" about the recent filming of *Oceans 11*.

After eating, they went next door to the Copa Room to catch the Clan's late night show. Parts of the performance were filmed from the rear of the showroom. Campbell was seated at a front table next to Ted, across from Jack. Also at the table to witness the scene was Associated Press writer Jim Bacon. Campbell had seen the show a number of times already, and so took the time to eye Jack.

"I could observe him without creating attention, and I must say that I was tremendously impressed by his poise and wit and charm. He talked to all the women at the table, and when he listened it was as if every nerve and muscle in his body was poised at attention."

On stage, according to Sammy Davis's account of the night, Frank poured a drink from the show's liquor cart and gave Sammy the honor of introducing "the next president." Senator Kennedy stood up into the just-turned spotlight. The film crew got it on celluloid for posterity, showing Kennedy turning, smiling, and waving to the applauding crowd. Into his mike, Dean Martin deadpanned: "Who did you say that was?"

When the show ended, Kennedy, Campbell, and the others in the group retreated to the Sands cocktail lounge. In Campbell's account, it was Teddy who made the first move on her. He asked her to show him the Strip and she agreed. A Vegas veteran, Campbell wrote that she and Teddy casino-hopped and drank, ending up at the lounge at the Flamingo hotel, where she was staying. She finally let married man Teddy see her to her room in the wee hours, where she insisted she firmly rebuffed his obvious advances. She declined his request that she fly with him on a campaign trip to Denver. The smitten Teddy called hours later to say he skipped his flight, but she turned him down again.

Campbell definitely preferred Jack to Teddy, whom she said "had nowhere near the charm and sophistication or just plain likeability of Jack." And so it was that the princess got the dream call she wanted. JFK phoned her room later that morning and asked her to have lunch at the Sands. Their reckless association was about to start.

When she arrived, Campbell said Kennedy interrupted a press conference he was giving in a hallway outside the Sands casino. "Judy, I'll be right with you, we're just finishing up," Campbell said he told her.

"I could have fallen off the bench in a dead faint," she wrote.

"All the newspapermen had turned around to look at me. Jack didn't seem to mind at all. He didn't even flinch."

Apparently unfazed, Kennedy switched his attention back to the reporters in the hall and their questions of complicated political matters, answering off the cuff and with apparent success. According to news accounts of the time, he said would not accept an offer to be vice president. He conceded that 200 Democratic delegates in New Mexico had come out for Johnson, and that Johnson was his toughest opponent. The main issue for 1960 would be "internationalism" and the next president would have to deal "with Russia and Communist nations, such as in the realm of nuclear weapons, Berlin, disarmament, and the United Nations."

Kennedy repeated his support for halting nuclear weapons testing only if the Soviets agreed to do so. He said France's decision two days earlier to explode its first nuclear weapon at the Nevada Test Site—ninety miles northwest of Las Vegas—in only a week's time "would be one more alarm bell in an already dangerous situation. Then again, there is the curious situation of pressure against France to halt their testing whereas the United States, Great Britain, and Russia have tested in the past. The situation then created is another nation in the nuclear club and possibly others soon making testing all the more difficult to control."

Kennedy added that he'd drop out of the race if he could not win in the upcoming primaries and would "concentrate on my Senatorial duties."

As soon as the reporters left, JFK turned his attention back to Judy. He proposed that they eat outdoors on the patio of Frank's ground level personal suite at the Sands. Frank came through again. "I want a chance to talk with you without the interruptions we would get in the restaurant," Judy said he told her, without acknowledging his rakish maneuvering.

They entered the three-room suite, went outside and sat under a metal awning on the patio, overlooking a large lawn and a small swimming pool, bordered by a high cement-block wall. It was an unseasonably warm afternoon. They talked for about three hours.

"It was lovely on Frank's patio," Campbell related. "There was not another soul around. I don't have the faintest recollection of what we had for lunch . . . I do remember a great deal of what we discussed because of his attentiveness and what seemed an almost insatiable interest in what and who I was.

"The main topic of conservation, once I had given him my family history, was religion," she went on, still playing coy to Kennedy's ingratiating, playboy routine. Campbell, herself raised Catholic, told him she figured his Catholicism would influence him as president.

"That's why I have to expose myself to as many people as possible as soon as possible," she quoted him, which if true amounted to setting up a potential new girlfriend. "The issues I'm interested in have nothing to do with religion. As I see it, it's basically a question of educating non-Catholics."

Campbell then told on little Teddy. "I recounted Teddy's antics about my going to Denver with him . . . Jack thought it was hilarious. 'That little rascal . . . You'll have to excuse his youthful exuberance. He's still quite a kid in many ways, but his heart's in the right place. He's a little immature, but time will cure that.'"

Campbell noticed the time and saw she had only an hour to prepare for the reception to be held at the convention center honoring Kennedy.

About 200 people attended the ninety-minute event. The smiling Kennedy found himself surrounded by overdressed members of the local Women's Democratic Club. Campbell said Kennedy kept coming by her side throughout the reception, "making my heart skip a beat."

It also made her nervous. In her book, Campbell engaged in hindsight about an affair with a celebrity that she did not discourage, "The fact that he was married, that he was a public figure, with all the dangers that implied; the fear that I might fall in love with him and be hurt again; or perhaps it was just a passing fancy; the fear that we would have an affair and it would become serious, or that it would not be serious; the fear that I was heading for a hard fall . . . I saw myself as a rudderless ship in a storm . . . without the slightest bearing on where I was headed . . ."

Jack told her he had set up "a date at eight o'clock" for them. He'd arranged with Sands hotel executive Jack Entratter to give them his private booth in the rear of the Copa Room to watch the Clan show again. That night, they sat together in the booth behind everyone, and each time JFK "reached for his drink, he gave me a love pat or a squeeze. I was terribly impressed with him . . . I could tell the feeling was mutual."

But after the show, at the edge of the Sands casino, Judy's nemesis, Gloria Cahn, swooped by with another older lady and separated her from Jack, taking him to a private dinner party.

"I watched him being propelled across the casino, with the crowd around him getting larger, and I remember Gloria turning to give me a last smug look just before they disappeared in the lobby."

She went back to her room at the Flamingo and acted out her disappointment by kicking the furniture around, thinking she wouldn't see him again. Then Jack called asking where she was.

"I almost died when we got to the restaurant and I realized you weren't there," she recalled him telling her. "I asked a couple of people but they didn't know. Gloria said you had other plans for the evening."

"'That doesn't surprise me in the least,' I said, wondering why she was working so hard to do me in."

Kennedy persuaded her to come back over and meet him outside the Copa Room to catch Frank's late show. When she arrived at the entrance to the Copa, Gloria and the other lady were standing next to him. They all sat down in Entratter's booth. "Gloria looked daggers at me" while, Judy claimed, Jack focused his attention only on her for the entire show.

Sammy Davis would recall that Kennedy and his friends went and had drinks privately with the Clan cast after the late show. Sammy never mentioned Campbell. Sammy related that later, an aide to Kennedy said the senator had to leave to catch a plane in six hours, and that Kennedy "was enjoying himself. 'Don't worry about me, (Kennedy said). I'll sleep in the plane.'"

Davis claimed that Peter Lawford whispered that Strip resort owners—mob-connected and otherwise—had made a huge contribution to JFK. Lawford, Sammy said, quietly told him: "If you want to see what a million dollars in cash looks like, go into the next room; there's a brown leather satchel in the closet; open it. It's from the hotel owners for Jack's campaign."

But Sammy said he "never went near it. I was told there were four wild girls scheduled to entertain (Kennedy) and I didn't want to hear about that either and I got out of there. Some things you don't want to know."

In Campbell's account, she and Jack exchanged phone numbers before he left on his flight to campaign in Oregon. She then retired to her hotel room and soon heard the phone ring. This time it was Dean Martin, who wanted her to come down and chat. Dean had used her as a sounding board other times for his suspicions that his wife Jeanie was having an affair. These conversations with Martin, which Campbell said had become frequent, bored her, but she humored him. She liked that Dean joked with her but didn't come on. She went back down and talked with Martin briefly, then went back to bed, alone, thinking girlishly of Jack.

"Something wonderful was happening to me. I was lying in bed and smiling at the ceiling. I was almost giddy . . . I slept well and woke up feeling like Scarlet O'Hara the morning after Rhett Butler carried her up the stairs."

After leaving Campbell at the Sands, an excited Jack Kennedy apparently became obsessed with her following their sexless meetings in Vegas.

"From that moment the calls never stopped," claimed Campbell. "He called me almost every day, no matter where he was or how tired."

In their subsequent interludes, Jack would arrange to pick her up in his private jet, the Caroline (named after his three-year-old daughter). Their first bedtime together occurred at the Plaza Hotel in New York on March 7, 1960, a day before Jack won the first-in-the-nation New Hampshire primary. Other reported trysts took place in Palm Springs, Chicago, and even—while Jackie Kennedy was out of town—in Kennedy's Georgetown home in Washington. Campbell complained that while she was an expressive lover, Jack was a get-it-over-with-quick, selfish one.

The affair continued after Kennedy was elected in November 1960, until 1962, when the FBI's Hoover told the president—for the second time—that Campbell was also seeing Giancana, identified by the FBI as one of the "top hoodlums" in the United States. Campbell, whose revelations in *My Story* could never be truly verified, wrote that Jack was jealous about Giancana but had also claimed that "Sam works for us." Campbell also insisted that JFK and Sam used her as a courier to deliver about ten large envelopes that she never opened.

White House phone records of the time showed that by early 1962, Campbell's phone number had been logged seventy times. FBI agents tailed her in Los Angeles and placed taps on her phone and her parents' phone. Hoover had learned of Giancana's ties to the unsuccessful CIA operation to kill Castro. The plot remained alive through 1961, although there is no evidence that Kennedy had known about it before 1962. The problem was obvious: the president could be compromised politically, even blackmailed, by Mafia dons Giancana and Rosselli who knew both about his affair with Campbell and the failed CIA plan to kill the Cuban leader.

JFK finally realized that his presidency meant more than good sex. After a private lunch with Hoover on March 22, 1962, there were no more calls from Campbell's number at the White House (Campbell swore that his calls to her lasted until June 1962). At the urging of his brother, Attorney General Robert Kennedy, JFK immediately cut his ties to Sinatra. But Jack was only all too ready to move on. Just two days later, on March 24, President Kennedy was in Palm Springs for a weekend stay, not at Frank's house, as he and Sinatra had originally planned, but at the home of singer Bing Crosby. (A furious Sinatra blamed Lawford for the change and cut all future personal and professional relations to him.)

While in Palm Springs, Kennedy would spend Saturday night—in front of a handful of guests—at an evening party with another old girlfriend, actress Marilyn Monroe. He spent the night with her in a private cottage. Kennedy had moved on already, and into another potentially damaging liaison.

"Marilyn was there and the President was there, and they were obviously together," Philip Watson, a Los Angeles politician at the 1962 party in Palm Springs, told author Anthony

Summers in 1985. "The president was wearing a turtleneck sweater, and she wore a kind of robe or something. She obviously had a lot to drink. It was obvious they were intimate, that they were staying there together for the night."

In May 1963, J. Edgar Hoover gave the Justice Department a thick document titled "The Skimming Report," which contained transcripts of secret, bugged recordings of conversations in the homes and offices of two dozen mob-connected executives of Las Vegas hotels discussing how cash was skimmed from the casinos. Though it would not come out until 1964, the FBI, through a front called the Henderson Novelty Company, had leased twenty-five local telephone lines in Las Vegas to tap into conversations at the Desert Inn and other hotels over eighteen months. The justification offered was that only through such recordings could the feds learn about how the mob was breaking laws. Not only was the bugging of the conversations illegal in Nevada, each installation, not based on a court order, involved illegal trespassing by FBI agents. Unfortunately, a copy of the report was somehow leaked to Mafia leaders, and the recordings were halted. In one case, the wife of Sands hotel executive Carl Cohen had a nervous breakdown after discovering their bedroom had been bugged.

President Kennedy, whose national poll numbers had been unusually high for most of his presidency, saw those ratings drop in the early fall of 1963 amid the turmoil caused by the growing civil rights movement. When he visited Las Vegas for the last time that fall, he became the first president to deliver a speech there. Kennedy perhaps knew the town better than any other president as he had visited Vegas while a senator as a guest in the spacious home of Desert Inn casino partner Wilbur Clark in 1954 and 1956.

It was hot and sunny on Saturday, September 28, 1963. Kennedy, whose wife and kids were at Camp David, was scheduled to make a ten-minute speech in the so-called "space age," flying saucer-like rotunda of the Las Vegas Convention Center. A week earlier, he spoke before the United Nations in New York, calling for a joint U.S. and Soviet expedition to the moon, and won a relatively rare legislative achievement: his tax cut bill passed the House of Representatives.

Las Vegas was the last stop in a five-day, eleven-city tour of federal property that started in Grand Forks, North Dakota. Afterwards, Kennedy would spend the rest of the weekend again at Crosby's home in Palm Springs.

Kennedy described the tour as "non-political," but Republicans in Las Vegas complained the trip was a disguised campaign swing. On the Friday night before the president arrived, Nevada Lt. Gov. Paul Laxalt, a Republican, delivered a blistering anti-Kennedy speech at a GOP fundraiser at the Stardust hotel on the Strip. Laxalt (later elected governor and U.S. Senator) called Kennedy's civil rights bill "flagrantly unconstitutional" and said that Nevadans "are fed up with (Kennedy's) wishy-washy, gutless, liberal-type government."

Kennedy had spent Friday night in a small cabin at Lassen National Park in northern California. That night was made famous, when news reporters—in cabins surrounding the president's—would recall hearing a young woman's voice from Kennedy's cabin exclaim, "I don't care if you *are* the President of the United States!"

The next morning, after dedicating a dam in Redding, California, Kennedy had the pilot of Air Force One fly over Lake Mead and Hoover Dam, thirty miles southeast of Vegas, before landing at the town's new McCarran International Airport, at 12:35 P.M. Nevada's Democratic Senators Bible and Cannon, and California Governor Pat Brown and Interior Secretary Stuart Udall, deplaned with him. Nevada Governor Grant Sawyer, also a Democrat, greeted him on the ground.

The president's customized, convertible Ford Lincoln limousine, in which he would be mortally wounded only weeks later, was unloaded from a separate plane. He would be in Las Vegas for ninety minutes.

Inside the open limo, JFK immediately asked Governor Sawyer, "What are you guys doing to my friend Frank Sinatra?" Just two weeks before, Sawyer and officials from Nevada's Gaming Control Board announced that Sinatra could lose his casino license for playing host to Sam Giancana at Sinatra's Cal-Neva Lodge at Lake Tahoe. Sinatra had said he would talk to the president about it, and apparently he had. Sawyer's glib answer: "Well, Mr. President, I'll try to take care of things here in Nevada, and I wish you luck on the national level."

Security around the president was tight. Both the *Las Vegas Review-Journal* and *Las Vegas Sun* reported seeing scores of Secret Service agents, sheriff's deputies, and other law enforcement officers during JFK's visit. There were also more than sixty news reporters and a portable "hot line" phone with the presidential seal.

It was standing room only, as 7,000 people in the rotunda handed JFK a thirty-second standing ovation. With outside temperatures in the nineties, some spectators, in keeping with the informal, lax standards of dress permitted by Las Vegas resorts, wore shorts and even bathing suits into the crowded hall. Outside the rotunda stood 1,000 other people who arrived too late to get in. A police officer described the scene outside the convention center as "the worst traffic jam in the history of the city."

Rancho High School's band played "Hail to the Chief," Las Vegas High School's band played "The Star Spangled Banner." Some 2,000 stadium seats behind Kennedy in the rotunda were blocked off for security reasons. His ten-minute speech was broadcast live across the country on the ABC radio network and by local radio station KORK-AM. Kennedy talked about conserving natural resources and for preserving Lake Tahoe's shoreline. He bemoaned the nation's high school dropout problem and stressed better childhood education. He spoke in favor of his landmark 1963 Nuclear Test Ban Treaty, for maintaining U.S. military strength, and even for reducing the forty-hour work-week.

"We have been fortunate that we have made in the years after the second world war the proper decision that this country could not be free and secure unless there was a free and secure world," he said.

Ad-libbing from his prepared text, Kennedy called Nevada "a product of people having become so mobile in this day and age." He then asked native Nevadans to raise their hands and only a handful did. Then, at his request, non-natives raised theirs, numbering in the thousands, and laughter filled the auditorium.

A statement about investing tax dollars in natural resources turned out to be an ironic one for what would befall him in November. "The fact of the matter is, as a general rule, every time we bet on the future of this country, we win."

Kennedy left the podium, shook hands with spectators for a few minutes, and thanked local police officers as he made his way out of the building. As he entered his limo in the motorcade outside, a group of teenaged girls screamed while running after him "in the fashion reminiscent of days when young American females swooned over a crooner," observed the *Las Vegas Sun*.

At 2:05 P.M., as the local TV and print media watched, Kennedy's plane took off for Palm Springs.

On Black Friday, November 22, the casinos on the Strip shut down for an hour before starting back up again. On the national day of mourning, November 25, Vegas hotels, lounges, and showrooms across the Strip were closed from 7 A.M. to midnight. Blackjack tables and roulette wheels were covered across town, as gambling and other entertainment were halted in honor of the dead president. For that brief time, the neon on the Strip went dark.

Shaken by Kennedy's death, Campbell retreated to a hotel suite set up for her in West Hollywood by Johnny Rosselli, and stayed for several days, downing drinks until she passed out. Rosselli came by and convinced her to go with him to Palm Springs. At a country club, she sat at a long table that included Sinatra and Martin, who, she wrote, both treated her coldly and said nothing. She never saw Frank and Dean again.

On New Year's Eve 1963, Campbell, still upset, took another free trip to Vegas, this time to the Desert Inn hotel, courtesy of Rosselli, who knew the man behind the resort, mob-connected operator Moe Dalitz. At a New Year's party, she got drunk and argued with Johnny. When Dalitz butted in, Campbell slapped him. "Nobody smacks Moe Dalitz across the face," Rosselli laughingly told her the next day. "Do you realize how hard you hit him? You nearly knocked him flat on his ass. You pack a mean wallop, sweetheart!"

In 1965, after an aborted suicide attempt, Campbell, out of wedlock, gave birth to a baby boy. Ten years later, she was subpoenaed to testify in Washington before the U.S. Senate Committee on Intelligence Operations, investigating covert assassination-related activities by the CIA and the FBI, in particular the Rosselli-Giancana plot against Castro. Campbell, now married to a man named Dan Exner, sought to be circumspect during her appearance on September 19, 1975. After all, Giancana, on June 19, 1975, had been murdered in his Chicago home only days before he was set to testify himself under subpoena. Judith told the committee she'd had affairs with Jack, Sam, and Johnny, but knew nothing of any assassination plans.

Rosselli testified in detail about the Castro plot, out of the public's eye, on June 24, and again on September 22, 1975. A year later, Rosselli was killed and mutilated, his body placed in a steel drum and dumped in the ocean outside Miami. Investigators suspected Miami mob boss Santo Trafficante gave the order.

Judith Campbell Exner survived the ordeal. She died, at age sixty-five, of breast cancer in 1999.

13

Holding Up the Customers
LENNY BRUCE

After a drunken, irreverent night in 1960, in a city that fawns over its entertainers, rebel comic Lenny Bruce settled into his room at the Flamingo hotel to take a dump. While still on the bowl, he heard loud banging on the guest room door. The door burst open and several security guards rushed into the bathroom. They unceremoniously picked Bruce up off the can, his pants still down at his ankles, and dragged him into the hallway to see the hotel manager. Only minutes before, Bruce had humiliated black singer Pearl Bailey in front of a crowd in the Flamingo's showroom. Bailey refused to perform unless management kicked Bruce out. It did. As the guards forcefully pulled Bruce to the elevator, the manager promised to mail him his baggage. "Well, at least let me get my pants up!" Bruce protested.

By all accounts, Lenny hated Las Vegas, even though as the "sick" but well-known comic (he'd appeared on NBC-TV's *The Tonight Show*) he could have made a great living—$5,000, $10,000, or more a week—in the popular hotel lounges on the Strip in the early 1960s. That is, if he'd played it reasonably straight and not punched his routines with the profanity and politically and religiously incorrect comments he was famous for. His usual act would have offended the mainstream, Midwest, and Southern sensibilities of the mainly middle class guests who filled Vegas's hotels and lounges. He'd shocked audiences elsewhere by saying things like "cocksucker," "I'm going to piss on you," and "We Jews killed Christ and if he comes back, we'll kill him again!" Bruce knew the people who liked his dirty stuff, goofy irony, Hitler jokes, and jibes at 1960s American society were different than the commoners: the hip, urban sophisticates of New York, Los Angeles, Berkeley, San Francisco, whose faces were fewer and far between in Vegas. One of his popular standup routines, based on his 1960 trip there, was titled "Vegas Tits and Ass." In his favorite routine, called "The Palladium," recorded live in San Francisco in 1959, Bruce played a bombing Brooklyn Jewish comic whose first joke was always, "Well, I 'jes got back from Lost Wages, Nevada! Funny thing, 'bout working Lost Wages, folks . . . the way to make a lotta money there . . . when you get off the plane, walk right inna the propeller!" The town in the early 1960s still preferred humor with technically clean, subtle double entendres about sex and race like Frank and Dean made famous. Swear words and outright dirt, with few exceptions, were reserved for private gatherings. That night in the Flamingo lounge, Lenny took his humor too far, and then some, for Vegas to handle.

Bruce, who'd never been to Las Vegas before, decided to make a visit as a tourist in the summer of 1960. He had met Morris Lansburgh, one of the partners in the Flamingo, in Miami, and Lansburgh (who at the time headed mob chief Meyer Lansky's secret skimming operation at the Flamingo) invited Bruce to stay there for free. Lansburgh put Bruce and his wife Honey up in one of the Flamingo's overly fancy high-roller suites. It would become what Albert Goldman described, in his Bruce biography, *Ladies and Gentlemen, Lenny Bruce!!* as "one of the most self-destructive sorties of his career."

That evening, Bruce and Honey, already loaded, were treated to ringside seats at the Folies Bergère showgirl prance show at the Tropicana hotel. Bruce overheard a man next to him refer to "tits and ass," providing for him the material he'd use later to lambaste what he felt was the town's hypocritical exploitation of sex. Bruce stood, pulled Honey up the aisle to the exit and yelled "Ahla fungoola!" He approached a Tropicana boss named Frankie Ray and demanded he take them to see comic Shecky Greene in the hotel lounge. Once seated, Bruce played the heckling drunk part at Shecky, and the two pros deftly exchanged insults that got bluer and bluer. Bruce then spotted Ben Jaffe, the Trop's landlord. "Look at that guy," Bruce said. "When he's not standing around here holding up that post he's holding up the customers!" Shecky playfully admonished him not to berate Jaffe, saying that Bruce might be working there as a comic himself someday. "I wouldn't work in this shithouse!" Bruce yelled. Jaffe then summoned hotel guards to remove Bruce, who shouted, "They're throwing me out!"

Following a cab ride to the Flamingo, Bruce's celebrity got him another front seat, this time for Pearl Bailey's performance in the showroom. Bailey's bandleader spotted Bruce and convinced Pearl to bring him on stage. Bruce at first refused, then gave in when a spotlight was turned on him. But as Pearl sang a song, trying to get him to sing along, Bruce slapped her expansive rump, drawing laughter from the audience.

"Whatchoo do that foh?" Pearl asked in her trademark black slang.

"I told you not to get me up here," Bruce answered.

As Pearl tried to distract him with a new song, Bruce distracted the audience by walking across the stage like Holly-wood's old stereotypical shuffling black man, Stepin Fetchit. He grabbed a fire extinguisher backstage—he'd once played with them with his mates while in the Navy—and promptly sprayed Pearl in the face, to more laughs. Stagehands trying to grab Bruce slipped on the foam and fell to the floor. Pearl, out-raged, viewed the episode as a racist slur. The audience, believing the slapstick was all a joke, stood and cheered. Retreating to her dressing room, Pearl found a note from Bruce: "Dear Pearl, I couldn't take your act. All the Uncle Tom bits you did like a lazy Negro." Pearl had enough and gave management an ultimatum: either he is thrown out of the Flamingo, or I stop performing.

The black news media and the American Guild of Variety Artists later chastised Bruce, but Goldman wrote that the Vegas episode convinced Bruce that his future as a comedian lay in controversy. "In Fun City, controversy was out of the question. Tits 'n ass, that's what sold there. Tits 'n ass, and a few feeble jokes . . . Why mess with fat bald zhlubs in the fucking casi-nos? The apes with the crew cuts who stood there at the tables at 6 A.M. pissing away their mortgage money with a Bloody Mary in one fat hand? . . . He would have to go another way . . . The time would come when he would be seen in only a few top rooms in a dozen cities. He would be a cult figure, a hipster genius. People would pay a lot to hear him say the unspeakable . . . The Vegas thing was not simply a goof. It was a message. The message read, 'Go right on, baby, and don't worry about the assholes.'"

Bruce's rebellion would gain him fans. But it also would land him in jail on obscenity charges, even in hip San Fran-cisco, and for buying illegal drugs. Broke, obsessed with free-dom of speech issues, and drug abuse, Bruce died of a heroin overdose in the bathroom of his home in Los Angeles, in 1966.

14

Landmark Pharmacy

ELVIS PRESLEY

In 1969, Las Vegas rescued Elvis Presley's career, as it had the flaccid careers of many other show biz veterans. But the town and its unethical medical professionals also served as his faithful drug pushers, facilitating his addictions to buffets of uppers and downers that surely contributed to his fatal heart attack at just age forty-two. Whenever Elvis needed to replenish his supplies of prescribed stimulants and depressants to cope with his grueling performance schedule at the Las Vegas Hilton and elsewhere, he could always rely on his Vegas connection, the pharmacy at the Landmark hotel, where he would spend a half million dollars on drugs into the mid-1970s. The store was conveniently located right across the street from the Hilton, so his local doctors could rush over, write him up a pile of orders, and have the Landmark Pharmacy deliver the vials of capsules, pills, and injectable liquid to his hotel room door. The handy Landmark would also mail him packages containing bottles with hundreds of pills to any city he wanted during his tours. These drugs were not used to deal with a medical condition or to recover from surgery, they were to keep Elvis's moneymaking engine running: uppers to keep him high, happy and motivated on stage, downers to induce sleep.

Thanks to his longtime, sadistic manager "Colonel" Tom Parker, Elvis played Vegas 837 times—excluding cancellations due to drugs or sheer exhaustion—while chained to the International (renamed Las Vegas Hilton) from 1969 until 1976, a year before his death. In 1970, he signed a five-year contract to play two months a year for the high-rolling gamblers and average folks at the Hilton. During the eight years after his '69 comeback in Vegas, the overworked Elvis—exploited by Parker, with the consent of Elvis's dad, Vernon—transformed into the drug-addicted fat slob he was known for when he died.

The major episode in Elvis's Vegas-induced tumble came in late January 1973, when he and girlfriend Linda Thompson arrived in town for his one-month stint of two shows a night at the Hilton. This particular trip, with the broadest smorgasbord of drugs he'd ever had, would turn Elvis into a crazy, paranoid freak on stage and in his personal hotel suite.

Only eleven days before, Elvis had made his famous Honolulu performance, a live satellite broadcast seen by more than a billion people worldwide. To get into shape, Elvis slimmed down to only 165 pounds, looking good in his white jumpsuit and jewels, and eschewed drugs during the rehearsals. But he didn't stay clean long; the day after the show, he resumed some of the mind-numbing drugs he'd been taking for years. His introduction to legal drug use actually started during a visit he made to Vegas, as a tourist back in 1956, when by chance he met and befriended an eighteen-year-old, beautiful blonde showgirl named Dotty Harmony at a bar in the Sahara hotel. While he drove her in a car on the Strip, Dotty watched as the still low-key pop star stopped and changed a flat tire for a stranded motorist. But Dotty would provide Elvis with his first sleeping pill, which he took during a trip to Memphis. He got used to using drugs while in the Army in the late 1950s, and during his early 1960s film days, all strictly legal stuff like Dexamil, Dexedrine, Placidyl, Percodan and Seconal.

When he and Linda entered the sprawling, top-floor Elvis Suite at the Hilton in '73, the bellboys drew the curtains to keep it totally dark inside, as Elvis liked it. While Linda unpacked, Elvis called the Hilton's doctor, Dr. Thomas "Flash" Newman, who could be counted on to dash upstairs with prescriptions for any of Vegas's highly paid performers. Flash went to the Landmark drug store and came back with bottles of the powerful painkiller Dialudid, the upper Dexedrine, and tranquilizers Valium and Valmid. Elvis had been prescribed this kind of stuff before on his Vegas trips, but he received more than ever this time and began a dangerous entry into mainlining. He received a doctor's kit with a syringe so that he could inject liquid Valium or Dialudid into himself. The liquid Valium came in a variety of doses but the liquid Dialudid was as addictive as heroin, so much so that it was nicknamed the "poor man's heroin."

Elvis took pills from three of the bottles from the Landmark and went to sleep. Linda separated the drugs by potency and put them under the bed. During each of his early performances, Elvis received two pre-show injections of an upper from Dr. Flash—into Elvis's butt, right through his pants—and two of a downer afterwards. If Flash wasn't around, Elvis would go nuts asking where he was. Soon, the drugs landed him in the hospital. While in bed there, with no access to his drug supply at the Hilton, Elvis called another supplier, Dr. Sidney Boyer, who gave him the prescriptions but lectured Elvis about addiction. Boyer refused to sign for any more prescriptions, even after Elvis sent him a new Lincoln automobile.

Paranoia was setting in from the uppers. Elvis went ape during a midnight Hilton show and started beating and choking some South American men who went up to the stage and tried to give him a gift. "I'm sorry I didn't break his goddamned neck!" Elvis told the crowd, to standing applause. In his suite later, he ranted that hit men were after him. He picked up the M-16 rifle he owned and screamed he would kill the man who stole his estranged wife Priscilla Presley from him years before (he married her at the Aladdin hotel in Vegas in 1967 and they divorced in mid-1973). He said he wished he could hire a hit man to kill the guy, and asked whom he could get to do it. His entourage notified another local doctor, Elias Ghanem, that Elvis needed downers to counteract the Dexedrine uppers that put him into hysterics, but Ghanem—one of Elvis's legal pushers in Vegas—never arrived.

That same night, Elvis nearly died from an overdose in his hotel suite. Linda, monitoring his breathing in bed, panicked when he started to slip away. Dr. Flash was summoned and could see that Presley had lapsed into a coma due to an overdose of his liquid Dialudid. To avoid publicity at the request of Colonel Parker, Flash ordered oxygen tanks and transformed the Elvis Suite into an emergency room. A tube shoved into his mouth got his lungs working again and the doctor dripped Elvis's stomach with a rapid antidote to the painkiller Dialudid.

The King woke up four days later. Elvis made another Vegas comeback! He had taken about 100 highly potent uppers over three days in the suite. He would suffer through three more overdoses that year. Another doctor who treated Elvis later discovered Elvis's drug expenses at the Landmark had reached $500,000.

After a break in Tennessee, Elvis was back in Vegas, where the pressure to perform prompted him to take Valium to sleep, but he also had to wear diapers because the drug took away his bowel control. He'd even sleep in the Hilton suite while eating and Linda estimated she saved him from death about eight times by pulling out food caught in his windpipe so that he could breathe.

Near the end of 1973, an Alabama doctor hired to free Elvis of his drug habits, Dr. George Nichopoulos, convinced Parker and the Hilton to reduce Elvis's performances in Las Vegas to only two weeks at a time and one show a night except for two on Saturday. He played two months in Vegas and more than 150 shows elsewhere that year. He still had his crazy moments while in Vegas, like the time he fired a gun at a Hilton light switch. The bullet exited the wall and just missed Linda, who was getting ready for bed in the other room.

Dr. Nichopoulos struggled to reduce Elvis's drug use and overeating in Tennessee. Elvis went to Vegas to partake in a so-called sleep cure for weight gain involving papaya juice. But Elvis ended up drinking lots of it and gained fifteen pounds. Dr. Nichopoulos succeeded in curbing the King's drug use, but things fell apart when Presley returned to the Vegas Hilton in 1975 and his former drug-providing doctors hooked up with him. Off the wagon again, he couldn't even perform at all, and he left town. Even then, his Vegas connections followed him. Once, Dr. Nichopoulos confiscated an envelope from Vegas with 100 caps of Empirin with codeine. When the doctor admonished Parker to cut back on Elvis's shows, the "Colonel" staunchly refused.

Now bloated from overeating, Elvis wore bigger clothes than his trademark jumpsuits. The Hilton ordered no more photos to be taken of Elvis in the showroom. On August 20, 1975, Hilton patrons watched a stoned Elvis garble the words to his songs. With his makeup dripping, he apologized sorrowfully to the crowd, fell down and had to be carried off stage. His show was cancelled.

In the plane on the way back to Memphis, he had a seizure and the pilot made an emergency landing in Dallas. He survived but had to receive more drugs to feed his addiction to prevent another seizure. By 1976, he was living on cheeseburgers and his pills. His final Vegas performances took place from December 2 to 12, 1976.

On a whim in early 1977, Elvis flew his new girlfriend, Ginger Alden, to Vegas where he bought her a large diamond bracelet. He took her to his suite at the Hilton, where she accepted his marriage plea and an 11.5-carat ring. Parker booked him for seven more U.S. tours, telling handlers that Elvis's shows were all that mattered. Parker set up two concerts that showed an exhausted Elvis televised by CBS-TV. Crowds and critics were shocked by his bloated appearance and poor performances.

At Graceland on the early morning of August 16, 1977, while on a crash diet, Elvis played racquetball for two hours, took three packets of downers and went to the bathroom. Six hours later, Ginger found him slumped off of the toilet—head first on the floor, gripping the carpet, and dead. The original cause of death—his heart stopped due to clogged arteries—was a cover-up by his family. Drugs surely did him in. The remains of 14 different prescription drugs—including painkillers and opiates—were found in his blood. Estimates put his weight at from more than 250 pounds to (less believably) as high as 350 pounds.

Colonel Parker, a shrewd and manipulative former carnival worker, certainly spearheaded Elvis's career, but also limited it to his own convenience. In the mid-1970s, Elvis chatted with and considered an offer by singer and actress Barbra Streisand to star in her movie, *A Star Is Born*. But the Colonel didn't like competing with Barbra and turned it down. Parker, afraid of having to apply for a passport, had refused to allow Elvis to expand his career, such as with a tour outside the States or better movie roles, in favor of U.S. tours and easy Hilton shows. He blocked other agents from contacting Elvis. It was Parker who got the King his first Vegas gig, two weeks at the Frontier, in April 1956. Unappreciative, middle-class dinner crowds at the Frontier gave young Elvis and his band the cold shoulder, but it wasn't Elvis's fault. He was put on stage like a circus act, the freak show among acts that were completely inconsistent with his: a floor show with the totally squaresville Freddy Martin playing—incredibly—Tchaikovsky numbers, followed by the Borscht Belt comic Shecky Greene.

For many years, he was a respected "legend" in Vegas and other entertainment circles. But Parker's life was darker than they knew. He was an illegal immigrant from Holland named Andre van Kuijk who, based on new research in the 2003 book *The Colonel*, by Alanna Nash, may have fled to the United States in 1929 after beating a twenty-three-year-old woman to death during a robbery attempt in a grocery store in his former hometown of Breda. Once in the States, Parker immediately joined the cheats and conmen in a traveling carny, where it'd be easy to work without papers, starting out as an elephant's groom and selling the droppings as fertilizer. In the Army in the early 1930s, he was discharged after suffering a nervous breakdown with symptoms of psychosis. The Colonel would later become well known among Elvis's "Memphis Mafia" for his crazy temper tantrums. After the Army, Parker rejoined carnivals, learning how to rip off patrons with fake "foot-long" hot dogs (the tips of meat protruded with the middle filled with sauerkraut) and adding brown food coloring to hide the small amounts of meat in his hamburgers.

The most embarrassing moment in Parker's career took place in Vegas, in 1953, two years before he met Elvis. Parker had served as manager for the popular country singer Eddy Arnold, who sold thirty million records under Parker's watch, with the Colonel getting a 25 percent cut. While Arnold was at the Sahara hotel, he learned that Parker was trying to manage competing singers Hank Snow and Tommy Sands. Eddy confronted Parker in the Sahara's coffee shop and had to be restrained from punching him. He fired Parker immediately.

Though Elvis would tell people he followed the Colonel's every wish and regarded him as a father, Elvis was just business to Parker. When the Colonel showed up at Elvis's funeral at Graceland near Memphis, the other men in the room were dressed formally in coats and ties, but he sauntered in wearing a Hawaiian shirt and cowboy hat and didn't even view the body. When questioned many years later about Elvis, Parker would only say the same thing, time after time, about his insomniac former client, while stomping his cane on the floor, "I sleep good at night!"

15

Jail a' Go-Go

JIM MORRISON

On a warm night in early 1968, people milling outside the Pussycat a' Go Go acid rock music nightclub on the Strip just north of Spring Mountain Road (now occupied by the Wynn Las Vegas property) watched a security guard throw out The Doors vocalist Jim Morrison, who fell hard onto the sidewalk. The hippies in the crowd recognized the famous singer right away. Morrison, who'd been drinking for the past ten hours, put his arms up to defend against attempts by the guard to whack him with a bully club. A friend tried to grapple with the guard and got clubbed in the head, as did Morrison. The guard was inflamed after Morrison went by, faking like he was smoking weed, and asked the guard if he wanted a hit. Not funny. That kind of hip was reserved for Sammy's private suite at the Sands. There was no quarter for 1960s hippies in Vegas, which still had the mentality and lack of patience for "longhairs" of a small Southern town. Police arrived and stuck the bleeding Morrison in the rear of a squad car with his longhaired buddy, Bob Gover, a former Vegas resident who was on assignment from the *New York Times Magazine* to write about Morrison.

On the way to jail, Gover tried to quiet Morrison, who taunted the cops with shouts of "chickenshit" and "pig." Both were booked for misdemeanor public drunkenness, but Jim received additional counts of vagrancy and no identification. Now it was their turn to be taunted. The officers laughed at their hair, called them girls, strip-searched them, and led them into a holding cell. The cell had tall bars that reached the ceiling. Morrison climbed up the bars, saw officers in the adjacent room, and yelled, "Hey Bob, aren't they the ugliest motherfuckers you ever saw?" One cop walked over, told Morrison that he was getting off at midnight and would take him into a private room for "a date. See ya later . . . sweety." Gover later related that Morrison barely dodged a beating by Vegas cops when a friend arrived to bail them out only minutes before midnight. The Vegas incident had become for him "a typical scene," his biographers wrote in 1980. "In the first months of 1968, Jim's drinking accelerated at a pace that had the other Doors alarmed." Morrison had only three more years to live, dying of apparent heart failure in a bathtub in Paris, hours after a drinking binge, at age twenty-seven.

16

Smack Down

SONNY LISTON

$\mathcal{S}$onny Liston, one of a family of twenty-four kids in Arkansas, was an ex-con who learned how to box in prison. He knocked out champion Floyd Patterson in just one round in Chicago to win the world heavyweight title in September 1962. While champ in July 1963, the powerful Liston came to Las Vegas to defend his title for the first time, in a rematch with Patterson at the Convention Center. Liston again knocked him out in only one round, sending Patterson down three times.

But in his next bout after the Vegas fight, in Miami in February 1964, Liston quit after six rounds, complaining of a shoulder injury, and lost the crown to his new nemesis, Cassius Clay (later Mohammad Ali). In their rematch, Liston would lose in less than one round to Ali in Maine the following year. The Maine fight drew controversy, as Ali said he didn't hit Liston very hard before he went down for the count. Some thought Liston, rumored to have known several mob figures, took a dive for the short money. The FBI investigated reports that the fight was fixed, but drew no conclusions.

His career in decline due to talk about the Ali fight, Liston fought in Sweden and then in the States, winning thirteen straight fights, including one at the Vegas Convention Center in May 1969. That fight got him a shot at the just-created North American Boxing Federation heavyweight title, set in Vegas at the new International Hotel (now the Las Vegas Hilton), in December 1969. Liston fought Leotis Martin, who KO'd the thirty-seven-year-old Liston in the ninth of the twelve-round fight. But Martin couldn't hold the title. Liston's punches detached one of his retinas and he had to retire.

Liston won his last fight in New Jersey in July 1970, but left boxing that year to settle in Las Vegas, and into drug addiction. He had only several months left to live in Sin City.

It was said he was used occasionally as a part-time muscle man for local hoodlums. But the mystery about his death on December 30, 1970—the most cited theory is that the mob killed him—has persisted for years. As it turns out, there was no mystery, not really. No big deal, no sensational Mafia plot to keep him quiet. Liston died of heart and lung failure, following an overdose of heroin that he'd bought in Vegas. His man for it was Red Rodney, the white "Albino Red" jazz trumpeter who had toured with the famed Charley "Bird" Parker in the 1940s and 1950s. Rodney, himself a longtime junkie, supplied Liston with the heroin the ex-boxer died from.

According to Rodney's son, Mark, who was a teenager in late December 1970, Liston knocked on the door of their Vegas home, smiled, and went with his dad into Red's bedroom. Liston soon left. A few days later, Red told his son that Liston's wife had found her husband's moldering corpse—after he'd been dead for a couple of days—in Liston's bedroom. Red feared that the police investigation would lead to him, but it never did. Red soon skipped town anyway. He died himself in 1994, shortly after playing in a jazz band that performed for President Clinton on the White House lawn. Meanwhile, Sonny lies in a graveyard next to Vegas's McCarran International Airport.

17

Audition in My Hotel Room

TOMMY SMOTHERS

In 1981, during the lax administration of Clark County Sheriff John McCarthy, it was said that prostitution in Las Vegas was so rampant that streetwalkers on the Strip would solicit a man even while he was holding hands with his wife. That year, the Nevada legislature passed a law designating so-called escort services as "privileged occupations," giving Clark County—which called the dozens of escort businesses in Las Vegas "modified brothels"—the go-ahead to try for the umpteenth time to close them down (the effort would ultimately fail, again).

Meanwhile, dozens of "house girls"—prostitutes assisted by front desk clerks, bell men, pit bosses, and other employees—bided their time in casino bars sipping their token drinks or "correct Cokes," to look like a bar patron but really waiting to strike up a chat with a conventioneer or a drunk gambler before taking the elevator to his room.

That year was also when the comic singing pair, the Smothers Brothers, were on the road to another comeback, using a venue many top entertainers resort to when their careers are on the wane: a Las Vegas showroom. In the Smothers's case, it was the 7,500-seat Aladdin Theatre for the Performing Arts inside the Aladdin hotel.

While Dick played the "smarter" straight man à la Bud Abbott, Tom Smothers was the seemingly ditzy Lou Costello. But Tom was no ditz. Older by a couple of years than Dick, Tom managed their career to stardom in the 1960s. He did so well that in 1967, he convinced CBS to give him creative control over *The Smothers Brothers Comedy Hour*, which became a ratings hit. The edgy variety show ran for only three seasons, taken off the air by CBS brass, angry about the brothers' suggestive jokes and their use of then-controversial words on the air, like "bra." But the Emmy-winning show became a TV classic for the controversies it caused. Even so, for years thereafter, the clean-living, dumb-but-cute stage persona that Tom cultivated throughout his career still held sway with American audiences. In the early morning hours of June 28, 1981, that image would be put to the test.

After a Saturday evening performance with Dick at the Aladdin, Tom had a fateful meeting with two women in the casino. The women told him, incredibly, that they were comedy writers and, more incredibly, Tom believed them. "I was walking around with my road manager and a couple of girls came and said our act was kind of slow and were we interested in a couple of jokes," Tom later related to United Press International in Las Vegas. "I said, 'Sure.'"

"They said it would cost me $50," he added. "I said that was reasonable for a couple of jokes. I asked them if they were professional writers and they said yes, they were professionals. We went up to my room and had a couple of drinks, and I asked them for the jokes. Then they said, 'We can show you a trick for $200.'"

So Smothers gave the two "professionals" a couple hundred.

The women, of course, turned out to be hookers. What happened next is that one of them, described by Tom as a little lady in red, announced she felt sick, then made off with $600 in cash from his wallet. Tom, feeling woozy himself, said he was able to punch her in the face—on his way down to the floor. The women had slipped a mickey into his drink and he'd slipped into darkness, sleeping for hours after the ladies split the scene. Vegas police told Smothers he'd been the victim of a trick-roll, a classic cocktail mixed for nervous johns and a problem that plagued Strip hotels for many years. "I didn't know the trick was they would take my money," Tom gamely went on to explain, after admonishing the UPI reporter not to "make me look too silly."

These days, Las Vegas remains a venue of choice for the Smothers Brothers (Dick himself moved to town in the mid-1990s). When they headlined the Las Vegas Hilton showroom in 2003, they included in their skits a yo-yo wielding Dick playing "The Yo-Yo Master," teaching the ditzy Tom—aka "The Yo-Yo Man"—some classic tricks, at one point telling Tom he was going to show him how to "do the Sleeper." As if.

18

One Night in Vegas

DAVID STRICKLAND

$\mathcal{I}$n 1999, TV actor David Strickland seemed to be on the road to stardom and perhaps a lifetime of fat, *Seinfeld*-like residuals from coast-to-coast reruns of *Suddenly Susan*. The once-obscure actor was one of the principals on the popular NBC sitcom, which starred his close friend Brooke Shields. Writers of the show intended to put Strickland in the enviable position of playing Shields's love interest during the 1999–2000 season. He also had a part in the brand new movie *Forces of Nature*, the Ben Affleck and Sandra Bullock vehicle that briefly topped the box office that winter.

But Strickland, now twenty-nine, was a cocaine addict. He got caught with some in 1998 in Los Angeles, got convicted, and was sentenced to three years' probation and mandatory rehab, with the opportunity to clear his felony record. Five months later, he was due in court to show he was clean, but another force of nature awaited him. In March, he arrived in Las Vegas to spend a lost, sleazy weekend before his Monday morning court hearing back home. He headed to one of the most rundown sections of South Las Vegas Boulevard, between the Strip and downtown, the home of dive bars, titty shows, pawn shops, wedding chapels, and cheap, post-war cinder-block motels. For lodging, he chose the Oasis Motel, which rented rooms for twenty bucks an hour, with adult films on the TV. He picked up a pile of free local magazines advertising the literally thousands of Vegas call girls who masquerade as "entertainers" or "nude dancers." Right off the bat, he ended up in a room with a local girl named Jasmine who lived at the motel. She buttered him up by telling him he looked like a movie star. Their encounter in her room lasted as long as a Vegas wedding—15 minutes. Jasmine went and told the motel clerk: "He's acting a little weird" (which, for her, was probably saying something). Strickland later joined fellow TV sitcom actor/druggie Andy Dick at a small downtown topless bar, the Girls of Glitter Gulch, where David paid for a personal dance by a girl stage-named "Bunny." But David's low self-esteem would not budge. He returned to the Oasis and said little to the motel clerk, who charged him $55 for the night. He bought a six-pack at a nearby 7-11 and entered his room. He removed a bed sheet and walked into the bathroom. He twisted the sheet, stood atop the toilet, tied it to a ceiling fan, and jumped, but the fixture ripped out and he fell to the floor. Then he spied a wooden beam in the ceiling of the bedroom, stood atop a bed table, tied the sheet on the beam, and jumped again. His feet hit the floor, but he slowly asphyxiated. When the clerk opened the door at 10:30 the next morning, she found a neat row of beer bottles on the floor, aligning the same bed table he'd leapt from.

19

Momo's Moll Flips

PHYLLIS McGUIRE

Rancho Circle was Las Vegas's first exclusive residential enclave, a gated private neighborhood a mile west of downtown, with sprawling lots and ranch-style homes from the late 1950s and 1960s, when fancy white rocks on the roof meant class. For Vegas, class also meant showing how rich you were by indulging your bad taste in interior design as much as possible, with stuff like green shag carpeting, Astroturf, smoke-mirrored walls, spiral staircases, wrought iron fences, gaudy table lamps and paintings, and faux Greek statues. That era of loud excessiveness, which flourished in the 1970s and into the 1980s, is largely over but lives on with some of the town's rich old-timers still obsessed with impressing others. One of them is one of the three singing McGuire Sisters, Phyllis McGuire, the city's queen of celebrities and charity events whose life and travails in Vegas have become legendary. In her expansive, aging home in Rancho, she'll point out to guests and magazine writers the forty-four-foot tall model of the Eiffel Tower that fits beneath the ceiling of her living room. On a tour described by *Vanity Fair* celebrity toady Dominick Dunne in March 2005, the seventy-four-year-old McGuire also boasted about her "fifty-five bergere chairs . . . a lake with black swans in it, five gardeners, a putting green and waterfalls you can turn on and off. She also possesses one of the world's greatest collections of serious jewels and once told me that maybe a few Saudis were better customers of Harry Winston's than she was."

Phyllis was still swinging at age sixty-eight in January 2000 as lead singer with her fellow McGuire Sisters, Dorothy and Christine, who—following very tight matching face-lifts—took their disingenuous 1950s song and sequins act to the off-Strip Orleans hotel, where other elderly entertainers perform for old times' sake, striving for as few embarrassments as possible. The three January 2000 performances were to mark the sisters' fiftieth anniversary in show biz.

During the peak of their stardom, the McGuire Sisters embodied the clean-living, white middle class values of the 1950s. The products of a female ordained minister in Ohio who forbade them from listening to anything but church music, the sisters got their start singing hymns, then broke loose from mom. They made it big when they replaced a gal group on the highly rated *Arthur Godfrey Talent Show* on TV in 1952, becoming regulars on the program into the late 1950s. They used their harmonizing skills to win a string of top-forty hits, all saccharin numbers like "Sugartime" (a gold record), "Sincerely" (number one on the charts for ten weeks in 1955), and "Something's Gotta Give." They weren't song writers; all of their songs were cover tunes. On the national nightclub circuit, they took their false innocent spiel to Las Vegas. The tall blonde Phyllis, considered the most attractive of the trio, defied her repressed upbringing by taking up with the short, bald, and decidedly ugly Sam Giancana, the wealthy Mafia boss of Chicago listed by the FBI back then as one of the top leaders of the national crime syndicate. By the late 1950s, Giancana, said to have ordered dozens of hits on rival hoods, had been a suspect in three murders, had served six years in prison, possessed a rap sheet with more than 70 arrests and held interests in prostitution, drugs, extortion, loan sharking, counterfeiting and other illegal rackets. He also enjoyed hidden points in the action at the Desert Inn, Sands, Dunes, Stardust and Riviera hotels on the Strip, holdings that earned him untold millions in criminally skimmed cash.

So notorious was "Momo" Giancana that in 1960, when Nevada started a "Black Book" list of hoodlums barred by law from even setting foot in a casino, he was one of the first ten men put on it. With the heat hotter in Vegas, Momo secretly visited the Cal-Neva Lodge up north at Lake Tahoe and stayed in a bungalow with Phyllis while she performed there (the lodge was co-owned by Momo's buddy Frank Sinatra, with Dean Martin and investor Hank Sanicola).

But later that year Giancana started doubting his girl's faithfulness. Momo secretly traveled to Las Vegas and asked CIA representative Bob Maheu, as a favor to a fellow public servant, to place a bug in Phyllis's Vegas hotel room. He told Maheu he wanted to see if she'd blab about a then-CIA plan to involve Momo and another top mobster Johnny Rosselli in a plan to assassinate Cuban leader Fidel Castro. Momo had foolishly revealed the plot to her during pillow talk, and he wanted to see if Phyllis might tell Dan Rowan, of the comic nightclub duo Rowan & Martin, about it. But, really, the tough guy mob man wanted to find out if his girl was carrying on with the tall, sophisticated, good-looking Mr. Rowan. Maheu arranged for a guy named Arthur James Balletti to plant the listening device, but Balletti surprised a housekeeper and was soon arrested by Las Vegas police before he could install it, thus putting the top secret CIA operation in Cuba into jeopardy (it was cancelled in 1962).

Still without the absolute truth, Momo followed Phyllis on her singing tours until they made it back to the Cal-Neva in 1963, when he and Phyllis's manager, Victor Collins, got into a bloody fistfight in her cabin. FBI agents tailing Giancana reported the incident to the state Gaming Control Board, and fed-up Nevada authorities pressured Sinatra to surrender his gaming license for the lodge and his interest in the Sands in Las Vegas, for illegally hosting a Black Book member.

Phyllis moved to Las Vegas in 1964 and went on seeing Giancana. After the McGuire Sisters split up in 1968, her sisters left to tend to their kids, while the childless, less-wholesome Phyllis chose an uneventful solo career. As for Momo, his life with the sword ended after even the mob grew weary of his infamy and news about the CIA plot against Castro. He was gunned down from behind—some believe by a young Tony Spilotro, who became a mob enforcer for Chicago in Las Vegas the 1980s—in the basement of his Windy City home in 1975. Ten years later, the McGuire Sisters reunited and resumed touring. Phyllis remained a fixture in Vegas's high-end social circles (often peopled by the newly rich and flaky, typical of Vegas society). In the mid 1990s, Phyllis shacked up with another wealthy beau, the controversial former Vegas World casino owner Bob Stupak, whose face had only recently required reconstruction following a near-fatal, face-first motorcycle accident in Las Vegas (which shattered all of his teeth), but who had a net worth of at least $50 million. A few years later, she threatened to file suit against producers of the HBO movie on her life with Momo, *Sugartime*, starring Mary-Louise Parker as Phyllis, claming it distorted her relationship with him.

In January of 1999, the McGuire Sisters performed at Nevada Governor Kenny Guinn's inaugural ball, and were inducted into the Casino Legends Hall of Fame, an over-hyped hole-in-the-wall (old photos, hotel matchbook covers, etc.) at the Tropicana hotel, a month later.

But on March 24, 1999, Phyllis hoisted herself on her own petard, pulling a vainglorious, Zsa Zsa Gabor diva turn with Vegas Metro police officers during a night of excessive drinking. That evening, police detectives were staking out a potential criminal suspect in a supermarket parking lot when they spotted a man later identified as Gerald Earl, McGuire's twenty-eight-year-old bodyguard, walking through the lot. Earl and the suspect exchanged a piece of paper and Earl got into McGuire's white Cadillac. Police followed the car as Earl drove, flashing their lights and turning on the siren. The Cadillac took a U-turn, sped away as if to escape, and parked outside McGuire's mansion. Police approached Earl and soon discovered he was legally packing a semi-automatic, .45-caliber Glock pistol. While searching the car for other weapons, they noticed Phyllis in the front seat. Officers asked her to leave the car and just go home, but she refused. One officer tried to move a bag Phyllis was reaching for. That's when the fun started.

"She appeared to be very intoxicated, slurring her words and smelling strongly of an unknown alcohol-based beverage," a police officer wrote in a report. "She began yelling and cursing at officers and also began yelling at her driver, telling him he was fired for cooperating with us."

She exited the car, started waving her arms wildly, and "struck me in the right shoulder," the cop said. He grabbed her arms and "repeatedly asked McGuire to settle down and at one point McGuire began to quiet down." The officers insisted she would not be arrested if she stayed calm, but she didn't. They turned on a tape recorder to get it all down. McGuire "suddenly lunged backwards, striking me in the right cheek with her head. I informed McGuire that she was under arrest for battery on a police officer."

It didn't stop there. While handcuffed in the police car, she kicked the arresting officer and tried to kick the other cops. Outside the county jail, she refused to leave the car, so "corrections officers removed McGuire from my vehicle and McGuire struggled with them all the way into the booking area. Inside the booking area, McGuire again became violent and was restrained."

Phyllis would not look into the camera for her mug shots, so a corrections officer grabbed her by the chin to get a picture of her face, an image that would appear prominently in the *Las Vegas Review-Journal* two days later.

Booked and sent to a holding cell on a count of obstructing a police officer that could get her six months in jail and a $1,000 fine, and a count of battery on a police officer (a year in jail, $2,000 fine), Phyllis got out of jail quietly early the next morning. The police said she intentionally assaulted them. Her attorney, John Moran, Jr. (son of a former Clark County Sheriff), filed a not guilty plea and defended Phyllis as "a completely innocent victim of an irrational and irresponsible police action," and alleged that officers "mistreated her and mishandled one of Las Vegas's most respected citizens and one of the world's most talented and beloved entertainers." The young cops involved said that even after finding out who she was, they'd never heard of her.

By her court appearance in April, McGuire had it all figured out. She flew in her personal attorney from New York for the hearing, which she did not attend. She committed herself to performing for free at an annual benefit for the local Nathan Adelson Hospice, where she'd already put in forty hours of volunteer work as part of a deal with the district attorney. She pledged $5,000 to the Injured Police Officer's Fund. The district attorney's office cited her advanced age as another reason to drop the charges, and the Justice of the Peace promptly did so. A month later, Phyllis served as the opening attraction for the hospice's $35 a ticket yearly fundraiser featuring medical doctors performing amateur music acts.

In late 1999, just before the McGuire Sisters' anniversary performance, Phyllis had put her life into a spacey, New Age perspective. "I have reached a point in my life right now," she related to a Las Vegas magazine writer, whose story did not mention her arrest, "where I have an inner peace that I haven't had in my whole life because I've been working a lot on going from within and thinking of light and what my thoughts are. Canceling negative thoughts. That brings me to these thoughts. We should be in abundance and not struggle. I think we manifest what we say. I've been struggling for so long and I just don't know what's going to happen next, that's a negative. You'll manifest that. So think abundance, joy, be up, think success, and happiness. That everything is good. That will change your position in life. The turning of the century and the new millennium is going to be a bright light, in a new upbeat direction for all of us. I really believe that."

20

Whipped Cream Dreams

ROBIN LEACH

The fourth floor of the Lied Library at UNLV houses what's called UNLV Special Collections, a large and respected compilation of donated papers, ranging from interesting (100 boxes of documents from Howard Hughes's longtime publicist) to boring and practically useless. It houses tens of thousands of photos, antiquarian books, casino press releases, news clippings, and miscellaneous bric-a-brac from Las Vegas's past.

One of its most recent bequeaths, hailed by the *Las Vegas Sun* newspaper as a "cultural coup" but more likely in the "useless" category, came from local resident Robin Leach—475 tapes of his 1980s syndicated TV show *Lifestyles of the Rich and Famous*, just in time to qualify for the 2004 tax year. Of what particular use the collection would have for scholars of Las Vegas history was glossed over by the library's handlers, who insisted that it might prove useful as pop culture perhaps 100 years from now (we'll never know). Leach's show came off as a pre-packaged, weekly video press release, taking his subjects' "lifestyles" at face value. But to hit home the usefulness of the donation as journalism, Leach himself appeared in 2005 at a news writing class at UNLV from a college department named, with unintended irony, the Hank Greenspun School of Journalism (after the late publisher of the *Las Vegas Sun* who shamelessly used his newspaper as a club to bash his enemies and as a PR machine for his friends and relatives). Leach told the wide-eyed kids: "If you are going into this business for money, you are never going to find it" and to make it, they'd have to "eat it, sleep it, and drink it." He added that as long as the students "are hungry, I'll put food on the plate in front of them."

Leach no doubt viewed the donation also as a comeback of sorts for the public relations disaster he took part in at the new Venetian hotel on May 31, 1999. Leach, who is never shy to flaunt his celebrity, frequently socializes at restaurant openings and elsewhere in town with an entourage of women in tow. On that night, Leach, who had been hired by the Venetian as a paid consultant to lure swank eateries to the Strip hotel-casino, hosted a private grouping with five party girls in a windowed room at Delmonico's, a restaurant owned by famous TV chef Emeril Lagasse. Sheldon Adelson, chairman of the Venetian hotel company, was also in the restaurant that night, but couldn't see Leach's party room. At about 9:30 P.M., Leach's party dolls got giddy and started stripping off their clothes and bouncing their breasts around at kitchen employees, who could see them through the windows. Several of Emeril's employees then entered the room to join the party. The now-naked girls caressed each other, sprayed whipped cream on their fun bags and rubbed up against several men while Leach looked on, cracking up. The festivities continued for ninety minutes before someone finally told Leach to end it, but only because the eatery was about to close.

When word leaked out to the media, the town treated the incident as more than simply another celebrity bad boy's wild night in Vegas. Self-righteous pols—seeking to tag along with the publicity it attracted—and bureaucrats demanded an investigation. So did the restaurant's absentee-owner, Emeril. Leach insisted reports of what happened were "a gross exaggeration," and he described what happened as "a harmless, fun whipped cream fight that lasted less than two minutes when dessert was served." But the short-haircut dowagers at the Clark County Department of Business License concluded that Leach himself and his girls were guilty of "lewd conduct." The County Commission, led by an outraged, news coverage-seeking Commissioner Erin Kenny, threatened to pull Emeril's liquor license. The chivalrous Emeril took responsibility for what he determined was "a breakdown in command. Who would ever dream something this bizarre would happen?" He also took action, firing the employees who partied with Robin and issuing warnings to others. He barred Leach from Delmonico's for life! In August 1999, the commission opted not to revoke Emeril's license, but reprimanded his crew and ordered them to take a "crisis management" class to learn how to avoid such things. Kenny chided Leach during the meeting for not showing up to apologize.

As of 2005, Leach has tied his future to Las Vegas, the capital of second and future chances. He's got an online gossip site about celebrities on the Strip, and he's been trying to corral interest in an all-Las Vegas, all the time, cable TV channel.

Vegas Politics

21

Harry Reid's Favorite Sons and Daughters

The "G-Sting" bribery scandal that broke in 2003 was named after a combination of the G-strings topless dancers use to cover their crotches, and the sting operation by the FBI that trapped former County Commissioner Lance Malone, topless club bigwig Mike Galardi, and three Vegas elected officials: County Commissioners Erin Kenny, Dario Herrera and Mary Kincaid-Chauncey. What was even more disgusting about the topless club scandal for Las Vegas Democrats was that two of their top prospects were on the Galardi topless club bribery gravy train even as they were running for higher offices: Kenny for Lieutenant Governor and Herrera for Congress in 2002. Kenny and Herrera both shared something else: each was re-cruited to run personally by Nevada's soft-spoken but quick-tempered senior U.S. Senator, Harry Reid. After what happened to two of his handpicked candidates in 2002 (neither Kenny nor Dario Herrera were honest with him beforehand about their actions with Galardi), Reid bowed out of further candi-date-recruiting during the 2004 contest. He may have unknowingly rid the party of two bad apples, but he certainly achieved his main goal: to get Herrera to give up his seat on the commission so Harry's son Rory could take it over and have his foot in the door for governor, Congress, or the Senate. Rory attracted big name-recognition money and did take Herrera's seat in a Republican year.

"Who is Harry Reid?" read the message on the bottom of the TV screen on the conservative Fox News Network during a news story on Nevada's juicy senator. The question was a good one for all but the most politically involved outside Nevada. The reporter was standing on a craggy bluff overlooking Reid's hometown of Searchlight, a desolate and dusty mobile home park and highway truck stop about forty miles south of Las Vegas. The sixty-three-year-old Reid had just been elected Minority Leader of the Democrats in the Senate, another coup in a remarkable career that has arguably put him in the company of only the late Senator Pat McCarran, a political power on Capitol Hill in the 1940s and 1950s, as the most influential senator in Nevada political history. Of course, the Democrats had the lowest number of senators in years, only forty-four, and so few others aside from Reid—the expert vote counter for the party's defeated former leader, Tom Daschle of South Dakota—were interested in the job. For now, higher-profile Democrats in the Senate like New York's Hillary Clinton and Christopher Dodd of Connecticut were satisfied to watch Harry with polite smiles and applause as he fought the good PR fight on the Hill against radical rightwing GOP judicial candidates on behalf of a vulnerable, rebuilding national party.

Actually, the conservative-liberal Reid ended up coming off quite well in the late 2004 Fox broadcast, as the successful product of a humble, small desert town, the son of a hard-working miner who tragically killed himself in 1972. But several months later, the Republican National Committee would use the same "Who is Harry Reid?" title in a long political hit piece e-mailed to a million GOP members and various news reporters. The Republicans painted Reid as to the left of Ted Kennedy and Al Gore, a fake opponent of abortion (in keeping with his Mormon faith, he is pro-life), a big supporter of "Hillarycare," a tool of Democratic lobbyists, "just another tax-and-spend liberal" who voted against child tax credit increases and marriage penalty relief, an "extreme" environmentalist, and a limousine-type with a $750,000 condo in Washington. The e-mail also bashed Reid as a "friend of trial lawyers" whose contributions to him totaled $1.1 million from 1999 to 2004, double his second-highest contributor group, casinos and gaming companies, which sent him $549,000.

Reid, who complained about the e-mails, knew full well why the RNC did it. After all, he, like President Bush in this case, had worked behind the scenes directing his party to bash political opponents while simultaneously negotiating backroom legislative and other deals with them.

Reid is a soft-spoken but tough former amateur boxer, an ambitious veteran political scraper and bankable candidate. Reid eloped with his high school girlfriend, an Orthodox Jewish girl, in 1959. Both soon converted to Mormonism and moved to attend college in Utah. In the early 1960s, Reid was already a dad of two kids while attending the George Washington University law school. Broke almost to the point of quitting, he turned to the Mormon Church in Vegas for financial aid and never forgot its generosity. The church would later prove crucial to his political success with money, influence, and, of less importance, their votes.

Back in town later in the 1960s, Reid also rose to prominence with the backing of his former history teacher and boxing coach, mentor and Roman Catholic, Mike O'Callaghan, later a two-term governor of Nevada. While his patron, O'Callaghan arranged to get young Harry a patronage job as a Capitol policeman while Reid went to law school in Washington. After graduating in 1964, Reid's ambition took him from city attorney in the small town of Henderson to state legislator to Lieutenant Governor and, later, chairman of the Nevada Gaming Commission. After he was elected the youngest Lieutenant Governor in Nevada history, at age thirty-one, in 1970, he flew too high like Icarus, running for the U.S. Senate in '74. He lost to the popular northern Nevada conservative Republican and former Governor Paul Laxalt. The still-young Reid blamed the media in the northern end of the state for his loss.

Within only a year's time, he'd run for governor, senator, and Las Vegas mayor. During his well-funded run for Vegas mayor in 1975, he took his opponent, the incumbent and lovable ribbon-cutter Bill Briare, for granted. Reid lost at the polls and his political future seemed bleak. But his old political patron and Nevada Governor O'Callaghan rescued his career via appointment, to the prestigious position of chairman of the Gaming Commission in 1977, a truly surreal time in Las Vegas casino history. Mafia chiefs from Chicago and Kansas City had set up cash-stealing schemes at the Stardust and Fremont hotels. The infamous Anthony "Tony the Ant" Spilotro—on whom Joe Pesci based his character in Martin Scorsese's 1995 movie about the era, *Casino*—ran street crime for Chicago mob interests. The hidden boss at the Stardust was Frank "Lefty" Rosenthal, who ran the secret cash skimming there for the Chicago and KC mobs.

Despite pressure in the provincial Vegas community to let bygones be bygones for the town's tired, poor, and overtaxed mob guys, Reid successfully helped kick out Rosenthal, the biggest fish in the caper, in 1978. Rosenthal, who undoubtedly used his skimmed cash reserves to hire local mob lawyer Oscar Goodman, accused Reid of accepting a free lunch at the Stardust with Brian Greenspun, an executive with the *Las Vegas Sun* and the son of *Sun* publisher Hank Greenspun. Rosenthal had a fit at the commission hearing—fictionalized in *Casino* with Robert DeNiro as the Rosenthal character and comedian Dick Smothers playing Harry's part—after the commission rejected his plea for a "key employee" license to work as a Stardust casino executive. While the TV mini-cams ran, Lefty got Harry to admit to the free lunch and that Rosenthal was in the Stardust's café during it. It didn't change the outcome, but Rosenthal and his cohorts stayed angry. Reid later claimed that the mob tried to bribe him, made threatening phone calls, and put bombs in his car that didn't work. But that wasn't all. Joe Agosto, a blustery, big-nosed mob character out of Hollywood's central casting or an old Mickey Spillane novel, was heard on an FBI-taped conversation saying: "I gotta cleanface in my pocket." Investigators theorized that the connected Joe—a front to help the mob swipe cash at the Tropicana hotel—was referring to Harry, and launched a five-month probe, only to find out that Agosto was only doing what mob sociopaths like him do best: bullshitting to impress.

Reid allowed himself to become part of a sting operation in 1979, after two California men, Jack Gordon and Joe Daly, told him they'd bribe him and another member of the Gaming Commission in exchange for approving a new kind of gaming machine. With the FBI videotaping the transaction, Gordon handed Reid $12,000. When agents moved in to arrest Gordon, Reid angrily dove after him and grabbed him by the throat. Agents had to remove Reid from the choking suspect. Gordon, who served six months in prison, married pop singer LaToya Jackson in 1991 but she later charged him with assaulting her.

When O'Callaghan, normally a straight arrow, once used campaign cash to buy gold wristwatches for his cronies, Reid privately sighed to a local politico that he regretted some of the people he had to put up with because he owed them favors. But Reid needed and held onto his powerful and popular buddy, nicknamed "Boomer." In 1982, Reid was elected to Congress. Only four years later, Reid succeeded in reaching the U.S. Senate and, thanks to a skill for shepherding Democrat votes on bills, rose to Majority Whip fifteen years later. He survived a big scare in 1998 when he beat challenger and GOP Congressman John Ensign by only several hundred votes statewide (Ensign ran for Nevada's other Senate seat and won two years later). Reid won big in 2004 with token opposition thanks to an early edge in campaign cash reserves: $1.8 million from political action committees of all kinds. Top Vegas casino firms were among his contributors: MGM Mirage ($102,000), Mandalay Resort Group ($83,000) and Harrah's Entertainment ($67,000). The 2004 landslide only helped elevate him to Minority Leader soon after the election.

Reid didn't waste much time in his new position of power, meeting with top Democratic lobbyists on Capitol Hill. In fact, in January 2005, within hours of being sworn in, Reid went to a D.C. steakhouse where top lobbyists lavished attention on him. A reporter for the daily Capitol Hill publication *Roll Call*, in an article titled "Reid to Enlist K Street," wrote: "It was like a scene out of *The Godfather*," said one lobbyist at the reception. '(Reid) was in the back room and people were lined up to greet him and pay homage.'"

But for Reid, the lobbying game has been a family affair. As usual, Las Vegans would have to read about the extent of his family ties in an out-of-town newspaper. In a now-famous front page story, "In Nevada, The Name to Know Is Reid," on June 23, 2003, the *Los Angeles Times* described the extent to which members of Reid's extended family have become Washington lobbyists—the very people who, as directed by their benefactors, pressure and cajole members of Congress to pass or block legislation.

One is Reid's son Key Reid, a lobbyist in D.C. for the largest law firm in Nevada, Vegas-based Lionel, Sawyer & Collins (the other three Reid sons, Leif, Josh and Rory, also work for the same firm). The firm's clients include the cities of Las Vegas and Boulder, Colorado, and the Olympia Land Corporation, a company that was part of a group of unsuccessful bidders for 1,710 acres of federal land in Nevada for private development in 2005. The winning bid at the Bureau of Land Management auction was $510 million. Senator Reid's own Clark County Conservation of Public Land and Natural Resources Act, legislation he sponsored that passed Congress in 2002, triggered the land sale.

Key Reid charged his clients about $220,000 in 2002 for his lobbying services. The other Reid family member is Steven Barringer, Senator Reid's son-in-law, married to his daughter, Lana. In 2003, Barringer's MGN, Inc. firm lobbied on behalf of clients such as American Electric Power, the National Mining Association, and Verizon.

The L.A. *Times* observed that the Clark County Conservation of Public Land and Natural Resources Act—touted by Reid as a victory for the local environment—turned out to have benefits for land developers and commercial interests including those represented by Lionel Sawyer. Indeed, because of that legislation, a controversial land deal near McCarran International Airport, in which investors made a quick $5 million profit, prompted investigations by the county, Las Vegas police, and the FBI in 2005.

"What Reid did not explain was that the (Act of 2002) promised a cavalcade of benefits to real estate developers, corporations, and local institutions that were paying hundreds of thousands in lobbying fees to his sons' and his son-in-law's firms, federal lobbyist reports show," *Times* reporters Chuck Neubauer and Richard T. Cooper wrote. "Other provisions were intended to benefit a real estate development headed by a senior partner in the Nevada firm that employs all four of Reid's sons."

The appearance of conflict of interest—that he used his position in public service to aid his family's careers and help enrich their business clients—wasn't lost on the Senator. Reid told the paper that conflicts were the natural order of things. "My kids are well-educated. They are nice young men. My daughter is a lovely young woman," the paper quoted Reid. His son-in-law, he said, is a "brilliant lawyer."

"I have done, I think, everything I can to protect myself and to protect my boys. The only thing I could do to help myself is to have fewer kids."

Further, the *Times* story claimed that Reid also had close relationships to lobbyists for Nevada's top industries, gaming and mining, which was not surprising and far less convincing a point. "So pervasive are the ties among Reid, members of his family, and Nevada's leading industries and institutions that it's difficult to find a significant field in which such a relationship does not exist."

After he was interviewed for the story, Reid made sure that his son Key and son-in-law Barringer were barred from talking to his staff and from even entering his D.C. office while working for their lobbying clients. When asked about the move, Reid's press aide described it as a "coincidence" unrelated to the *Times* story.

Back in 2002, Reid got his son inserted into the County Commission by urging the commission's chairman, Dario Herrera, to run for the new Nevada Congressional District #3 against Republican Jon Porter. Herrera turned out to be a disaster as a candidate. He was eventually indicted by a federal grand jury on nineteen felony charges of soliciting bribes and other allegations, and shipped to federal prison. Herrera's vulnerabilities as a candidate should have been known before he was chosen and hundreds of thousands in out-of-state donations from the national party and elsewhere were bestowed on him. In 2001 and 2002, the senator found himself embracing a rare successful Hispanic candidate in Herrera, who could help inspire Vegas's generally politically uninspired Hispanic residents to turn out for him and later for Reid. After Herrera tanked, Rory ascended and is in a position to one day succeed his dad in the Senate.

Reid's loyal representatives run the county and state Democratic organizations. The vast majority of its members are over age 60, with little interest in recruiting anyone younger. Many are a coffee klatch of cranky, former activists from the 1970s who are now the keepers of the crypt.

Harry set a new record for fundraising by a Nevada U.S. Senator, taking in $8.4 million since 2003. Over six weeks in late summer 2004, Reid garnered $477,000 in campaign money while his kamikaze GOP counterpart, Richard Ziser (father of the anti-gay marriage ballot proposition that carried Nevada in 2002) panhandled just $38,000.

Undaunted by public criticism, Reid continues to take advantage of his political clout. In early 2005, he helped his daughter-in-law, Cynthia Reid, Rory's wife, get appointed by Republican Governor Kenny Guinn to the State Board of Education. John Hawk, who had held the seat, had just resigned after the state Ethics Commission determined that his work at a Las Vegas school funded by the state board amounted to a conflict of interest. Cynthia herself insisted that family connections had nothing to do with it. Instead, she claimed the governor simply chose her on the basis of her education (English

degree from Utah's Brigham Young University, a master's in education from UNLV) and her teaching high school and community college courses.

"They (her family) didn't earn my master's degree or teach
my classes," she told the *Las Vegas Review-Journal*.

22

Democrats and Daiquiris

SHELLEY BERKLEY

*I*n true Las Vegas fashion, Shelley Berkley, the liberal Democratic Congresswoman from the First District, has proved her mettle as an expert in promoting herself and changing in the face of new realities. The former Shelley Levine, a proud member of the Vegas Jewish community, retained her anglicized last name via her first marriage (as did Lieutenant Governor Lorraine Hunt) despite her current one to a Vegas doctor, Larry Lehrner. Her deep understanding of the local politics of influence peddling would haunt her in 1998, the year she won election to Congress even after an embarrassing ethics scandal and questions about her truthfulness under oath.

Underneath that ethics scandal were uncomfortable truths about how things get done in Vegas. Berkley, who grew up in Las Vegas while her dad worked as a waiter at the Sands hotel, was elected student body president at Valley High School, became a lawyer, member of the State Assembly, and mother of two boys. By the mid-1990s, the well-connected Shelley was working as "vice president of government and legal affairs" for casino developer and political opportunist Sheldon Adelson, a blowhard former Bostonian who was planning his $1.5 billion Venetian Hotel out of the ashes of the imploded old Sands property on the Strip. When it came to trying to influence local politics, Sheldon was completely, shamelessly—and without knowing it, comically—obvious, often to the detriment of his own cause. He made blunt, self-serving public statements and spent $2 million in Vegas to sway the 1998 election, to mixed results. He produced outlandishly negative TV ads attacking those he didn't want elected (one showed a squeaky-voiced boy in a school uniform and cap, meant to represent County Commission candidate Dario Herrera, who was twenty-five years old and won anyway). Like Howard Hughes, but on a smaller scale, Adelson brazenly sought to control the political processes in Las Vegas and Nevada through money and inside political deals, even when they seemed out of proportion to his needs.

Shelley served him well as an advisor. In 1996 and 1997, communicating privately with Adelson in ways similar to how Bob Maheu did with Hughes more than twenty-five years earlier, she wrote memos and made phone calls to her boss suggesting how to curry favor with elected officials on the County Commission through contributions, job offers, and business concessions.

Shelley and Sheldon soon had a parting of the ways—frequently the case with Sheldon and his former executives in the 1990s—in May 1997. While a member of the state university's Board of Regents, Shelley ran for Congressional District 1 in 1998. Some of the written and taped evidence of her advice to Adelson dropped into the lap of the news media, and suddenly, Shelley, who was the acknowledged frontrunner thanks to weak opposition and her ability to raise funds, was on the defensive.

In a 1996 memo, she advised Adelson to consider laying some bread on some local judges because it tended to work, although which judges and which contributors she knew who were later "helped" via their contributions, she did not name. "In the past two weeks, I have contacted three judges to help us with legal problems . . . Each judge was instrumental in dismissing tickets, reducing the charges, lowering the fines, and reducing the points against their (contributor's) records . . . (Judges) tend to help those (who) have helped them. If we want to be able to continue contacting the judges when we need to, I strongly urge that we donate to the judges that I recommend."

Next, Berkley urged her boss to insert himself into the shady politics of the Clark County Commission. In a recorded conversation in May 1997, Shelley advised that it would have been a good idea to hire the uncle of Commissioner Erin Kenny to get her to vote for what Sheldon wanted. "That's how you could have gotten Erin because she would have been very, very grateful."

Another remark caught on tape came close to destroying Berkley's political career. Berkley suggested that if Adelson wanted to ensure future votes from Commissioner Yvonne Atkinson Gates for building permits for the Venetian project, he'd have to give the commissioner what she wanted: a lease at his new hotel for Atkinson Gates's business, called Fat Tuesday's, a bar dispensing frozen daiquiris.

"Yvonne wants money," Shelley said on tape. "She wants a business." She also explained to him that Atkinson Gates "asked me to approach them about a daiquiri, I don't, she's got some little daiquiri things, you know."

Later that year, Adelson complained to the news media that Atkinson Gates had approached him twice in 1996 about granting her space at the Venetian for her daiquiri business, including one time two weeks after she had voted against permits for the hotel. Atkinson Gates would later admit to talking to executives of the MGM, New York-New York, Circus Circus hotels, and that her partner, longtime Vegas investor Ed Nigro, had talked about leases for Fat Tuesday with a company that brokered retail space in malls at the Caesars Palace and Stratosphere hotels. Adelson told the *Las Vegas Sun* in October 1997 that he "was just shocked it was a public official who would say that." He added that he asked Berkley if what Atkinson Gates did was okay, and he said Shelley replied, "absolutely, everybody is doing it." In the same story, Berkley told the reporter she remembered Adelson did not appear shocked at all and instead had told the commissioner that he felt "that it would be better to do (a) coffee (business)."

Adelson, who claimed to be outraged by Berkley's advice, granted none of her requests, but got his yuks from the political fires Berkley's written and taped words stoked during the 1998 Congressional campaign. However, in the face of potential case evidence, the local district attorney, the FBI, and U.S. Attorney's office passed on investigating the corrupt judges Berkley alluded to, or Commissioners Kenny and Atkinson Gates, or Berkley herself.

Although Berkley dodged a political bullet that might have hit and killed someone with fewer powerful friends in town, another major cause for concern soon appeared. Her taped comments about Atkinson Gates seemed to conflict with her sworn testimony in January 1998 before the Nevada Commission on Ethics. The ethics panel was investigating whether Atkinson Gates broke state ethics codes by trying to subtly peddle influence with Strip hotels in exchange for landing space for her daiquiri franchises. When the panel asked Berkley if Atkinson Gates had ever requested her to urge Adelson to grant her the daiquiri concession, Shelley answered: "She did not." This is not what she indicated on the 1997 tape, released in June 1998, four months after her testimony to the ethics board.

But Shelley got lucky again. Vegas didn't seem to mind, and the FBI and the local authorities were either asleep, didn't care or decided the tape and memo couldn't be used as evidence. One thing's for sure: if she wasn't exactly telling the truth in public to the ethics panel, she was being forthcoming in telling it like it is about Clark County politics to Adelson in her memo and on the phone.

The liberal Democrat-leaning *Las Vegas Sun*, a Berkley supporter, predictably downplayed the whole incident and published an interview with her on June 9, 1998, days after the tape surfaced. She apologized, described the situation as "a bump in the road," said "most of all, I've disappointed myself" and that she had "inadvertently contributed to the cynicism that permeates the political process." She said that an unidentified friend or someone recorded her phone conversation illegally. Who that was, who might have committed a felony under Nevada law by recording a phone call without her consent, was never revealed.

She then turned it further her way in the *Sun* story. "Someone is trying to keep me out of Congress and silence my voice on important issues. This just makes me fight harder for what I believe in." Lastly, she implied Sheldon had been behind the leaks.

But the Rush Limbaugh-conservative, pro-Republican *Las Vegas Review-Journal* condemned her in an editorial on June 5, 1998.

"Ms. Berkley pleads pragmatism in defending her advice to Mr. Adelson and insists she adheres to high ethical standards. But that's weak," the *R-J* declared. "One who advocates corruption can't later claim with any moral authority to be an innocent bystander. If this is how the system works, the last thing we need are more people in power who wink and nod as they wade into the muck rather than strive to make changes."

"At the very least, these revelations raise ugly questions about Shelley Berkley's judgment and integrity. But they also bring us close to that fine line between outright bribery, and the cynical delivery of political contributions by those who assume they can buy access and preferred treatment."

"Perhaps the district attorney should find out which side of that line Shelley Berkley is on."

District Attorney Stewart Bell didn't bother. "It's not a crime for people to believe that by making contributions to persons in authority that they can curry favor," Bell told the Associated Press in Vegas. "The important thing is for the elected officials to have the integrity that that not be a reality." Berkley dodged comment on it, but Craig Walton, an expert on ethics at UNLV, told the AP that "to undertake to corrupt a person is certainly wrong. If (Berkley) is teaching newcomers to town (Adelson) that this is how we live around here, it's bad advice."

Berkley won the 1998 race, by 49 percent to 46 percent, against a hapless GOP opponent, Don Chairez, in the general election in November. Shelley had amassed a six-to-one advantage in campaign money over Chairez, $882,000 to $153,000. Chairez, who got a $15,000 donation from Adelson, had decided to give up a six-year district court judgeship—after only eighteen months into the term—to run against Berkley.

Berkley won a tough and dirty campaign in 2000 waged by Nevada state senator Jon Porter, an insurance salesman and former Boulder City Councilman, who brought up the memos and tape again. It mattered even less that time.

By the early 2000s, Berkley's ability as a fundraiser was considered formidable by national standards. She'd also received a huge advantage after Nevada was awarded a third congressional district following population gains in the 2000 census. Horse trading by both parties in the State Legislature, in charge of writing new district boundaries, bestowed a very "safe" Democratic district for Berkley, and an equally impregnable one for the GOP Rep. Jim Gibbons covering a piece of Las Vegas and everything else to the predominately right-wing northern Nevada up to Idaho. The new third district was made to be roughly even in registration, around Berkley's and extending south to the Arizona border. Still, her opponent in the Year of the Republican, 2002—Las Vegas Councilwoman Lynette Boggs McDonald, hailed by the GOP for being black—lost by only 11 percent in Shelley's district despite the wide Democratic registration edge.

Relatively secure in her district but without much chance for higher office—given the Reid dynasty and right-wing-conservative northern Nevada—Shelley has tended to cling fast to bread-and-butter liberal issues like protecting Social Security. Her commitment to veteran's affairs is no doubt based on good political advice. She remains a staunch opponent of the proposed national nuclear waste dump in Yucca Mountain, 100 miles northwest of Las Vegas, and an outspoken supporter of Israel, which she frequently visits and incessantly defends. She can be prone to making inappropriate remarks in public, such as when she used a microphone to complain to the band of her high school alma mater for failing to play a song she wanted. When Senator John Kerry came to Vegas to campaign in 2004, Shelley introduced the national party's Presidential nominee with a long string of remarks about her district: "my district leads the nation in growth of labor members, my district leads the nation in growth of seniors, my district leads the nation in . . ." etc., etc. Each time, the politely smiling Kerry expected to be handed the microphone but had to wait. When she finally handed it to him, he might have been thinking that Shelley's district perhaps also led the nation in platitudes.

23

GOP Rocks the Vote

Republicans in Vegas have generally had their share of political maladies and private-life embarrassments in recent years,
except they are typically a whole lot blander and boorish than
the Democrats. One example came in 2005, when the state
Democratic Party in Vegas howled at Congressman Jim Gibbons, the GOP's right-wing frontrunner for governor in 2006.
Gibbons stubbed his toe while trying to be glib to a like-
minded audience way up in Elko, one of northern Nevada's
many hick-town bastions of loutish anti-liberalism. Gibbons,
as boorish as they come, first said "liberals" in the entertainment industry were "trying to divide this country" over the Iraq
and Afghanistan wars, then put his foot into it.

"I say we tell those liberal, tree-hugging, Birkenstock-wear-
ing, hippie, tie-dyed liberals to go make their movies and their
music and whine somewhere else . . . Can (these) possibly be
the same people who are for abortion? They are the same people who are for animal rights, but they are not for the rights of
the unborn."

Gibbons later apologized, not for the content, but for the
fact that what he said—word for word—had been lifted without credit from a verbal screed given by the virulent anti-liberal

Beth Chapman, Alabama's state auditor, at a Bama rally in March 2003, to standing ovations. Later known as "The Speech," it was so popular Chapman copyrighted it. Thing is, Gibbons didn't need anything resembling a real speech to appeal to his supporters in the so-called cow counties of upper Nevada, where the comparatively few registered Democrats try to hide their affiliation from their neighbors to avoid embarrassment and open ridicule. A northern Nevadan, the married Gibbons, while campaigning in liberal Las Vegas, would embarrass himself even more after cavorting in Vegas with a drunken, buxom cocktail waitress, just three weeks before the election (he'd win anyway).

The state's Republicans have at times outsmarted the Dems in some ways since the mid-1990s. Nevada had been a solid Democratic state—with some liberal and some rather conservative Democrats—for decades. That changed in 1994 when creeping Republican registration gains in suburban Vegas and Henderson—many of them disgruntled, overtaxed former Californians—helped kick the lackluster Democratic Rep. James Bilbray out of office, and almost unseated Senator Reid in 1998 (who may have been saved by his largely conservative Mormon brethren). John Ensign, who took out Bilbray in 1994 and nearly beat Reid in 1998, became junior U.S. Senator in 2000 when Senator Richard Bryan, "Mr. Integrity" throughout his long political career, decided not to run after two terms. Bryan's decision was unfortunate for Senate Democrats trying to cling to the slimmest of majorities that year, but he left in favor of cashing out as a gaming industry attorney for the influential Vegas firm Lionel, Sawyer & Collins. His first effort as a casino attorney was to track the possibility—via legislation in Washington—of the Vegas industry's entry into Internet gaming.

Nevada's GOP senator with the permanent tan, Ensign is a father of three and former veterinarian whose legacy includes opening the first twenty-four-hour pet hospital in Vegas. He is an attractive political candidate in a state not used to them. As the conservative website Redstate.com observed: "Ensign has the advantage of fitting the Zoolander definition of being really ridiculously good-looking by Senate standards." His pedigree is good by Vegas standards, too: he's the son of Mike Ensign, a longtime Vegas casino partner, executive and multimillionaire. Not surprisingly, in 1996, Ensign topped all freshman Congressman in fundraising with almost $800,000, with gaming firms Station Casinos, Harrah's, Circus Circus, and Primadonna Resorts among his largest donors. Almost a year before the 2000 Senate race, Ensign had already raised $2 million (he'd raise $5.2 million in the end). Months before his race against Harry Reid in 1998, Ensign told the *Las Vegas Sun* that he learned about the highway congestion on Interstate 15 (between Las Vegas and Los Angeles) while working for his dad's casino company in Jean, Nevada, just outside Vegas.

"I can tell you that on every weekend, and especially on busy weekends, motorists know they'll be backed up at Barstow and so they leave Southern Nevada earlier and earlier and earlier. And because our gaming business really involves renting time at a slot machine or a blackjack table, the less time they're here, the less money comes into our economy."

Conservatives like most of Ensign's conservative stances, like his switch from pro-choice to pro-life before deciding to run for Congress in 1994 at age thirty-six. His money and looks work for him and override his tendency to make inopportune, even silly statements. Once in 1998, he referred to environmental groups as "socialists." But after his Senate win in 2000, his right-wing friends chided him for his political alliances with Harry Reid on Nevada issues like his opposition to the proposed Yucca Mountain waste dump. He didn't court their favor either when he told *USA Today* about Hillary Clinton: "With some of my folks back home, I have to be careful how I say this, but I like her." It was Ensign, while a Congressman, who originally wrote the Southern Nevada Public Land Management Act of 1998, which sends 15 percent of funds earned from federal land sales in the Vegas Valley back to state education and local water programs, and the remaining 85 percent to acquire "environmentally sensitive" lands. It had generated $2 billion by 2005, although President Bush said he wanted the money sent back to Washington for deficit reduction.

Ensign, known to fly back to Vegas to be with his family each weekend, probably courted the most controversy in February 2002, when he'd made himself conspicuously absent from the Nevada political scene for weeks. His press secretary told the media that he "has asked everyone for privacy." When his colleagues said it had to do with his family, there were murmurs from Washington about a fall from grace, an affair that jeopardized his marriage to his wife, Darlene. This from a guy described by the *Washington Post* in 1999 as someone who "will not be alone in a car with a woman" to avoid the potential fallout. But Ensign's people kept the lid down tight and it went away. He was reelected in the Democrat year of 2006, helped the GOP retain two Nevada House seats, and was picked by his party to head the National Republican Senatorial Committee.

After losing to Shelley Berkley in 2000, Jon Porter was already the frontrunner for the GOP nomination for the new Third District. When Harry Reid determined in fall 2001 that Dario Herrera would run for the seat, GOP opposition researchers— led by Mike Slanker, a former Ensign campaign chief who specializes in fighting dirty—went into action like the White House Plumbers, eventually spoon-feeding the conservative *Review-Journal* boxfuls of nasty stuff they'd uncovered on Herrera in the months before 2002. For Dario, it would result in one of the biggest political belly flops in local history. They unearthed private things about Herrera's stupidity that had to be seen to be believed. He cast votes on the county commission that benefited his wife's billboard business contacts; he accepted a no-bid contract from a crony involving tens of thousands in federal housing funds for public relations services he could never prove he provided (a federal investigation followed); he borrowed money for his home from a man convicted of crimes involving Eastern mobsters; there were rumored infidelities and trips to topless clubs that nearly cost him his marriage; on and on. The worst news of all—his associations with admitted briber and topless clubman Mike Galardi, and accepting unreported cash payments from Galardi while running for Congress—was unknown at the time except to the FBI, which was taping his phone chats with Galardi's front man, Lance Malone. Dario at the time was changing his cell phone number each month, to no apparent avail.

All the bespectacled, squeaky-clean, somnolent Porter, from sleepy Boulder City, had to do was sit back, relax, and let Dario beat himself in 2002. There was no party registration edge to overcome this time. The Democratic Congressional Campaign Committee had placed the Third District in its top ten winnable House races in the country, and so devoted lots of valuable money, Washington staff time, and political power to Dario.

In 2001, Dario was only twenty-eight and won comparisons to a young John F. Kennedy—youthful, attractive, articulate and ethnic, with powerful backing. At one point in the 2002 race, the national Democrats had Dario make their weekly national radio broadcast. But nothing Dario could do, even in desperation, could bring him up in the polls amid the publicity about his many missteps. At one point, he announced that he was converting from Catholicism to his wife's Mormon faith (which was also mentor Harry's), but the obvious cheap trick didn't gain him much except added distrust. Dario spent hundreds of thousands provided by the national party, used many young, inspired white and Hispanic volunteers to walk precincts and paid hefty salaries to former Al Gore campaign pros, but garnered a humiliating 19 percent of the vote against Porter. In the end, the campaign was all about Dario and who-knows-what about Jon.

Not one of Congress's greatest or standout members, or one to attract much controversy, Porter was able to win his voter-reg even district again in 2004. His Democratic opponent was a politically inexperienced, wealthy former Caesars Palace casino executive, Tom Gallagher, who ran—with no base or name ID—late in the year after no one else (with his access to money) would. Gallagher opened up his considerable bank account, spending $486,000 of his own funds, and raised about $1 million. Porter raised $2.2 million of other people's money. Republicans pointed out that Gallagher had once donated $10,000 to the GOP. Union people donned T-shirts at Gallagher's media performances, top Democrats parroted each other talking him up, he touted a rags-to-riches, here's-my-family, now-vote-for-me shtick. But Gallagher's paint-by-numbers campaign was one of those "wake me up when it's over" types: predictably futile. Porter won easily. One of the few controversies about Porter was an ear ailment that has prevented him from traveling by air, only meaning it might take him longer to return home, if anyone's paying attention. Moderate and loyal Republican Jon Porter proved, by his reelection in 2006, there was still white-bread power to burn in Vegas.

24

Bad Girls, Sad Girls

Elected politics in Las Vegas was almost the exclusive purview of men for decades, but the city added more women to the establishment than ever in the 1990s, especially to powerful seats on the Clark County Commission, considered a steppingstone to statewide office or Congress. The spark began with Jan Laverty Jones, who made a name for herself by appearing in TV promotions for local car dealerships owned by her then-husband, Fletcher Jones, Jr. (with the refrain, "Nobody is cheaper than Fletcher Jones"). In 1991, the city's controversial mayor, Ron Lurie, was ready to leave office and make his fortune, in slot machine sales for the Japanese company Sigma Game. Local moneymen and women rallied around the wealthy Jones and convinced her to run, despite her lack of experience in public office. She agreed and won, becoming the city's second female leader in more than eighty years and the first since the 1950s.

Meanwhile, more and more professional women arrived in town from out of state, joining law firms, the government bureaucracy, and private business. All of a sudden, like a changing tide, female residents made themselves heard in the ballot box, supporting and sweeping girl candidates into office. Little-known attorneys—good and not too good—were elected to local judgeships because, pollsters found, many Las Vegas women voted for them simply because of their female first names on the ballot. But a surprising number of these new lady pol-ettes were quickly caught up in foolhardy ethical or corruption scandals, some involving their strange male bedfellows, on the commission, city council, and in state government. They proved they could be just as tough, and possibly even more corrupt, than the all-boys club. They broke through the glass ceiling of political sleaze and influence peddling. By 2005, the once-promising political careers of many of these "Nineties Women" had been cut short, victims of their own ambitions, misjudgments, rigidity, or greed.

Perhaps the biggest bungler of this class was Erin Kenny, elected to the county commission in 1994, though barely over thirty years old. An attractive, blonde mother of four, Kenny was catapulted into office with little political experience and she did it in only a few short years. She and her chiropractor husband John Kenny moved to Vegas from outside Chicago in 1989, when she took a job at the Imperial Palace casino on the Strip as a waitress. Her first experience in politics came in 1992 when she won a State Assembly seat. Animated and talkative during commission meetings, Kenny evolved into a popular, aggressive, and for the most part, respected local politician. Re-elected in 1998, Kenny had her eyes on higher office. She began to ally herself with big donors, developers, labor leaders, and other special interests. When the anti-union Wal-Mart sought to build big-box grocery stores, Kenny courted union support in passing a county law banning them. Then she started to overreach. She unsuccessfully pushed laws banning smoking in restaurants and motorists from using their cell phones, and laws that required car dealerships to close on Sundays. Worse, she sought to cut the residence of a candidate for her seat out of her district. At one point, she denied allegations from county employees that she ordered them to break into the office of Commissioner Mary Kincaid-Chauncey.

Details about Kenny's less attractive private side began to leak out. Demanding and temperamental with her staff, Kenny was resented by developers and their handlers for frequently changing her commitments to their projects at the last minute. People wondered why the home she shared with her husband, in the upper-middle class Rhodes Ranch housing community in southwestern Las Vegas, had so many expensive improvements done, given her family's relatively modest income. She also started to propose requests made by Rhodes Ranch developer Jim Rhodes.

By 2002, the blush was off the rose. It was clear she was headed for a fall from grace, and she decided to bail out of rough-and-tumble Clark County Commission politics. But few knew what she really had to hide. Senator Harry Reid, recruiting local Democrats for Congress and state offices, convinced her to run at the last minute for Lieutenant Governor against incumbent Lorraine Hunt, a former Vegas lounge singer. Kenny's handlers ran an incredibly inept campaign, but she would have lost to Hunt anyway as Nevada voters, in a pro-George Bush mood like much of the rest of the country in the months after 9/11, sent Republicans into all six statewide offices.

But the feds were waiting. They'd held off until after the election to file the nineteen felony charges against Kenny in the G-Sting topless club, buy-a-vote scandal. Kenny turned out to be topless clubman Mike Galardi's point lady on amendments to the No Touch Ordinance (later known as the Limited Touch Ordinance) regulating how customers at the clubs could lay their hands on the dancers. In 2002, Kenny agreed to make sure health inspectors okayed Galardi's new Jaguar's club, and to ask the county staff to "recraft" the No Touch law to include amendments to permit tipping in dancers' G-strings and dancers to be under the age of twenty-one where liquor is served, in exchange for payoffs to her campaign. On March 17, 2002, Galardi was heard on the FBI wire telling his lobbyist, former Commissioner Lance Malone, to give Erin "another five" ($5,000) and that she'd receive a new Denali SUV if she got the ordinance on the March 19th agenda. On August 13, 2002, a few weeks before the primary for Lieutenant Governor, Erin accepted $10,000 from Malone. A week later, she voted with Commissioners Dario Herrera and Mary Kincaid-Chauncey (both later indicted with her) to suspend enforcement of the No Touch Ordinance.

As the clock ticked down on the 2002 statewide election that Senator Reid convinced her to enter, Kenny got more demanding. On the phone to Malone on October 16, she needed new campaign cash so bad she told him: "I'm ready to cry uncle! But I, if I cry uncle, it's gotta be substantial . . . I mean it. I mean it. And it has to be today." On October 28, days before the election, she called up Malone and said: "Tell me what I've got to do, but I've gotta have money from him . . . I'm begging now . . . I'm on my knees begging!" Two days later she called and really shook Malone down, saying of Galardi: "He's gonna be asking me to do the biggest thing in the world for him right now, you know what I mean? And that's, that's what I'm doing." On November 1, Malone gave Erin a $10,000 donation. Even though she lost the election, a few weeks later on December 3 she joined her later-indicted chums Herrera and Kincaid-Chauncey and voted to amend the No Touch law to permit G-string tipping.

In 2003, the federal grand jury charged Erin with extortion, wire fraud, and conspiracy (her husband was also indicted). The prosecution charged she solicited and accepted money provided by topless club maven Galardi, and then voted to help his clubs and interfere with those of his rivals. Unlike her fellow former politicians who were similarly charged, after learning the feds had it all on tape, Kenny pled guilty. Things got a little worse for her in 2005, when it was reported that she had facilitated some controversial land deals near McCarran International Airport years earlier, one that resulted in a quick $5 million profit for its investors. Seems she arranged to have the land, meant for development as a graveyard, changed to a commercial designation. The FBI jumped into probing that one, too. During Las Vegas's centennial year, it was hard to imagine how she could escape time in state prison.

Of the female politicians elected in the 1990s, Kathy Augustine was perhaps the most abusive, emasculating, and arrogant, traits that contributed to her impeachment as a state office holder in 2004. Her overbearing personality was evident clear back to when her political career began in 1992. With a B.A. in political science from Occidental College in Los Angeles, and a master's in public administration from California State College, Long Beach, she ran as a Republican for a Democratic party-majority, mostly white State Assembly district seat in Las Vegas against an African-American woman named Dora Harris. Kathy promptly used a campaign mailer showing the blonde Kathy beside a lousy, grainy shot of Harris. With obvious racial overtones, the photos had this caption: "There are two women running for Assembly in this district, but . . . there is a real difference." So there was, and it helped Kathy win.

Underhanded tactics would soon serve her well again. After one term in the Assembly, she got elected to a Vegas seat in the State Senate, also in a Democratic-majority district, in 1994 after besmirching her Jewish-American opponent, Lori Lipman Brown. Brown, the Democrat incumbent and more than a trifle self-righteous, had insisted on leaving the senate chamber during the outset of the 1993 legislative sessions at the state capitol to say her own prayers each time the Legislature began the proceedings with prayers by a Christian clergyman who mentioned Jesus, although she joined her colleagues during nondenominational prayers. Leaders of the senate had no problem with her decision, but Augustine pounded Brown during the 1994 campaign, saying Brown "actively opposed prayer" at the sessions, and claimed that Brown had refused to salute the American flag.

The religious and patriotic exaggerations were effective, as Augustine prevailed in the general election. Brown later sued Augustine over the allegations in Vegas but Augustine settled it privately. She sent an apology letter to Brown, later released to the public, in which she agreed that Brown had prayed separately as a result "of your discomfort praying to Christ each day." Kathy explained that her inaccurate statement about Brown failing to recite the Pledge of Allegiance "was my way of characterizing information received from other senators who recounted a few occasions in which you were delayed entering the chambers. The term 'refused to participate in the pledge of allegiance' was an unfortunate choice of words developed during the heat of the campaign." Yadda, yadda. But the yuks were reserved for Augustine, as the loss in 1994 ruined Brown's political career.

While in the state capitol, Augustine turned off her colleagues in the senate with her mean disposition and abrasiveness. Her ambition quickly took her attention away from the senate in 1998 to run for controller, the least distinguished statewide office that collects debts owed the state and shares bill-paying duties with the state treasurer. It was a statewide office and political springboard, nonetheless. Augustine defeated her Democratic rival, becoming the first woman in Nevada history to hold the office. During her term, stories about her bitchiness and the abuse heaped on her staff on a daily basis—such as throwing paper at them during numerous, screaming pissy fits they nicknamed "the wrath of Kath"—circulated from Carson City to Las Vegas. Employees said privately that she made the controller's office the worst office in the state to work in and that morale couldn't be lower.

When Augustine ran for reelection in 2002, she looked like the weakest entry on the Republican ticket. Rumors circulated that her controller staffers illegally worked on her campaign inside a tiny office at the Grant Sawyer state building in Las Vegas. Democrats tried to use it against her but failed to prove it, or convince anyone in the local media to investigate it. The Democratic party, which ran John Lee, a state senator from Las Vegas, against her, chastised Augustine for spending campaign money to take a government course at Harvard University and recycled the old stories about how her staff couldn't stand her. However, she benefited from the GOP landslide in the wake of 9/11. Republicans swept all six statewide races, although Augustine received the lowest margin of victory.

She triumphed over tragedy the following year, this time outside of politics. After Charles, her second husband, died following treatments at a hospital in Honolulu, Kathy waited a few weeks before marrying a male nurse who'd tended to Charles there.

In 2004, abused employees took state's evidence concerning her behavior to the Nevada Commission on Ethics, overseer of the state's ethics code that rarely goes beyond wrist-slapping wayward politicians. Augustine's case would prove an unusual one. Her former workers provided statements and proof that in 2002, she ordered the public employees to use state computers, phones, and faxes for campaign work such as writing her speeches, preparing election mailers, keeping tabs on contributions, and filing her financial disclosure reports.

One ex-state employee, Jennifer Normington, said she worked full-time on campaign duties in the controller's office from September to November 2002, confirming rumors Democrats heard two years earlier. Normington described Augustine as so demanding that she refused to permit Normington to visit her grandmother on weekends or to leave work to inject her cat with the insulin it needed. Normington said Kathy once deadpanned to her: "That cat's interfering with your life. You need to kill it."

Augustine at first offered to resign to avoid the charges, but the state attorney general, keen on proceeding, rejected the offer—unwisely as it turned out. The ethics commission found Augustine guilty of violating ethics laws and really threw the book at her, levying a fine of $15,000, the highest in state history. Nevada's Republican big boys, Governor Kenny Guinn, U.S. Senator John Ensign, and Congressman Jim Gibbons, all urged her to step down. But now her fur was ruffled. Augustine, who admitted to the deeds alleged, thought she was punished enough and threw up a firewall, saying she'd tattle on other elected officials who did what she did. Guinn then directed the legislature to convene a special session for her impeachment. In November, every member of the state assembly voted in favor of three counts of impeachment—the first impeachment of a state officer in Nevada's 140-year history—and a trial began in the senate in Carson City to consider kicking her out. She hired influential Las Vegas defense ringer Dominic Gentile, and lawyer John Arrascada, of Reno.

Augustine's impeachment trial, televised live in Carson City to be seen in Las Vegas, ranged from fascinating to bizarre. Normington and other former workers testified, as did the head of the ethics commission, who described Augustine's conduct as the worst ever reported to the commission. Augustine, suspended but still collecting her $80,000 annual salary, usually sat frowning, with her arms folded. Arrascada projected Power-Point slides, one showing a painting of a guillotine surrounded by a mob of people, and another of Joan of Arc with a halo. He argued Augustine's transgressions were minor and didn't rise to removal from office. He attacked both the former employees and the attorney general's office for bringing the case.

In the end, Augustine made out much like Bill Clinton did five years earlier. Conviction required fourteen votes, two thirds of the twenty-one-member senate, on each count. But she was convicted on just one count—misusing state office machines, a misdemeanor crime—by a fourteen to seven vote. The senate dismissed, by eleven to nine, the count she forced Normington to do election work, and only eleven voted to convict for misuse of Normington's state computer. Her office saved, the forty-eight-year-old Augustine burst into tears. One supporter, Senator Bob Beers, a Las Vegas Republican, told the *Las Vegas Sun* that the attorney general's case was weak and that computer discs used to show the state computer had been used for campaign purposes "could have been manufactured."

A triumphant Augustine likened what the Senate did to a parent bawling out a kid. She vowed she would manage her employees the way she always did and left open another run for office in 2006, even for Congress. The good news for Augustine was compounded a few days later when Art Ingram, her former chief deputy, withdrew a sexual harassment suit he filed in federal court against her that summer. Ingram charged Augustine with "sexually stalking" him at the controller's office, and that she showed "outright hostility" towards him after he rejected her "sexually inappropriate conduct." Ingram insisted that the controller would have fired him had he not been called to active duty in the U.S. Army. He dropped the suit after an attorney hired by the Nevada attorney general's office to represent Augustine claimed to have found a 1964 federal law specifically exempting elected officials from sexual harassment claims. Reckoning the need to clarify some inconsistent laws, given the weird results of Augustine's impeachment hearing, legislators introduced bills during the state's 2005 session that would explicitly outlaw the use of public computers for campaign work by state office holders. But Augustine's luck ran out in 2006, when she was murdered by her male nurse husband, who injected her with a deadly dose of a muscle relaxant.

During the 2002 election season, none other than conservative syndicated columnist George Will mentioned Las Vegas Congressional candidate Lynette Boggs McDonald as a new, modern kind of up and coming Republican—notably because she was an African-American woman. Will's comments were given the jaundiced-eye treatment in Las Vegas, since most observers believed that Boggs McDonald, a Las Vegas City Councilwoman, had little chance against the better-financed Democrat incumbent Rep. Shelley Berkley, whose party enjoyed a wide margin in registration thanks to the many working-class blacks and Hispanics in the district.

A former Miss Oregon of 1989, and the mother of a young boy, Boggs McDonald had worked for the city as an assistant manager in the 1990s before she was appointed to the City Council in 1999. That same year, she began a controversial relationship with the powerful local casino operator and prolific developer, Station Casinos. She accepted an expenses-paid trip from the company to attend a football game at Notre Dame, where she'd received her bachelor's degree. She listed it as a campaign contribution. The junket got her in hot water with the state ethics board, which cleared her of wrongdoing in 2001. In 2003, she accepted an appointment to Station Casinos' board of directors, prompting conflict of interest concerns. She promised the *Las Vegas Sun* that there would be no true conflict, since "just two of the eleven Stations (casino) properties are in the city limits."

A devoted Catholic, Boggs McDonald startled some at a council meeting in 2002 when during a disagreement with Councilman Larry Brown, she blurted out, "We are a Christian people and God will be my rock, my sword, my shield. I will not be intimidated or deterred . . . I send you right back into the fire in the name of Jesus Christ."

In the Republican election year of 2002, she pulled within 11 percent of Berkley in 2002, despite the more than twenty-point edge in registered Democrats in the district. Berkley's much bigger campaign account and expensive field operation involving a crew of full-time, paid operatives who walked the same precincts in her district five or more times for months during the campaign also made a difference. Boggs McDonald's impressive showing in defeat was a bit surprising, since she seemed unable to attract attention to her candidacy aside from GOP donors and friendly write-ups from outside the district. Boggs McDonald also had shown she could bring in the dough, too, raising about $1 million.

However, her reputation after three years on the City Council had preceded her. Insiders already knew her as someone who voted for permits and zoning either before or after cashing large campaign donations from home and commercial developers and other companies with business with the city. According to city voting and campaign records, Boggs McDonald received $117,000 from developers and businesses asking the council for beneficial votes from 2000 to 2002, with $32,500 coming before she even voted for their requests. Two of the valley's top developers, Howard Hughes Properties and the Focus Commercial Group, each donated $5,000 following favorable votes in 2000 and used the same carrot to garner future favors. Hughes fronted her another $20,000 for seven favorable votes between 2000 and 2002, while Focus dropped her $8,000 in 2001 following one vote. She also got $12,000 from construction firm Poggemeyer Design Group in 2001 after she favored two of its projects.

Her reputation became notorious in 2004, when she ran for election to the seat on the County Commission. In March of that year, GOP Governor Kenny Guinn had appointed her to serve the rest of the term of a commissioner who left office. It was District F, the same area where Station Casinos had proposed three new casinos. But she had to run for the office—two years were left on the four-year term—that November. Her Democratic opponent, longtime Assemblyman David Goldwater, son of a powerful Vegas lawyer, dubbed her "the queen of the special interests" and aired campaign ads about her pro-development stances, her defaulting on a home mortgage, and her refusal to release her tax records. He also chided her about allegations that she tried to save her husband from being fired (for chronic absenteeism, although the reason was not publicly released) from a cushy patronage job with Nevada's Republican state treasurer. But Goldwater made things worse for himself, and more lucrative for Boggs McDonald, by claiming he favored a "slow growth" policy for the booming Las Vegas Valley.

During her side of the contest, Boggs McDonald would viciously skewer the equally vulnerable Goldwater with even harder-hitting TV ads, including ones replayed many times showing Goldwater's mug shots from a 2002 DUI arrest. She also mentioned years-old sexual harassment whines about him from Republican female legislators (for pinning up girlie pictures in his capitol office) and his alleged role in a 1994 bar fight.

Knowing where the butter was, local developers and gaming interests with developments in mind pushed their chips toward

Boggs McDonald, while some hedged by stacking far less on Goldwater. By the September 2004 primary, Boggs McDonald's camp led with $876,000—$357,000 of it from development interests—to Goldwater $223,000 for Goldwater, who got only $78,000 from builders and casinos. The biggest development and casino "whales" showered funds on Lynette's side, including her patron Station Casinos ($35,000), Hughes ($20,000), J.A. Tiberti Construction and Coast Casinos ($15,000 each), MGM Mirage, the Palms Casino and four others ($10,000 each) and Boyd Gaming and seventeen home developers and development firm attorneys ($5,000 each). By the end of the 2004 campaign, Boggs McDonald had pulled in $1.3 million, an all-time record for a Clark County Commission seat. She dispatched Goldwater on Election Day, 52 percent to 48 percent. Her political reputation remained intact—in Vegas, development cash is king! She started to gear herself for another run, and campaign account, in 2006.

She went right to work. A month later, on December 8, 2004, Commissioner Boggs McDonald, over the objections of residents, made the motion to approve the zoning for Station Casinos' planned Durango Station casino on sixty-one acres in southwestern Las Vegas, and to avoid a "design review" that would have delayed it. All she asked was that Station cut the casino from a breathtaking 196,000 square feet—as big as the MGM Grand on the Strip—to a still-huge 120,000 square feet. She prevailed on all three motions without opposition from her colleagues. Then, on December 14, despite pleas from neighbors that it was too tall, she approved an 80-foot-high LED sign for Station's new Red Rock Station casino, also in her district. Commissioners voted seven to nothing on that one, too. It seemed greater heights surely awaited her, not to mention her patrons. But her petard would hit the glass ceiling—she lost the election in 2006, and in 2007 was charged with four felony crimes, such as perjury and falsely claiming she lived in her commission district.

In December 2004, the County Commission gathered to say a few kind words and goodbye to Commissioner Mary Kincaid-Chauncey, after her eight years on the board. The matronly, high school librarian-type mother of eight was leaving office following her defeat in the September primary election, another victim of the temptations of sinful, growing Las Vegas. In May 2003, she was indicted on nineteen felony counts by a federal grand jury that charged her with taking bribes from topless club owner Mike Galardi. Mary's husband, former Vegas cop Robert Chauncey, was also indicted. She denied the charges and refused calls for her to resign in late 2003. The guy who beat her easily in the 2004 Democratic primary (and won in the general election), Assemblyman Tom Collins, ran promising to reform county campaign money laws.

"You exemplify a great public servant," Chip Maxfield, the commission's chairman, politely told Mary at what was her final commission meeting.

"I want to again thank you for your service through the years for the citizens," Commissioner Boggs McDonald told her. "Although 10,000 may be against you, with God on your side, you will always be with the majority."

"I am really looking forward to retirement," the sixty-six-year-old Kincaid-Chauncey said with understatement. "You'll still see me around. You'll still see me in the community doing all kinds of things."

One of those things was continuing to deny she did anything wrong, even after being found guilty in 2007 on 13 felony counts, and going to federal prison. While some were taken aback, even saddened, by her indictment, under her nice-lady façade, Mary Kincaid-Chauncey was as calculating as they come with the moneymen. A member on the local boards of the Boy and Girl Scouts, and Boys and Girls Clubs, she knew a lot more about county politics than most believed. Her political background extends to her election to the city council of North Las Vegas in 1977, back when that town was a small, little-known sometimes corrupt Mayberry where backroom deals were the norm. She fit right in there. Her only real political problem came in 2001, when the state ethics board considered, then dropped, a complaint that she used county employees to work at her flower shop and on her reelection campaign. Fact is, Mary and her former commission colleague Erin Kenny— also indicted on similar charges involving Garladi—used to be the fundraising champs of the county, each taking in more than $1.2 million. Kenny did the trick back in 1998, and Kincaid-Chauncey in 2000, before Boggs McDonald topped them by a hundred grand in 2004.

After hearing the evidence from the infamous 2003 "G-Sting" probe, the federal grand jury charged Mary with extortion, conspiracy, and wire fraud. Prosecutors said they had her on tape asking for $15,000—to pay for tuition for her grandson's skiing school—from ex-Commissioner Lance Malone, who represented topless club owner Galardi. Mary even got her daughter in the act. On June 5, 2002, she sent her daughter to serve as a bag girl for $4,000 from Malone, meant for the grandson's tuition.

Mary was charged with accepting money for votes from Galardi on four occasions from 2001 to 2002. She voted in December 2002 in favor of Galardi's plea to allow patrons to place tip money in G-strings, a favorite activity among locals and visitors to town. She also agreed to Galardi's request she oppose an uncooperative building inspector chief's bid to become the permanent head of the department. In 2003, she failed to list

Galardi's donations on her financial disclosure statement. Mary also asked that her son and his friends be treated to a visit to Galardi's Cheetah's topless club, where they later received free beers, and her son got a hundred dollars' worth of free lap dances.

She denied taking money or soliciting favors, and suggested she intended to place Galardi's money in some kind of trust account she created to benefit some of the kids she knew (she'd been a foster mom to more than twenty kids). She blamed the media, then she claimed she was set up by the FBI, which leaked damaging details to reporters and "lied" to her by saying she was not a suspect when they first questioned her. She insisted she was still a straight arrow.

"I never even had a traffic ticket before," she sniffed at a news conference.

When she was elected to the county commission in 1992, Yvonne Atkinson Gates just about had it all. She was attractive, black, articulate, bankable, the wife of a district judge, Lee Gates. She seemed destined soon for state office or Congress, Harry Reid or no Harry Reid. But her career would be tarnished before her first term was up, after a fateful chat with a neighbor and friend, the politically connected local investor Ed Nigro, in 1996. Nigro suggested she go into the frozen daiquiri business in Vegas. "I'd never been in business before," she'd explain years later to skeptical officials. "I was excited."

Yvonne did enter the drink biz, with Nigro as her partner, but instead of pursuing it like anyone outside of politics would do it, she foolishly chose to approach some Strip hotel operators, directly, about giving her a franchise on their properties. She'd talked it over with the District Attorney's office, which instructed her to get a decision first from the state Ethics Commission. But she waited eleven months to do that, after first talking it over with the casino landlords. Her business with Nigro won a signed lease with the MGM Grand hotel in August 1997, after she and Nigro both met with the hotel company's chairman, J. Terrence Lanni.

Her improper behavior soon leaked out to the media and Yvonne found herself up on charges before the ethics board. She compounded her problems by giving misleading testimony to the panel, telling them that she was actually a "silent partner" and had not been involved with negotiating leases with anyone. In January 1998, the ethics crew found her guilty of violating a pair of state ethics laws: her misleading testimony and lobbying the casino people about drink franchises while serving as an elected official.

"You are not a stupid woman," the panel's chairwoman, Mary Boetsch, told her. "But sometimes I get the feeling you are in the ozone."

Atkinson Gates, crying, said that she "never owned a business. I am not a businessperson. I went to a friend who I relied on and trusted. Just because I didn't know how much I was going to invest doesn't mean I'm in the ozone." She also played the race card, stating that: "Being a female and being black hasn't helped."

But that wasn't all. The ethics people were also looking into other potential conflicts of Yvonne's that came to light after the daiquiri charges. This time, it was about three lucrative concessions at the new D Gates at McCarran International Airport that she both recommended and voted in favor of awarding in August 1997. Two of the businesses went to her paid campaign advisor, Michael Chambliss, and another to a company that included Judy Klein, a friend and donor to her campaign. In August 1998, the commission found her guilty on six counts of failing to disclose her relationships with Chambliss and Klein, and for voting in favor of them. It also found Commissioner

Lance Malone guilty of putting a friend of his on the list of concessionaires and voting for him. In response, Yvonne circled the wagons and brought Democratic Congresswoman Maxine Waters, an African-American from California, to town for support and statements to the media.

But in their decision, ethics officials said that Yvonne "knew exactly what effect her recommendations might have" on the selection process at the airport. "A process that was designed to be apolitical and merit-based was rendered entirely political and cronyism-based by Ms. Atkinson Gates with her little list," they snapped.

Meanwhile, Yvonne survived two failed attempts to recall her from office. And, she would survive her ethics crisis as well. A state judge ruled that the ethics laws cited by the commission in the airport case were vague and unconstitutional, and he threw her case out.

The thing went away as far as she, and Las Vegas voters, were concerned. Atkinson Gates was re-elected in 2000 and 2004. In 2001, she complained publicly about the elevation and Harry Reid's "anointment" of County Commissioner Dario Herrera to run for the new Third Congressional district Nevada got from population increases. She felt she'd been snubbed, kept from the big campaign money people in Washington. Senator Reid could well have been concerned that had Yvonne been elected to Congress, she might have made a strong candidate against Rory to succeed his dad in the U.S. Senate. In any case, the spotlight on Yvonne's political career had dimmed considerably by 2005, when she became a general contractor to build custom homes. But trouble was on the horizon (and, yet another potential corruption scandal for Las Vegas) in January 2007. She said she would resign her seat in March, and boasted she never was really found guilty of wrongdoing while in office. But weeks after her resignation, she faced investigations by the FBI and Las Vegas police on a list of things, such as her home valued at $2.4 million, why $356,000 from her campaign fund was paid to her son's company in 2004, and how she voted to give cash grants to a non-profit group without revealing she was building a custom home for the group's vice president.

Since the early 1990s, Las Vegas City Councilman Michael Mc-Donald, a former Las Vegas cop, had been powerful and controversial in his ward in the western part of the valley. But by 2003, voters had had enough of his tarnished reputation, including an association with topless club owner Rick Rizzolo. But who could beat the well-financed and well-known McDonald? No prominent candidate emerged. So Janet Moncrief, a veteran registered nurse and mother of a twenty-two-year-old daughter, entered the race. When the election came down to him and her, McDonald set forth a nasty, negative campaign that included leaking info about Moncrief's DUI arrest and seeing to it that her mug shots were published by the *Review-Journal*.

The forty-three-year-old Moncrief, yet another political novice, hitched her wagon to a pair of local political ne'er-do-wells: former Vegas World casino owner Bob Stupak and one-time Vegas Councilman Steve Miller, who served as her advisors. Stupak, a failed candidate for mayor in 1986, helped Moncrief raise campaign funds. It was Stupak, after the returns showed he lost the 1986 contest, who was photographed, standing on a car, making a drunken speech at the headquarters of Ron Lurie, the man who won the election. Miller, who claims his dad invented the tacky Vegas souvenir, the dice clock, was the landlord of a topless cabaret and well known as a loose cannon.

As the race went on, McDonald could see he was losing

ground, and he was, thanks to problems of his own making. Some people thought he'd be indicted along with others in the G-Sting topless club corruption case. He wasn't, but voters remained wary of him. For one thing, his buddy Rizzolo's club had been raided by the FBI.

Moncrief beat McDonald in the primary, 48 percent to 43, and outpolled him in the bitter June 2003 run-off. She'd walked many of the precincts herself, sometimes dressed in her hospital scrubs. But her problems began almost immediately. McDonald's campaign manager, Jim Ferrence, went nuts after losing the councilman as a client and filed a complaint alleging Moncrief violated state laws by sending illegal mailers and underreporting what she spent on her campaign.

Steve Miller and Peter Christoff, a Moncrief campaign worker who had run against her and McDonald in the primary, filed ethics complaints against Janet on the day she was sworn in. Miller, the local gadfly, filed a sworn statement saying he helped advise Moncrief for much of her campaign appearances for free, but that she failed to note his donated services in her disclosure reports. He admitted his motivation to file was partly because he was offended that a new political advisor had urged her to dump him. He insisted that Janet's camp was responsible for a political dirty trick—distributing an anti-union mailer that appeared to come from McDonald. Christoff, an equally loose cannon, acknowledged that he prepared the mailer, timed so voters would receive it on Election Day.

Janet denied the allegations, but constituents unhappy with her launched a recall drive. After an investigation, Moncrief was found to have indeed underreported some campaign charges, but the allegations appeared way overblown: she didn't report expenses and contributions from Miller and costs of a loaned van and the anti-union fliers. But she was also charged with perjury for allegedly signing deceptive campaign reports. After little more than a year in office, Janet was indicted in August 2004 by a grand jury on five counts of allegedly filing false campaign reports.

The recall succeeded and Janet was turned out of office, replaced by Lois Tarkanian, the longtime local politician and former wife of former UNLV basketball coach Jerry Tarkanian. Moncrief visited Lois's campaign victory party that night and tearfully congratulated her. She insisted that she would win her criminal case, but her remarkable and brief political career was in tatters, the result of taking on a vulnerable but powerful incumbent and trusting the people who'd already failed the smell test of a pungent Las Vegas political scene.

The Dunes hotel was a loser until the late 1950s when its desperate new owners brought in Minsky's, a cheap topless review that solidified Vegas as the capital of low-rent stage acts. Here a stagehand is too bored to even check out the tits.

As if topless, butt-floss and garter belt were not enough, this Minsky's dancer piles hats on her head and on some kind of fan thing on a pole, at Dunes hotel, late 1950s.

After his private outdoor lunch with Judith Campbell at Frank's suite at the Sands, JFK waves during a Democratic reception at the Las Vegas Convention Center for his run for president, February 8, 1960. Among the dowagers there, at far right, is dowager-in-chief, a local socialite named Dorothy Dorothy.

JFK shakes hands with Jack Entratter, who that night, February 8, 1960, provided Kennedy a private booth for him and Judith to watch the Rat Pack at the Sands.

President Kennedy, behind Ray-Bans, waves goodbye to Vegas from Air Force One, after giving the first speech by a president in Las Vegas, September 28, 1963.

Dean Martin once said: "You're not drunk if you can lie down on the floor without holding on." Here, Martin takes an unrehearsed pratfall on a Vegas stage, while concerned Sammy Davis, Jr., Peter Lawford (obscured) and Joey Bishop try to help him up, early 1960s.

Peter Lawford (standing) turns to a camera, mid-joke, playing to an audience including blonde Marilyn Monroe (front row center), and her one-time one-night stand, Milton Berle (at left), plus Dean Martin (at right, beside Liz Taylor and Eddie Fisher) and Sammy Davis, Jr. (behind Berle), at the Sands, about 1961.

In the Sands's Copa Room, Marilyn ogles Jack Entratter, who surely comped her flight, room, meals and show passes, because the PR was priceless, about 1961.

Tom Jones with Priscilla and Elvis Presley, late 1960s, after the Presleys wed at the Aladdin. Several years later, Elvis, in a jealous rage over Priscilla leaving him for another man, fired a bullet through the wall of his suite at the Las Vegas Hilton, barely missing his girlfriend in the other room.

Booking photo of Jim Morrison, vocalist for The Doors, taken by Las Vegas police in 1968 after his arrest for brawling with a security guard outside the Pussycat a' Go Go club, now part of the site of Wynn Las Vegas.

Mr. Las Vegas: The adored hidden mob guy, and always camera-shy, Moe Dalitz, left, listens to a guest during a party for Wilbur Clark's birthday, in 1956.

Kirk Kerkorian proudly poses in front of his International Hotel project, which in 1969 became the largest hotel in the world (1,512 rooms). He sought to outdo himself, opening the MGM Grand in 1973 (2,100 rooms), but cut corners on fire safety to do it, with deadly results.

The 1981 fire at the MGM Grand hotel was so hot that flames consumed cars parked out front. Stingy MGM execs had rejected a suggestion from fire inspectors to spend only $192,000 on fire sprinklers. Eighty-five people died in the fire.

A "Moustache Pete" Steve Wynn (second from right) watches the birdie with (from left to right), Toni (Mrs. Wilbur) Clark; Barbara (Mrs. Hank) Greenspun; an unknown Vegas-type idiot in a tux; and Elaine (Mrs. Steve) Wynn, at Steve's Golden Nugget hotel, circa 1970s.

Out of the carriage, but not out of the closet, comes Liberace, at the Las Vegas Hilton, late 1970s. A star on the Strip since the mid-1940s, Liberace's deadly case of AIDS in the 1980s was first reported in Las Vegas. His deathbed, gaudy costumes and pianos are displayed at the Liberace Museum in Vegas.

In disguises during a bit, Tommy Smothers (left) performs in Vegas with younger brother, Dick (right), in the late 1970s. Tommy would be drugged and "trick-rolled" by two hookers at the Aladdin in 1981.

Comic Shecky Greene, famous for his drunken crash into the fountains at Caesars Palace, mugs while sitting next to ex-Sam Giancana moll Phyllis McGuire, at Moe Dalitz's birthday party, circa 1980.

Workers place singer Wayne Newton's name on the marquee of the Aladdin hotel in 1980, when he and partner Ed Torres outbid The Tonight Show *host Johnny Carson to buy the hotel. But the Aladdin jinx (big losses) forced Wayne to sell out in 1982. The Aladdin filed for bankruptcy in 1984.*

High winds in 1991 knocked down the Strip neon sign of the old Vegas World hotel, once owned by former Phyllis McGuire beau Bob Stupak, and now the site of the Stratosphere hotel beside a seedy community dubbed Naked City.

Longhorns on the grill, circa 1970: Actor Chill Wills (left) in front of a Caddy owned by his buddy Benny Binion (right), a one-time killer and convicted tax cheater affectionately known in Vegas as the founder of the former Binion's Horseshoe casino and the World Series of Poker.

Gaming with the Future

25

The Bonfire of Kirk's Vanities

THE MGM FIRE

$\mathcal{L}$ike many other human beings, even including some in Las Vegas, *Arizona Republic* reporter Tom Fitzpatrick was outraged by the negligence shown by the operators of the MGM Grand hotel and county building inspectors preceding the devastating blaze at the MGM in late 1980. It was the second-deadliest fire in American history, and still the worst day ever in Las Vegas.

"They should change the name of the town," Fitzpatrick angrily wrote after the fire killed eighty-four people and injured 500 others (three more of the injured would die months later). "They should change it to Greed, Nevada."

Among the many reasons over the past century to nickname Vegas "Greed, Nevada," the infamous MGM fire certainly ranks at the top. As a result of the disaster, the state soon adopted what were then considered the strictest fire code laws and regulations for hotels in the country, but the laws came as little comfort to the hundreds of victims and their family members affected by the fire. Once again, Vegas did something sensible because it was forced to do it.

When it was completed in 1972, the MGM Grand was the

largest hotel in the world and gave its fifty-five-year-old owner, Kirk Kerkorian, yet another reason to boast—he'd done it for the second time running, since his International Hotel in Vegas became the biggest hotel when it opened in 1969. But like any other Vegas gambling joint that profits from slots and table games, the pressure was on to get it up and running so the revenues could start flowing in to pay for overhead costs before the inevitable profits. That's what's always mattered most, and still does. The only "built-in" advantage at the MGM was the house edge on the gambling, not its hapless patrons.

The MGM Grand fire could easily have been prevented if building and fire prevention procedures that existed in the early 1970s had been followed. But they weren't. Indeed, as Clark County's Fire Chief Roy Parrish told the news media hours after the fire: "They always knew something like this could happen."

Kerkorian's MGM Grand approached fire safety like something out of the 1974 film *The Towering Inferno*, in which fictional builders saved millions on a skyscraper in San Francisco by avoiding costly fire prevention measures. Only this time in real-life Las Vegas, MGM Grand execs rejected a suggestion from fire inspectors that the hotel spend a paltry $192,000 on fire sprinklers. The installation might have delayed precious early gambling revenue. Meanwhile, a compliant building official for Clark County agreed with the MGM—no sprinklers required.

The cause of the MGM Grand fire itself was unremarkable. Sometime during the early morning hours of November 21, 1980, something called an electrical ground fault—wiring that sent power to a compressor beneath a windowed case used to display pies in an eatery called The Deli—got hot, smoldered without detection, and evolved into flames. The fire department was called at 7:15 A.M., and firefighters from a station right across the street on Flamingo Road arrived in only four minutes, in time to see the fire flash. Within five minutes, flames consumed plastic and other flammable materials and raced across the casino at a rate of up to nineteen feet per second. Pressure from the fireball blew out the hotel's front doors all the way down to the northwest end. Flames raced into the covered porte cochere and valet area, injuring some bystanders and totally consuming some parked cars.

As the fire spread north through the casino, firefighters noticed that some clueless gamblers continued to feed the slot machines despite the flames, smoke, and fire hoses. Other customers, similarly oblivious, exited the casino and immediately entered others nearby to resume their gambling. Meanwhile, smoke and toxic fumes soared up the MGM Grand's stairways and elevator shafts. It escaped through the hotel's huge air conditioning system, which should have shut down in response to the fire, but didn't. Also, the fire alarms should have sounded, but didn't. Laundry chutes should have kept the smoke out, but didn't. Stairwells that were supposed to keep smoke out, didn't. Many of those who survived heard about the fire from fleeing guests yelling and knocking on doors in the smoky hallways. Most of the sixty people who died were overcome by smoke that traveled into the hotel's nineteenth to twenty-sixth floors.

Helicopters appeared and flew people off of the hotel's roof. Some trapped guests broke their windows to breathe, and one fell to his death as gawkers and prospective thieves on the street watched. Fitzpatrick complained about "the callous mobs who lined the sidewalks watching the fire, and who grew bored when people stopped jumping out of windows and when the helicopters stopped entertaining them by lifting people off the roofs."

"It is a town that has been indulging in an orgy of self-congratulation ever since the smoke died down," he wrote. "So they set up a few cots in the convention center and served coffee and doughnuts. And a few hundred residents showed up with old clothes. Big deal.

"They don't mention that this was a town in which the looters actually rushed into a burning building and began scooping up money and jewels from the abandoned rooms."

In a news conference, Chief Parrish estimated that about 8,000 guests and employees were in the hotel at the time of the fire (later reduced to 5,000). Parrish said that eighty-three were confirmed dead so far, then observed, incredibly: "That's only 1 percent of life."

"Beautiful," Fitzpatrick wrote. "We are given a reading of the odds. This is exactly what this town deserves; a fire chief who is not only a grandstander, but an oddsmaker as well."

Fitzpatrick wasn't the only outraged journalist. Hank Greenspun, the publisher of the *Las Vegas Sun*, asked in a column: "How can the public officials who are charged with the safety of the public explain to the orphans of parents who died in the fire that the deaths did not have to be?"

How indeed. When it was all over, some local lawyers got rich helping victims collect $223 million from scores of lawsuits. Fire investigators discovered yet more troubling news to go with everything else that went wrong at the MGM: the wire that ignited the conflagration had not been inspected and the compressor under the pies wasn't put in right.

For Vegas, it was a lesson learned the hard way. Nothing approaching the MGM Grand fire has happened since, thanks to stringent, anti-fire building standards. But the rest of the world learned a lesson about Vegas. As Fitzpatrick succinctly put it: "It is all so simple to explain. A rigorous enforcement of fire regulations only would have interfered with commerce. Why should anyone rock the boat? After all, the odds were right."

26

Binion Family Values

Downtown's original "carpet joint," the Binion's Horseshoe hotel-casino once served as a time capsule of the 1950s, a living reminder of Vegas's fun, post–World War II years and its crooked past.

Binion's Horseshoe, founded in the early 1950s by Lester "Benny the Cowboy" Binion, once boasted of the most dedicated gamblers on Fremont Street, but the Binion family dynasty couldn't hold onto the casino past the second generation. The once venerable Horseshoe had weathered recessions before, but Becky Behnen, one of Benny's three daughters, had to give up the property in January 2003 after an IRS investigation and the Culinary Union Local 226 insurance fund foreclosed on the Horseshoe's million-dollar debt. Casino giant Harrah's Entertainment Inc. bought, then sold Binion's after taking over its famous World Series of Poker—another storied innovation of Benny's, who made Texas Hold 'Em the perennial test of high stakes skill and luck—and moving it to the Rio Suite hotel off the Strip.

Just four and a half years after forcing her two brothers—veteran casino managers Jack and Ted—and her sister Brenda to sell their shares of the Horseshoe or face a court battle, the inexperienced and hapless Becky and her equally hapless husband Nick turned the Horseshoe upside down. The luck Benny found in Las Vegas since the late 1940s while on the lam for tax evasion finally ended. Under Becky, the Horseshoe sevened out.

In the history of downtown Las Vegas, the Horseshoe was arguably its most legendary casino. Tales of Benny's vicious gangster past in Texas, his willingness to take bets of almost any amount, and the family's clashes with the hated IRS, drew some of the most loyal Vegas customers ever, from local grinders to Southern yahoos (singer Willie Nelson who loved Benny despite his past, and white supremacist David Duke, a craps player at the Horseshoe) and the hardest of the heart-of-stone poker sharps. The Horseshoe's rough security guards added to Benny's outlaw persona with a reputation for beating up suspected cheats, even getting away with killing some of them.

The story of the Binion family's patriarch is so infamous it's on the continuous loop of retold Las Vegas lore. From the 1930s to mid-1940s, Benny was a ruthless, mob-connected, illegal-gambling baron on the streets of Dallas. He personally killed two people in his life at the very least and ordered killed who knows how many others. But in 1946, after a reform candidate defeated his political fixer in Dallas, he famously drove all the way to Vegas at age forty-two with his wife Teddy, his five kids, and $2 million in cash tucked in a suitcase.

In 1973, Benny told a Nevada historian he'd come to Vegas to bankroll some gambler friends, but he really meant to escape a grand jury indictment in Texas for running an illegal policy wheel racket, and hide from the IRS, which had demanded hundreds of thousands from him in back taxes. Locals admired his story, and would make him one of the most popular figures in Vegas history.

Vegas was just the spot he'd wanted: legalized gambling and

new crops of politicians and cops to buy. Plus, the crusty, pistol-packing Texan, who favored western garb and donned ten-gallon hats throughout his life, fit Vegas's tacky "Old West" fantasy just fine. Look-the-other-way Nevada public servants sanctioned the wealthy Binion by granting him a gaming license, and willing Silver State judges delayed his extradition to Texas.

"The most enjoyable place that you can imagine," Benny later recalled of Vegas in the 1940s and 1950s. "Everybody was friendly, and there wasn't this high jackin', there wasn't no stealin', wasn't nothin'."

In one famous bit of Vegas lore, when questioned by Nevada gaming officials in public about his Texas killings, Benny used the N-word to explain his reason for doing in his African-American bootlegging partner during Prohibition. Benny's white victim—whom he shot dead on a Dallas street—simply deserved it, he'd said. For years, that story drew howls of laughter from ball-capped rednecks in smoky bars throughout Vegas.

In the late 1940s, Binion invested in the Las Vegas Club, and then opened the Westerner Club, both downtown. During this time, he and his former Dallas gambling rackets rival Herb Noble engaged in a feud that would earn Noble the nicknames "The Cat" and "The Clay Pigeon" for avoiding numerous gunshot wounds from hit men Binion hired from afar in Las Vegas. At one point, Noble's wife was blown apart when she turned the ignition on Noble's car, which was fitted with nitroglycerine in one of Benny's hit attempts (Noble was seen hugging the upper half of his wife's body where it lay in his front yard). Benny's men finally blew Noble to pieces (as with his wife, only his upper body was found) with a case of nitro beneath his car outside his Texas ranch in 1951.

Benny himself ran into problems back in Vegas. He had to cough up his gaming license and sell the Westerner after a bodyguard of his shot and killed a street hood in the men's bathroom. In 1951, Benny was licensed again and opened the Eldorado Club casino on Fremont Street, then he leased the old Apache hotel above it and called it Binion's Horseshoe.

But Nevada or no Nevada, the IRS finally caught up to Benny and he was sent to the federal penitentiary at Leavenworth, Kansas, from 1953 to 1957 for tax evasion. The Horseshoe, meanwhile, carried on in his absence. When Benny got out, though his conviction was supposed to prevent him from running the Horseshoe, he ran it anyway behind the scenes with his friends' names on the license. Benny installed young Jack and Ted as dealers, then as bosses, and they slowly acquired pieces of the Horseshoe as they got older in the 1960s. After launching the World Series of Poker in 1970, Benny helped Vegas steal away the annual National Finals Rodeo from Oklahoma.

Benny became a suspect in the notorious, Herb Noble-like car bombing death of local lawyer and ex-FBI man William Coulthard in a Las Vegas parking lot in 1972. The blast blew off his head and legs. Seems that Coulthard, the first agent the FBI sent to Las Vegas during the investigation into Ben "Bugsy" Siegel in 1946, owned some of the land underneath the Horseshoe with his wife, and was ready to sell it to one of Benny's gaming rivals. But Benny had too much influence in town, having corrupted Sheriff Ralph Lamb with large cash loans. Lamb didn't pursue Binion as a suspect and the FBI, which believed for sure Benny arranged the hit, couldn't intervene in the local murder case. Meantime, the Binions kept the rival out and signed a 100-year lease on their dead landlord's former property. Benny lived another seventeen years until 1989.

After losing the Horseshoe for owing back taxes in 2003, things came full circle for the Binion clan. As Benny himself put it, he started the Horseshoe in '51 after "the Eldorado Club had a $870,000 tax loss, which was very attractive. So I took it and I built the thing (Binion's Horseshoe) here. And I put the first carpet on the floor here . . . that was ever downtown."

Still, the large bronze statue of a mounted, cowboy hat-wearing Benny, the first such distinction ever granted a gambling industry man in Nevada, still stands a block from the new Horseshoe casino, a solid monument to the city's legacy of corruption and hypocrisy.

Of Benny's five kids, daughter Barbara's life was the most troubled, tragic, and brief. A rebellious sort, she was a hippie before her time in the late 1950s and early 1960s, often seen by residents walking into shops and on streets downtown in her bare feet. She shot off part of her jaw in a suicide attempt, survived, and looked like a freak until her drug overdose death in 1983. Brenda is the most obscure. She received a share of the family fortune after Benny died in 1989 and $10 million when the casino was sold to Becky in 1998.

Jack, the thoughtful, sensible one, ended up with the most money. He sold his out-of-state Horseshoe Gaming riverboat casinos in the Midwest and South in 2003 for $1.45 billion (putting the Binions out of gaming for the first time since Benny's Dallas rackets in the 1930s).

Ted, regarded as the smartest of the lot, followed his dad's penchant for trouble with the law. Everyone knew he palled around town with the Las Vegas-based Chicago mob figure "Fat Herbie" Blitzstein (who was shot to death in the late 1990s). A heroin junkie for years, Ted was convicted of a drug charge in 1986. He also had a violent side—he was indicted in 1990 on beating, kidnapping and robbery charges brought by Horseshoe patrons (he was never convicted). He struggled to stay clean in the 1990s—he even showed up to a state-required drug test with every strand of hair shaved from his body to avoid detection. But due to his reputation as a drug user and his association with Blitzstein, the state revoked his gaming license in March 1998. That's when friends say he went back on the smack. He died six months later of an apparent drug overdose on September 17, 1998, after purchasing more than a dozen "balloons" of black tar heroin and the drugs Xanax and Valium, delivered to his Las Vegas home. One-time Las Vegas Mayor Jan Laverty Jones testified she went to Ted's home the day before he died and talked to him before walking out with his $40,000 contribution to her unsuccessful run for governor. When his sexy, live-in lover Sandy Murphy and her then-secret lover Rick Tabish—Ted's friend—tried to swipe his $7 million worth of silver bars and rare silver coins—melted from skimmed silver dollars from his dad's Horseshoe—they were arrested for attempted theft, and later, murder.

The widely publicized first trial of the Ted Binion murder case had all the markings of the old, pro-Binion bias from within the Las Vegas community, including an investigator paid by the Binion estate to interview 100 witnesses, the case's overreaching Judge Joseph Bonaventure, and journalists. The overarching factor: the Binion family's competition—Becky figured prominently in the drive against the defendants—with Murphy over Ted's $50 million estate.

Dubbed "Southern Nevada's trial of the century," the proceedings were circus-like and seriously flawed legally, with highly prejudicial, negative suggestions about Murphy and Tabish allowed by Bonaventure into the courtroom and the jury box. The Nevada Supreme Court threw their 2000 murder convictions out and a new trial was ordered. The second trial in 2004 would be far different. Sandy's flaky and bizarre behavior in the first trial—her chronic crying in court, her goofy mugging repeatedly for the cameras, her spray-painting a house-arrest homing device on her leg to match the outfit she wore to court—was well documented, but she was subdued and camera shy in her second trial. Without some of the controversial information allowed into the first trial, the jury was able to focus on challenges to theories of how Binion was killed by the defendants.

The authors of several best-selling books on the Ted Binion murder case were stunned to find out that Sandy and Rick were acquitted of murder in the late 2004 retrial (but convicted of felony theft and conspiracy charges). Now what would they do? Their books were based on the prosecution's apparently strong 2000 case that was a different case before the second jury. What, for instance, would *Positively Fifth Street* author James McManus do about all of the references to Murphy "killing" Ted via "burking"—sitting on his chest and covering his mouth until he died? Legally, she didn't do it. What about the completely unsubstantiated rumor that Murphy and Tabish had malicious sex on the carpeted floor beside Binion while he was dying?

The new team of defense attorneys for Murphy and Tabish discredited the case that the defendants suffocated Binion after they forced him to ingest his drugs. That was the case presented by the prosecution's star witness, HBO *Autopsy* show regular Dr. Michael Baden. During the retrial, new expert witnesses thoroughly discredited Baden's "burking" theory. Justice was finally done for the two foolhardy defendants and for their equally wacky dead friend.

27

Ginji's Aladdin Genie Loses $100 Million

$\mathcal{I}$n the mid-1980s, Japan produced an economic bubble like no other. Nippon banks loaned so much to speculators—more than $22 billion—that the value of commercial land in Tokyo grew by 110 percent from 1985 to 1987. During that time, Japanese investors bought an astonishing $18 billion worth of American real estate, including the sixteen most expensive office buildings in the United States.

One beneficiary of Japan's skyrocketing real estate market was Ginji Yasuda, a native of Korea. After World War II, Yasuda's Korean father moved his family to Tokyo, and changed his son's given name (Sam K. Park) to make it sound more Japanese and to avoid anti-Korean discrimination. After the death of his wealthy pop, Yasuda inherited a large apartment complex in Tokyo that was worth $120 million by 1985.

Thanks to his family's holdings, Yasuda was already a rich, young playboy by the 1960s, often spending his time racing custom-built cars. In Japan, and in Las Vegas, Yasuda was a high roller who earned a reputation as a big loser at Strip casinos, including a reported $2 million loss at Caesars Palace.

While on a Las Vegas visit in 1985, the fifty-three-year-old Yasuda was approached by Dunes hotel casino host Ash Resnick, an elderly former New England mob associate tolerated by local law enforcement and government officials. Resnick suggested Yasuda buy the then-bankrupt Aladdin hotel-casino across the street. It was the right time for another king-sized Japanese investment in American property.

The unlucky Aladdin property, originally the site of the failed former Tally Ho hotel in 1963, got its name and Arabian theme in 1966 from owner Milton Prell. A large, glittering model of Aladdin's lamp topped the hotel's sign on the Strip. Elvis and Priscilla were married there in 1967. Prell booked cheeky burlesque shows and comics, such as a young Richard Pryor, at the Aladdin's misspelled Bagdad Theater. Later owners included a parade of losers, notably, Mae George and other front persons who allowed Detroit mobsters like James Tamer and Vito "Billy Jack" Giacalone to soak the Aladdin of its excess cash until the late 1970s. Wayne Newton, the famous pop star and local lounge singer with a black belt in karate, along with former Rivera hotel boss Ed Torres, outbid *The Tonight Show* host Johnny Carson for the Aladdin in 1980. Management problems persisted, leading Wayne to sell his share in 1982 while Ed filed for bankruptcy in 1984.

Now it was Yasuda's turn to try to make a dollar out of fifteen cents. He sold his Tokyo apartment complex, and his $54 million cash bid for the 1,100-room Aladdin won the day in bankruptcy court. But when he took over on January 21, 1986, Yasuda had to close it down, as he didn't have a state gaming license yet. A year later, after spending $30 million on renovations plus $800,000 a month to keep some of the Aladdin's employees on the payroll, Yasuda became the first foreigner ever to be licensed for gambling in Nevada. The license, however, was for only two years with the condition he hire experienced casino managers.

Yasuda selected Dennis Gomes, a respected former Nevada gaming board investigator, to spearhead a promising casino management team picked by Gomes. But Yasuda soon blocked Gomes's levelheaded requests, such as marketing toward low-rolling slot players in addition to the high-spending whales. Yasuda thought slot players weren't classy enough. He was condescending to his experienced American casino advisors and refused to listen. After only five months, he dumped the Gomes group without replacing them and ran the casino himself.

Up in the Aladdin's large, top-floor high-roller suite, Yasuda lived the high life with his young, doll-faced trophy wife, Yoko, with whom he sat on the suite's long balcony overlooking the Strip. Yasuda reserved one of the hotel's guest room elevators for use by only himself and his wife. Yoko is said to have chartered the hotel company's private jet for impulsive shopping trips in New York. She was known to enjoy driving the hotel's black Rolls Royce down the Strip for shopping sprees at the Fashion Show Mall. Even their two dogs were pampered—they freely relieved themselves inside the suite, leaving yellow stains along the walls leading to the balcony.

By 1989, the Aladdin was still the Aladdin, an aging money pit. Yasuda had now frittered away more than $100 million on the place, including millions on extravagant surveillance and computerized race book equipment. As bad luck would have it, the Japanese government told him he owed $90 million in capital gains taxes on proceeds from the apartment building he used to buy his way onto the Strip.

The flame on Yasuda's lamp was fading fast. Japanese police alleged he accepted $6.6 million in loans from a Tokyo financial firm run by an associate of the Japanese organized crime group, the Yakuza. The gaming board said he failed to report the sources of $4.5 million in loans, which he'd used to pay the IRS. Yasuda hired Grant Sawyer, Nevada's venerated former governor, to help convince the gaming board to hold on until he could sell the hotel to a white knight.

But on August 28, 1989, facing foreclosure for failing to service the Aladdin's $40 million mortgage, and in declining health from lung cancer, Yasuda filed for bankruptcy. He listed $121.2 million in debts to 810 creditors and assets of only $82.9 million. The gaming board stripped Yasuda of his license for failing to tell them about the Tokyo loans, but agreed to let him transfer the license to Yoko Yasuda. A bankruptcy judge appointed a "debtor in possession" to manage the place and save its 1,700 employees. Meanwhile, the board ordered Yasuda to have no involvement in the casino's finances, and never to set foot in the Aladdin again.

But the state, citing Yoko's lack of experience running a casino, took her gaming license away only a week later and gave it to a brand new bankruptcy trustee. Yoko returned to her husband's side at their home in Beverly Hills, where he died in December 1989 at age fifty-seven.

In 2000, the Aladdin reopened after a massive, $1.2 billion infusion by investor Jack Sommer's family trust that subtracted the Aladdin's main hotel and casino and added 2,567 new rooms, plus a cavernous, maze-like interior shopping and eatery mall called the Desert Passage. But the curse of the Aladdin soon reared its ugly head and the new place fell into bankruptcy. For one thing, the owner botched the plans by placing the casino's entrance too far in from the street. Was the Aladdin in fact built atop an Indian burial ground?

By 2003—fourteen years, three owners, and an implosion of the old hotel building later—the Aladdin was set on a new journey with a planned new name, Planet Hollywood, thanks to another winning bid from yet another bankruptcy court. The new owners, former Hard Rock Café impresario Robert Earl and his New York-based partners Douglas P. Teitelbaum and Theodore W. Darnell, snatched the Aladdin for a steal at just $637 million while investing only $40 million of their own money. Earl was himself a veteran of financial towel-throwing. His fancy Planet Hollywood hamburger chain, which once featured actors Bruce Willis and Arnold Schwarzenegger among its high-profile investors, failed in an attempt to acquire the old Desert Inn on the Strip in the mid-1990s. He lost his celebrity partners and later emerged out of two bankruptcy filings, due to a lack of repeat business. In 2004, Earl embarrassed himself with the Gaming Commission by failing to pay the Nevada sales and use taxes his Planet Hollywood burger joint incurred at Caesars Palace, and having to admit he kept important information off of his casino license application. He was in trouble well before the new hotel's 2007 opening.

Earl's grand plan included stripping the Aladdin of its Arabian décor and basing it this time on his twice-bankrupted Planet Hollywood venture: adorning the insides with Tinsel Town movie memorabilia and inviting movie and TV people to plug their wares at the hotel.

So long, suckers.

28

Billionaire Sandboxes

STEVE WYNN VERSUS SHELDON ADELSON

Neighboring Strip casino moguls Steve Wynn and Sheldon Adelson did not see eye to eye on a whole lot in 2005, while Steve was developing his newest dream resort project, and Sheldon was building his underground parking garage and drug store right across the street.

Steve let it be known he didn't like Sheldon's insistence on anchoring a new little shopping mall with a Walgreen's, only a block from Steve's swank new $2.7 billion Wynn Las Vegas, the world's most expensive casino.

Wynn was readying things like a Ferrari and Maserati dealership, a sixty-car fancy used car lot, an eighteen-story faux mountain fronting the Strip, a small man-made lake with a water and image projection attraction, a new golf course, a crew of overpaid celebrity chefs, fashion shows with sexy models wearing Dior and Lagerfeld clothing, an expensive, brand new Broadway-type musical, 2,700 hotel rooms, and 111,000 square feet for gambling fun.

Steve was even accommodating superstitious Chinese patrons by taking the forties (unlucky numbers) out of his fifty-floor hotel—the floor numbers in the elevators stop at thirty-nine and resume at fifty. As he'd been doing so well on Wall Street—stock in his Wynn Resorts company had climbed by more than 400 percent since 2002—he decided to build a second, even more exclusive hotel-casino, called Encore, for another $1.4 billion, on the other side of Wynn Las Vegas.

However, the ever-stubborn Sheldon, who is used to getting his way (he's known for holding his telephone conferences with Wall Streeters from his home in Israel), prevailed on his Walgreen's.

Then there was the little thing about Sheldon owing Clark County about 11,000 more parking spaces than he had at his Venetian hotel and his convention complex, right across Sands Avenue from Wynn Las Vegas. To be technical about it, county codes required Sheldon to provide an astonishing 16,000 spaces, taking into account his plans to build another 3,000 hotel rooms on the corner of the Strip he controls. But the pliant county let him reduce that to 11,000.

Still, Sheldon stalled. His builders dug an immense, atomic bomb crater into the hard desert ground on the corner of Sands Avenue and the Strip. He wanted to install a six-level underground garage, but took forever to do it. His and Steve's $400-an-hour attorneys sniped at each other for months and months in public and in private. Steve's lawyers said it'd take Sheldon until at least 2006 to finish it, if then.

Steve wouldn't relent on this one. His new joint is next to Sheldon's Sands Expo Center, a huge convention building with no parking. Steve and his neighbors have howled that Sheldon's employees, guests, and conventioneers would be using their parking lots to walk over to Sheldon's Venetian.

"He has the world's third-biggest convention center . . . and not one single car parking space to serve it," Steve related to a *Las Vegas Sun* columnist in February 2005. "My garage and my door and my VIP entrance are directly adjacent to the Sands Expo Center. So what we will end up with is to have a police state to stop people from taking our parking for our guests and walking across the street."

"He has to build more parking and he has come to that conclusion, I think, reluctantly," he added. "But they are the most grossly under-parked facility in the history of Las Vegas. He has 4,000 rooms and (spaces for) 4,400 cars."

As for Sheldon, he remained silent in public and steadfast, to put it mildly, in private.

But one thing the pair of multibillionaires could definitely agree on is that 2004 was their best year ever, on paper at least.

Of the two, Sheldon got the best of it. By the beginning of 2005, Sheldon was worth $15.6 billion, ranking him nineteenth on the *Forbes* magazine list of the 500 richest Americans (he was briefly ranked #3 in the world in 2007). He was easily the richest in Las Vegas, well ahead of the resident Forrest Mars candy bar family, listed as thirty-second with $10.4 billion.

Actually, Sheldon's fortune rose higher than anyone else's in the United States in 2004. He took in $13.8 billion, topping the top-ten list.

Sheldon's climb to the peak in Vegas came on Wall Street. It began late in the year, on December 15, 2004, when shares of stock in his Las Vegas Sands company went on sale starting at $29. His timing, or luck, couldn't have been better—visitors to Vegas increased by 5 percent, but new rooms increased by only 1 percent, so supply and demand sent room rates soaring. The Vegas economy was on fire and investors knew it.

Within only hours, the price of Sheldon's stock rose to $44.50, more than 50 percent. That day alone, Sheldon's worth grew by nearly $9 billion. He'd socked away 88 percent of his company's stock for himself, a cool 308 million shares.

Investors on the New York Stock Exchange liked his cash-generating Venetian hotel on the Strip. They also appreciated the prospects of his overseas gaming hall at the Chinese gambling commune of Macau, where he became the first American to open a casino in 2004, well ahead of Steve's plans. Steve's place there, at a cost of $700 million, was to be completed in 2006.

Steve ranked considerably behind Sheldon on the *Forbes* list at 306th, with only $2.1 billion (behind even the bankrupt Donald Trump, who nonetheless held $2.6 billion at 228th). But his fortune did rise by a billion bucks, as he watched shares in his public company, Wynn Resorts, go from just thirteen dollars a share to peak at seventy dollars before receding a bit by early 2005.

However, both men know that their real futures, their greater fortunes, lie in China. Macau sits beside a gaming market of hundreds of millions of Chinese, who are known to be among the world's most obsessive gamblers. Wealthy and middle-class Chinese stand in lines several people deep in front of the crowded gaming tables and slots in Macau.

The profit margins from the cash flowing over the tables and through the machines in Macau are just tremendous. Steve told *USA Today* in April 2005: "In Macau, the average player at the table will lose twenty-five dollars an hour. The dealer makes less than twenty-five dollars a day."

Steve and Sheldon also know that the steady stream of millions from Chinese gambling losses will ensure that they'll never have to turn to American-style financing—selling stock on Wall Street or paying high interest on loans from banks or junk bond kings—ever again.

Meanwhile, both men were waiting for the private hangars for their corporate jets to be completed at McCarran International Airport. Both were expecting to park their Gulfstreams, the corporate plane of choice, inside the new $25 million airport complex.

Already flying high during Vegas's centennial year of 2005, Steve and Sheldon have now shifted their attention from the Strip to China, the new Las Vegas, where a billion new suckers beckon.

True Crimes

29

Three Women in a Cell

For nearly four months in 2000, three suspects in three of the most storied homicide cases in Las Vegas history lived together in the same jail cell at the Clark County Detention Center. That all three suspects were women made the situation all the more intriguing, aside from the fact that their living arrangement lasted for as long as it did until the third banana accused the other two—both former topless dancers—of getting too hot for her to handle. The verdicts on them would be the same: all three were found guilty in their separate cases, although two got their cases thrown out and reset by the Nevada Supreme Court, with one ending in acquittal in 2004.

The girl cell-mates were Margaret Rudin, age fifty-six, Jessica Williams, twenty-one, and Sandy Murphy, twenty-eight. It was Rudin who broke up the gang, after complaining to jailers that Jessica and Sandy were engaging in "inappropriate conduct" in one another's bunk beds, a charge that the younger girls vigorously denied: Sandy, they insisted, was only consoling the deeply sorry and remorseful Jessica.

Williams joined the cell with Rudin and Murphy on March 19, 2000, hours after her arrest on felony driving under the influence and drug charges following a horrific accident in which she fell asleep at the wheel and crashed into six teenagers on a median on Interstate 15 just west of the Strip. All six kids died while they collected trash as punishment for stuff they did in their Las Vegas schools. Williams, then working as a topless dancer in town, had been driving back to Vegas overnight from Los Angeles and had taken ecstasy and smoked pot in the car on the way over. After the horrible accident, Jessica had asked the girl who drove in with her: "Is this real?" Traces of pot in her system eventually got her eight assorted felony driving and drug charges.

In a bunk in their cell, Murphy hugged the shaken Williams and tried to get her to stop crying. She was there for her in the awful coming weeks as the funerals for the teens made the local news, and the charges against Jessica mounted. Rudin, another generation or two away from them, scoffed as the pair lay together in the same bunk. She didn't want to have to live with whom she regarded as a pair of lesbian lovers in her cell.

Rudin had considerable problems of her own that year. She was on trial for the slaying of her fifth husband, Ron Rudin, a sixty-four-year-old millionaire local businessman. His burned, skeletal remains were found on the side of a hill in January 1995 in a remote area near Lake Mohave called Nelson's Landing, south of Las Vegas. According to the case against her, Margaret, or a hired gun, shot and killed Rudin while he slept in the bedroom of his Las Vegas abode, in the evening of December 17, 1994: the very day Margaret held the grand opening of her antique store. To throw off investigators, she or someone parked Ron's 1993 Cadillac behind the Crazy Horse Too topless club a week later. Inside Ron's house, police found splatters of his blood on the wall. Ron's head was cut off and his body placed into a trunk—the same one seen earlier at Margaret's antique store—that was set ablaze near the lake. Was Margaret the kind of person who could chop Ron's head off? It seemed far-fetched that given her thin frame, she could have moved the body of a 220-pound man and dragged a trunk that far by herself. She likely had an accomplice, but whom? Their plan might have worked if they'd bothered to remove Ron's bracelet (with "RON" spelled out in diamonds) from his arm and the teeth from his severed skull, both used to identify the body. It would also have helped if they'd done a better job of disposing of the murder weapon; a scuba diver at Lake Mohave recovered the .22 caliber pistol with flash suppressor in shallow water about eight months after the murder. That gun had been Ron's, and he had reported it missing shortly after he filed for divorce against Margaret in 1988, only a year after they got married. The firearm stayed missing after they reconciled in 1989.

Her trial revealed her weird marriage to Rudin, a gun dealer, real estate investor, and himself a veteran of four other failed nuptials. It got rocky in no time. One evening, Margaret secretly listened on a phone extension as a drunken Ron complained to another woman that he wasn't getting enough sex. Margaret confronted him later and pulled a gun on him. Ron grabbed it and fired into a painting on the wall, then fired a round into the headboard of their bed. That sent her packing, but they got back together several months later and Ron cancelled the divorce.

Margaret remained curious about what the snarky Ron really thought. To satisfy her suspicion that he was either cheating or bad-mouthing her, she bugged his office with a pair of transmitters and tape recorders and listened in—for three years. She found out he was putting her down from time to time among his friends and business contacts. She wrote down what he said in a diary, including an account of a conversation with a woman in which Ron "tells her I've (Margaret) lost $50,000 in the antiques this past year (and) I'll probably stay another year so I can lose another $50,000. They laugh and make fun of me." A month before Ron disappeared, Margaret hired a private detective who reported seeing Ron and a girl-friend enter a condo he'd bought, where they stayed for a half hour before leaving.

Margaret was a woman scorned. Investigators said she re-moved Ron's head in the bathtub, put his body in the trunk, then enlisted her Israeli friend, Yehuda Sharon, to help her get rid of the corpse. Cops said it was suspicious that she didn't appear concerned about Ron's disappearance, was nonchalant about even reporting he was gone, failed to show for his memo-rial service, and quickly hired a workman to remodel the bed-room murder scene. Oh, and she stood to inherit most of his $11 million estate.

Margaret told police that she'd called her husband from her store that night and he quickly ended their conversation. When she returned home, he and his car were gone. She resumed her life but then fled town a few weeks before a grand jury indicted her on murder charges in 1997. Margaret successfully lived in hiding in a small town in Massachusetts, with a man, until No-vember 1999. Someone had seen her on *America's Most Wanted*. To ensure she didn't escape, cops put her in ankle and wrist chains during a prison bus ride to Vegas.

Eventually, while incarcerated during her trial, Margaret grew jealous of cell-mate Sandy who was allowed to wear civil-ian clothes to court, instead of the jail costume Rudin had to wear, and that Sandy had a "dream team" of attorneys on her case while Margaret had to use case-overloaded public defend-ers. The defenders were "up against impossible odds" due to the gravity and attention the case was getting, she complained to the judge in asking he appoint her a heavy-hitter.

"This is causing me extreme anxiety, worry, and apprehension that a horrid high profile case, as my problems have turned out to be, should become at the most opposite end of Lady Justice's scale from Sandy Murphy's 'dream team' defense. It appears as if justice is equal to whatever defense a client can buy."

The judge only let her wear a sweater over her jail togs, but it didn't help her case. He allowed her to hire a new attorney, but that didn't help matters, either. The public watched as her new Vegas lawyer, Michael Amador, made a bizarre spectacle of himself, preening for the news cameras, making an opening statement that made little sense, showing little or no preparation in his motions, failing to adequately interview witnesses. His legal secretary said he "was bragging about the many strippers he was dating."

After a jury found her guilty of murdering Ron, Margaret fired Amador and asked the judge to order a new trial, citing his lousy defense. The judge refused and sentenced her to twenty years.

Jessica Williams was also convicted. In 2002, she received a worse sentence than Rudin's, up to forty-eight years in prison for the accident that killed the six kids. She had to sit and listen to the family members of the victims recount their horrors during the sentencing hearing.

Harriet Booth, the mom of victim Jennifer Booth, dead at sixteen, said her daughter had told her "about the prom dress she had bought the week before, and could not wait to go to the prom. We buried her in her prom dress!"

Jennifer's dad remembered seeing his daughter in the hospital, where she died a day following the accident. "Instead of tears coming down her cheeks, she had tears of blood."

Another mom sat on the witness stand holding a box containing the ashes of her fifteen-year-old daughter. A third mom described how the death of her son, sixteen, had devastated her family: "There are no more holidays, no Christmas. In a year, I have not been able to sit my family at the table."

Williams, after hearing her dad, mom, and sister recount their pain for the victims and their families and requests for a lenient sentence, said: "There's never been a day that I have not recalled details of the accident. And since that day there has never been one day that I have not thought about those young people who are no longer alive."

Her conviction was thrown out in 2003—the judge cited a poorly written DUI law—but she was convicted again in 2004.

The luckiest of the three women in the cell was Sandy, save for the brief controversy over a pair of missing panties that she accused jailers of furnishing to the cops to extract DNA evidence. She'd been convicted in May 2000 with her former boyfriend Rick Tabish on murder charges in the 1998 death of her live-in boyfriend, Binion casino family black sheep, Ted Binion.

Taking on the powerful Binion family in Vegas proved overwhelming. The rich family, through Ted's estate, paid a private detective to provide additional evidence that Las Vegas police had "missed," and the prosecution relied heavily on it to file the charges. Though Murphy and Tabish definitely conspired to steal Ted's valuables, the murder case was shaky and prejudicial. The district attorney's office couldn't decide if Ted died via forced overdose or suffocation, so they said it didn't matter, whatever, take your pick, the accused did it. Prosecutors showed a videotape of a profane Sandy acting spoiled and bitchy in Ted's home after he died. The tape showed her picking up a wine glass—ah-ha, prosecutors said, proof that she used a wine glass to force drugs down Ted's throat. The publicity from leaks of unsubstantiated statements and rumors—the powerless Ted watched them have wild sex next to him as he lay dying, Ted had told a friend that if he died, Sandy did it—

mounted to the point where the only conclusion the outside world could make was that they were guilty. It was amazing that she and Tabish got through it alive.

The trial showcased Murphy acting like a silly bimbo who liked the attention but showed little understanding of what she was in for. There was the time when her attorney called her mother (also named Sandy Murphy) to the stand, prompting the defendant to stand up, fake like she was going to testify, and then say "just kidding!"

The tiresome, even embarrassing case resulted in convictions for her and Tabish on murder, theft, and conspiracy to rob Ted's millions in silver. Jurors were convinced by flawed prosecution testimony from forensic expert Dr. Michael Baden, who said that the heroin and the prescription drug Xanax in Binion's system wasn't enough to kill him, and that Binion died after one or both of them sat on his chest to halt his breathing. Judge Joseph Bonaventure's mistakes—overreaching rulings that helped the prosecution's case—were cited by the Nevada Supreme Court in throwing out the convictions.

Sandy and Rick had better lawyers the second time around. They discredited Baden's testimony and showed that Ted killed himself, accidentally, mixing heroin and Xanax. Just before the jurors delivered their verdict in a 2004 retrial, Sandy turned and vomited into a wastebasket. She and Rick got off on the murder allegations, although the theft charges stuck. Sandy eventually walked out with credit for time served, but Bonaventure tacked a few years onto Rick's term—he was already serving time on other felonies related to the Binion case—for good measure.

Now shed of her legal problems in addition to the millionaire lifestyle she once had with Ted, Sandy also shed herself of Las Vegas. She ended up moving to Los Angeles to work for William Fuller, the elderly guy from Ireland who had paid her enormous legal bills in the two trials.

Criminal Refuge

30

Vegas Confession

On the day before New Year's Eve 1959, Las Vegas police officers Ocie Pigford and Francis Macauley were downtown, enduring one of the coldest local winters on record, when they spotted a black and white 1956 Chevrolet parked by the main post office on Stewart Street, near police headquarters. The car, with one man in it, matched an auto reported stolen from a barn in Iowa and that might contain two convicts—and utter clods—suspected in the brutal murders of a family of four in Kansas.

The officers watched a second man leave the post office and enter the car with a cardboard box. Guns drawn, the officers arrested the two men, who indeed turned out to be the pair wanted for questioning in Kansas, Richard Eugene Hickock, twenty-eight, and thirty-one-year-old Perry Edward Smith. Police charged the former inmates of the Kansas State Penitentiary with violating parole. In mug shots taken at the Vegas city jail, both appeared disheveled, a Mutt and Jeff duo—Hickock's tall neck and wide forehead versus Smith's undersized head, sloping shoulders and small frame.

The five-week national manhunt for Hickock and Smith had ended. They had passed bad checks during an aimless trip from

Miami to Mexico and then to Perry's old apartment complex in Vegas. For Hickock, his capture ended a private, grandiose plan, the real reason he agreed to accompany Smith to Las Vegas—take the famous casinos along the Las Vegas Strip for a ride. After settling down in Smith's apartment, Hickock imagined slipping away in the 1956 Chevy to free himself of Smith forever. Then he'd play the part of high-rolling gambler up and down the Strip. Hickock's gambit would be to don a uniform and impersonate an Air Force officer, then use his skills in writing rubber checks to gamble across the tables of the big casinos. Instead, the pair's decision to travel to Sin City was their downfall.

From October 13 to November 11, 1959, Smith had lived in a sleazy, nine dollars-per-week rooming house—a former illegal brothel—just outside downtown Vegas. He sold his old Ford for ninety dollars to cover bus fare to Kansas City. Smith intended to return to Vegas from the start. He'd asked his landlady to store a box of his things, labeled "Beware, Property of Perry E. Smith," at the rooming house.

Both men had been paroled that year from the Kansas prison for sentences they received for felony crimes in 1956. Smith, out in July, had robbed a store. Hickock, released in August, was in for check fraud. Smith met Hickock in Kansas City on November 12. They soon hit the road and lived it up, thanks to phony checks. Now, in Kansas again, it was time to make a killing. While in prison, Hickock heard a bogus story from a fellow inmate about lots of money stored in a safe at the rural home of Herbert Clutter in Holcomb, Kansas. Ironically, it turned out that Clutter, a forty-eight-year-old grain and cattle farmer, religiously paid his expenses by check.

When the two ex-cons broke into the Clutter home at 1 A.M. on November 15, 1959, the family had already gone to bed. There was no safe and no cache of cash, only fifty bucks. Smith, who'd been polite and told the Clutters that no one would get hurt, went berserk. As Hickock watched, Smith viciously cut Herb Clutter's throat and shot him at point-blank range. He then turned his shotgun on Clutter's wife and teenage children. A week later, while the fugitives were prowling around Acapulco and Mexico City, the inmate who'd told Hickock about the Clutter house tipped off investigators.

Exactly why the killings occurred, detailed famously in Truman Capote's 1965 book *In Cold Blood*, is subject to speculation. Hickock said that as parolees, a robbery would send them back to the pen, so they had to get rid of the witnesses. Another theory: they were a gay couple and Perry went into a jealous rage after Hickock—a divorced father of three—wanted to rape Clutter's teen daughter.

Informed of the arrests, the Kansas Bureau of Investigation immediately sent agents to Vegas. Hickock and Smith were placed in different sections of the city jail to prevent them from talking. Next came the separate interrogations of Hickock and Smith by two Kansas agents, aided by Las Vegas's hardboiled Chief of Detectives, B.J. Handlon.

Things started to fall into place quickly, thanks to the suspects' own stupidity. In the cardboard box, local cops found pairs of boots owned by each suspect and said to match footprints in the Clutter home. Hickock also left the murder weapon, his .12 gauge shotgun, at his parents' home in Kansas for investigators to find.

Under the pressure of these facts, Hickock was the first to crack beneath the bright light during the long, pre-Miranda interview. On January 3, 1960, he burst into tears, confessed, and detailed Smith's role as mass murderer. While being led out of the room, Hickock lost it in front of a *Las Vegas Sun* news photographer. As Handlon and a Kansas agent struggled to hold him up, Hickock fainted, his arms falling limp to his sides.

In Kansas, a prosecutor filed murder charges against them. Smith, informed of Hickock's taped confession, admitted his guilt to an FBI agent from Kansas on January 5. The next day, a handcuffed Hickock looked defiant as he was led out of the Vegas jail and into a car for the long trip back to Kansas. Smith politely replied, "Yep" to a detective who'd said, "You're on your way back." Smith furnished a detailed statement of his crimes during the drive.

Their confessions did nothing for them. Eleven weeks later, they were convicted and quickly sentenced to death—by hanging in Kansas. The U.S. Supreme Court declined to consider their three appeals, and on April 14, 1965, witnesses watched the men's necks snap under the gallows. Capote attended the execution, but was seen fleeing the room before Smith died because, one detective maintained, he and Smith had became intimate on the sly during prison interviews.

31

Evil Spirits

Stanley and Jan Hershey put themselves into a trance and began to communicate with their spirit guides. The police in Surprise, Arizona, had found them and were preparing a warrant for their arrest. Both former teachers with master's degrees, Stan and Jan were true believers in the New Age cult of "channeling" or communicating with powerful spirits circling the earth's atmosphere. The spirits had guided them throughout the country in 1988 and 1989. They gave the couple assignments to follow. One was taking a motor home and cash from their new friend, Gordy Johnson, who was now a missing person. What would the spirits tell them to do now?

The answer came quickly: go to Las Vegas, the refuge of many other troubled spirits and fugitives from the law, figuring they can disappear in the sea of tourists and hotel rooms. On the door of Gordy's motor home Stan attached a note to a fictional "Martha" saying that Gordy was dying of AIDS in Las Vegas and they were going to visit him in the hospital there. He and Jan quickly unhitched Gordy's car from the rear of his RV and drove away in it, minutes before police got there.

On the way to Vegas, Stan and Jan arrived in Sedona, Arizona. A concerned Jan wrote in the notebook she used to take down what her spirits told her:

"Loves: Stan, being free from fear/doubts. Fears: 1. jail, 2. more assignments like the last one. 3. no love, 4. loneliness, 5. not knowing, trusting God, not trusting me. Preferences: 1. Staying with Stan, 2. do Spirit's work with Stan. Conditions: 1. can't harm anyone/take a life."

At last, they arrived in Vegas, their spirits' chosen sanctuary, in late February 1989. Driving in Gordy's car down the Strip, Stan turned into the parking garage of the Bally's Las Vegas hotel. They checked into a room and dropped off their belongings. Treated like high rollers, they went to see the Oak Ridge Boys country singing group in the big showroom. They played high-stakes blackjack. Jan played five dollar slot machines. They went to a shopping mall at Caesars Palace where Stan tried on and bought $8,000 worth of designer men's clothing. Jan also bought expensive new clothes.

A few days later, Las Vegas police found Gordy's missing car at Bally's. They notified FBI agents who arrived at the couple's hotel room. Stan opened the door and the agents arrested them. One agent found $5,000 cash inside Jan's purse and another retrieved the couple's spiral notebooks. A judge ordered Stan and Jan held without bail, saying that they might have killed Gordy Johnson.

On January 11, 1990, the two sat at separate tables during their hearing in the federal courtroom in downtown Las Vegas. Stan declined to say anything to the judge. Jan, now nine months pregnant, testified on her own behalf. She burst into tears and said she still loved Stan and had no intention of hurting anyone. Her parents wept in the courtroom.

Her attorney asked her if she still believed spirits guided her life. Jan replied that of course she did, that she would fall apart, her entire world would crumble, if she learned it wasn't true.

And what about the $1,000 in designer clothes she bought with Gordy's money in Las Vegas? The spirits told us to explore the casinos, and people treat you better when you dress well, Jan replied. Besides, they had no good clothes, she added.

Jan explained she was convinced Stan was telling the truth when he told her that Gordy had left by himself for Los Angeles, and was letting them use his $120,000 bank account, his new luxury motor home, and new car to further their interest in "channeling"—writing down messages communicated by invisible spirits, who tell them how they are destined to live. The spirits tell their followers they can't harm anyone or take a life, she said.

During final arguments, Jan's attorney told the jury that Jan was only passively following her husband, who was the real mastermind of the plot. Stan's attorney said he had no final argument, that he'd rest his case on the presumption of innocence. The prosecutor insisted Stan and Jan were guilty of fraud and theft. He warned the jury not to be swayed by the couple's story that Gordy was hiding somewhere. He said Gordy had been missing for more than a year and was probably no longer living.

The jury deliberated. The next day, the foreman read guilty verdicts on all eighteen felony charges against Stan and Jan—that they stole Gordy's money from ATM machines and drove off with his motor home and the jeep-like car it towed. Stan looked on blankly. Jan squeezed her hands tightly. She looked over at Stan for consolation, but he looked straight ahead. Jan's parents and her sister quickly left the courtroom. Stan and Jan were taken away at opposite sides of the room to jail.

The following day, Jan was in labor, writhing atop a gurney as attendants pushed it inside University Medical Center, the county hospital in Vegas. Nurses removed her orange jail-issue jumpsuit. She screamed as the baby was born. The doctor told her it was a girl. A jailer at the Clark County Detention Center in downtown Las Vegas walked over to Stan's cell and blandly informed him of the birth and sex of the baby. Stan nodded and looked down. He didn't look happy. He was preoccupied. Where were the spirits now?

The assistant U.S. Attorney in Vegas urged the judge to impose the maximum sentence on both—215 years—because Gordy was likely dead. The pair had spent nearly all of Johnson's $120,000 life savings during their criminal spree. The judge sentenced Stan to twenty years in federal prison, Jan to five years. Jan and her parents cried as she was led out. Stan didn't look at his wife.

Two years earlier in Santa Monica, Stan had told Jan that they were in for a big change. He reminded her that a spirit told him they should buy a motor home. He still wanted to drive across the country and teach others how to talk to their spirits. They shopped for recreational vehicles and looked at the bigger models with showers and living rooms, but those cost way too much. They settled on a smaller model that still cost a lot of money, $80,000. Jan wrote a check for $25,000 from her inheritance from her dead uncle as a down payment.

They left their jobs, stored their belongings, and started on their journey. They drove to New Orleans and Minnesota. During a stop in Jackson, Mississippi, Jan sat down to write in her notebook what the spirits dictated:

"We support you as you hold the fort and enable us to explore possible futures for the coming year. Wait a week or two and then sit with the phone book, continue asking around— you will find the appropriate person to add to our summer funds."

In Minnesota, they lived in an RV park near Minneapolis. They were discouraged and worried because they had no income and hadn't made a payment on the motor home in months.

But perhaps the spirits had delivered an opportunity for them. On September 12, 1989, a man in his early sixties parked a large new motor home into the space right next to theirs. It was Gordy Johnson. He soon met Stan and Jan. They found out they were both from Southern California and quickly became friends. Gordy explained that he drove there to visit his brother and sister who lived in Minneapolis.

Gordy showed them his forty-foot motor home, and his small dog, Rocky, living inside. The couple was amazed at its built-in shower, queen bed, living room, and big kitchen. Gordy's RV was much nicer than their narrow, cramped one. Stan politely asked Gordy how much it cost. $220,000, Gordy said. He paid cash for it after selling his home in Glendale a few months back. He also bought a brand-new compact SUV and hitched it to the rear of his RV. Gordy candidly added that he had to be frugal because he had only about $120,000 left in the bank that would have to last for all of his retirement years.

Gordy informed them he planned to drive to Oregon to have his RV repaired. Would they like to caravan along with him, through the Dakotas and Idaho? They had nothing else to do and happily agreed.

Stan and Jan privately remarked to each other their sense that something significant was coming, based on the messages their spirits were telling them to write. Is the next assignment finally at hand?

September 15, 1989. While channeling a message from his spirit guides, Stan wrote:

"As we approach the equinox and the time you assumed the next shift/assignment would surface—you grow increasingly restless as nothing appears. We suggest that your restlessness is the forerunner of the next assignment—clearing the space so to speak. Allow us additional time—don't hold fast to the 22nd. We are present. We are active—and there is more to do soon. When and where and what are the prizes of the scavenger hunt—you are well along to a solution but the final solution is not yet available. It will be."

Across from him on their tiny kitchen table, Jan read Stan's writing. She stared at the table for a moment, then picked up her pen and wrote what her spirits said:

"We ask you to be ever patient as things on our level take its course. You are not being toyed with—proper timing is as important as anything else. Continue to use this time for rest, reflection, as before you know it you will be wishing for these moments you see drifting past you now. We give you no hint of the next assignment just yet as we enjoy watching you both marvel as the way things just seem to 'set up.'"

A week later, on September 22, Jan wrote:

"So you feel pushed to hear our words. This fine day offers much to be examined. The plan is in action and ready to be executed. All that is left is the discovery of what Spirit has planned for the next part of our journey. Do not take the word journey literally. Money spent along the way should not be worried about."

Gordy invited Stan and Jan to eat dinner in his RV. They relaxed in his spacious living room. He let them use his shower. Stan and Jan now are all but convinced that the spirits intend for Gordy to be central to their next assignment. Stan told Jan they must be willing to do what the spirits assign them to do.

On September 26, Stan and Jan again sat down together to channel.

Stan went into his trance and wrote:

"You wonder with some disbelief at the info that seems to

be surfacing re: Gordy and his assets. You wonder at the wisdom of what seems to be implied. Let us say quickly that the judgments and considerations and fears that surface are the natural and expected—even predictable—results of your cultural environment combined with your natural regard for the sanctity of life."

"You have full permission to engage in any activity that will serve your interests—and that permission includes much that you currently find to be distasteful or clearly beyond the scope of our work. You need to remember that regardless of earth-based systems, no act or word or thought from either of you that could be judged as 'harmful' from your cultural vantage point accrues any harmonic consequences for you. There are no limits or prohibitions at your level of service."

Stan pushed his notebook over to Jan. She read the message. She appeared puzzled, concerned. She looked at Stan. Then she stared down, turned to her notebook and wrote:

"Shaken up by today's pieces is only on a personality level. Your true being is so sharply tuned to the job you're contracted to do. The task ahead, dear sister, is acknowledging/believing who you really are. There is no real trust unless you can trust the fact that you are part of Spirit. Acknowledge difficult moments—That's being truthful to personality. To take it further and claim you can't possibly get through an unpleasant task is nonsense. Did you not get through a year in New Orleans? Allow love and light to flow through you dear one—Remember that is what you are."

Over dinner the next night, Gordy said it would probably take several days or so for his RV to be fixed in Oregon. He wanted to get back to Los Angeles by the third week of October. They should all get on the road next week, by October 3, to leave enough time for the repairs, then they could all head down to Los Angeles.

Stan proposed that he and Jan drive alongside Gordy, and then take a detour south to Lake Shasta, California. It was where he grew up with his dad. Stan and Jan were to spend a few days by the lake and drive back up to Oregon and meet up with Gordy. That's fine, Gordy said.

The following day, September 28, Stan pulled out his notebook and wrote:

"This is a formal request for you to consider the proposal that has revealed itself. We add no additional details at this time—you know that specifics follow commitment in our line of work. Should either or both of you decline, other proposals will surface for consideration/action. No judgment attends rejection or selection—we simply need to know your willingness/distaste for this one.

"Be at peace—slowly and gently seek your own alignment— for it is surely there to be found. We are present—you are loved."

On the highway in Oregon, Stan and Jan followed behind Gordy's RV, then drove to Lake Shasta. That night, Stan turned to Jan and asked her if she would be up to the assignment. It's what is being asked of us, he said. Jan stared forward and nodded her head passively. She got up, went to the back of the RV and lit up a joint.

On October 10, 1989, Stan maneuvered their motor home into the RV park in Oregon where Gordy was staying. Gordy said the repair work was almost done. While on the road with Stan and Jan, Gordy went to a payphone on October 15 and called his sister in Minneapolis. He told her he was in Northern California on his way to Los Angeles. Gordy then retired for the night in his motor home.

Stan went over to see Gordy. Hours later, he entered the couple's RV and announced to Jan that Gordy had just decided to go on his own for a while and that he'd given them free use of his RV, car, and money to help further their channeling activities. Jan replied that it was very good of Gordy to do that.

Stan and Jan used Gordy's money to buy a plane ticket to Tahiti, and they drank champagne during the flight. In a hotel room on the South Pacific island of Bora Bora, Stan sat down and wrote: "Do not hold attachments to the need to preserve available funds for any set period of time. We will supply what is necessary when necessary. There will be times when you will seem to go through large amounts quickly—ego will raise alarms and argue for preservation/caution—etc. Do not be concerned—we are far ahead of you in terms of plans for activities and plans for support. We remain—as always—readily available for consultation and clarification."

Stan and Jan gambled away thousands at a casino in Lake Tahoe. Jan wrote in her journal how the spirits advised her to play the twenty-five-dollar slots.

In Minneapolis, Gordy's family members were worried. They hadn't heard from him for weeks. His sister opened one of Gordy's bank statements sent to her. It included the cancelled check drawn by Stan to buy the plane tickets. She called the sheriff's office near the RV factory in Oregon to report that Gordy was missing and someone else was using his bank account.

The sheriff of Shasta County, California, later stood overlooking the expansive shore of Lake Shasta with some deputies and other officers next to him. Stan Hershey had rented a boat on the lake on October 16, the day after Johnson disappeared. He must have dumped the body out there. But the lake is 500 feet deep, too deep to drag. It'd be as hard as dragging in an ocean. And no body would float to the surface from that depth—the water's too cold and it keeps the body down there.

On May 22, 1993, at Stan's murder trial in Redding, California, prosecutors believed that they could convict him even though Gordy's corpse had not been found. Jan, recently transferred from the federal pen to the Shasta County jail, got immunity for agreeing to testify against Stan. She no longer trusted him. She felt her husband betrayed her. It also meant she wouldn't be charged in Gordy's disappearance.

When it was over, the jury found Stan guilty of murder. He was sentenced to life without the possibility of parole, on top of his twenty-year sentence on the federal charges. Jan was transferred to a prison on the East Coast, close to New York. It was where her parents were taking care of her and Stan's daughter, whose birth certificate shows she was born in Las Vegas. Jan was released from federal prison two years later and divorced Stan.

Shasta County sheriff deputies still occasionally find human remains in the area of Lake Shasta, especially during drought season when the lake recedes. For them, Gordy's file will remain open until his body is found.

As for the spirits, Stan and Jan had left them behind in Las Vegas, where they'd apparently completed their last assignment.

Dueling Shills

32

Vegas's Little-Read Newspapers

Like many sizeable American cities, Las Vegas once enjoyed competing daily newspapers. Two morning papers, the *Las Vegas Review-Journal* and *Las Vegas Sun*, battled for nearly forty years. A third small daily, the feisty *Valley Times*, was run out of North Las Vegas and published from the 1960s until 1983, when editor and publisher Bob Brown—in legal trouble after borrowing money from Stardust hotel mobster Frank "Lefty" Rosenthal—killed himself.

The *Sun*'s publisher, Hank Greenspun, a law graduate from New York who moved to Vegas in 1945, founded the paper in 1950. He made himself rich over the years in television, cable TV, and real estate, using caustic editorials and his reporters at the *Sun* to bully his enemies in politics and business. He didn't want to be there when it happened, but he made a secret deal with the *Review-Journal*, that upon his death, the two papers would merge under a legal exemption from U.S. anti-monopoly laws, called a Joint Operating Agreement, reserved for struggling newspapers. Business operations and printing would be handled by the *Review-Journal*, with only the editorial department remaining from the *Sun*. The *R-J* agreed, only if the *Sun* switched to afternoons, and only five days a week. Hank's family didn't mind at all; without the overhead of printing, advertising, and circulation, they went from money-losing to money-gaining, through the *Sun*'s share of the advertising proceeds from the *R-J*. But after the 1989 merger, the *Sun* saw its circulation languish at only about 30,000. In 2005, the *Sun* lowered itself into becoming a mere section insert in the *Review-Journal*.

The largest paper in the state is the *Review-Journal*. Although daily circulation in 2004 was about 165,000, and 225,000 on weekends, it has had trouble adding readers during the week. In order to pitch growth to advertisers, the paper has provided an unappreciated gift for the thousands of non-subscribers in Las Vegas: an almost daily stack of slick advertisements and coupons—junk mail—stuffed into their mailboxes, and most likely, immediately trashed.

In the mid-1980s, the *R-J*'s daily circulation was in the 135,000 range. Greater Las Vegas back then had a population of about 750,000. In 2004, while the population grew by 100 percent to more than 1.5 million, the *R-J* managed to add only 30,000 readers, or two percent.

Just why the *Review-Journal* has been unable to penetrate the area's surging population since the 1980s is still an open question. Some cynics say it's the residents themselves—many of them in the casino and construction industries, a crowd not associated with reading newspapers—and the city's expanding Hispanic population, many of whom speak English as a second language. Yet another explanation is what many longtime residents (and resident non-subscribers) say about the *R-J*: "There's nothing in it!" The city's movers and shakers shake their heads over the big paper's lack of comprehensive news coverage and sophistication for an increasingly complex town. New arrivals from Los Angeles, New York and other large cities are surprised at how poorly the *R-J* compares to the "real newspapers" they used to read.

A truer explanation for the *R-J*'s quality lies with its owner. The paper is the flagship, and by far the biggest paper, of the rich but mediocre Stephens Media chain, the private Arkansas-based publisher of dozens of American newspapers, none with any real distinction. In 1999, Stephens had $5 billion worth of holdings in publishing, energy, and telecom firms, according to the *New York Times*. Stephens ranks with the Ingersol and Singleton news chains with money-grubbing combined with editorial cheapness and inadequacy.

Nearly all of Stephens's papers are in small, one-paper towns, many in the rural southern states. Without competition, these pubs produce fat profits from high advertising rates combined with the lowest editorial expenses possible, and so have little incentive or ability to produce quality journalism. The chain approaches the *R-J* the same way. The *R-J* is Stephens's cash cow, making scores or even hundreds of millions in revenues a year free from competition, although exactly how much it rakes in is hard to estimate since the company is private. With a staff far too small compared to papers in cities the size of Las Vegas, reporters are overworked. Underworked are some of its upper-level editors, who have been in place since the 1970s or mid-1980s, when Las Vegas was a much smaller town. The lack of "big picture" editorial oversight and the heavy workload tend to result in coverage that is neither aggressive nor demanding of sources. Stories about the area's dominant gaming and development industries, for example, normally have a friendly public relations tone to them, in part because some of the people writing them used to work in public relations.

In 2002, the *Review-Journal* raised concerns when it entered the hotel room sales business on the Internet, partnering with two major casino companies, Mandalay Resort Group and Caesars Entertainment. The paper planned to sell hotel rooms with the very resort industry it covers in its newspaper on the *R-J*'s profitable website, lasvegas.com. Its partner paper, the *Sun*, had already been doing that via "virtual tours" of the resorts on its website, vegas.com. The temptation to grab a share of Vegas tourism gold proved too much, and trumped journalistic integrity.

Recently, the *R-J* was happy to announce that it acquired two of the last independent papers in town, the weekly *CityLife* and *Las Vegas Business Press*, after wearing down Wick Communications, a publishing firm out of Arizona. That makes both of the town's "alternative" weeklies owned by either the *R-J* (*CityLife*) or the *Las Vegas Sun*'s owner, the Greenspun Media Group (*Las Vegas Weekly*). Thing is, Las Vegas readers really have no alternative.

BIBLIOGRAPHY

Chapter 1
Jameson, Jenna, with Neil Strauss. *How to Make Love Like a Porn Star: A Cautionary Tale*. New York: HarperCollins Publishers, 2004.

Moehring, Eugene P. *Resort City in the Sunbelt, 1930–2000*. Reno: University of Nevada Press, 2000.

Chapter 2
Ainley, Thomas "Taj" Jr., and Judy Dixon Gabaldon. *Las Vegas: The Fabulous First Century*. Charleston, SC: Arcadia Publishing, 2003.

Dawes, Amy. *Sunset Boulevard: Cruising the Heart of Los Angeles*. Los Angeles: Los Angeles Times Books, 2002.

Demaris, Ovid. *The Boardwalk Jungle*. New York: Bantam Books, 1986.

Demaris, Ovid. *The Director: An Oral Biography of J. Edgar Hoover*. New York: Harper & Row, 1975.

Farrell, Ronald A., and Carole Case. *The Black Book and the Mob: The Untold Story of the Control of Nevada's Casinos*. Madison: University of Wisconsin Press, 1995.

FBI. "Mafia: Section II, United States" (Confidential Report). United States Department of Justice: July 1958.

Glass, Mary Ellen, editor. *Robbins E. Cahill: Recollections of Work in State Politics, Government, Taxation, Gaming Control, Clark County Administration, and the Nevada Resort Association*. Vol. III. Reno: University of Nevada Press, 1977.

Gosch, Marin A., and Richard Hammer. *The Last Testament of Lucky Luciano*. New York: Little, Brown, 1975.

Hulse, James W. *The Silver State: Nevada's Heritage Reinterpreted*. Reno: University of Nevada Press, 1991.

Kennedy, Robert F. *The Enemy Within*. New York: Popular Library, 1960.

Lacey, Robert. *Little Man: Meyer Lansky and the Gangster Life*. Boston: Little, Brown, 1991.

Lyman, Michael D., and Gary W. Potter. *Organized Crime*. Upper Saddle River, NJ: Prentice Hall, 1997.

Maclean, Don. *Pictorial History of the Mafia*. New York: Pyramid Books, 1974.

Mahoney, Richard D. *Sons & Brothers: The Days of Jack and Bobby Kennedy*. New York: Arcade, 1999.

Messick, Hank, and Burt Goldblatt. *The Mobs and the Mafia: The Illustrated History of Organized Crime*. New York: Galahad Books, 1972.

Miller, Millie, and Cyndi Nelson. *Desert Critters: Plants and Animals of the Southwest*. Boulder, CO: Johnson Books, 1996.

Moehring, Eugene P. *Resort City in the Sunbelt, 1930–2000*. Reno: University of Nevada Press, 2000.

Pileggi, Nicholas. *Casino: Love and Honor in Las Vegas*. New York: Simon & Schuster, 1995.

Porrello, Rick. *Corn Sugar and Blood: The Rise and Fall of the Cleveland Mafia*. Ft. Lee, NJ: Barricade Books, 1995.

Rappleye, Charles, and Ed Becker. *All-American Mafioso: The Johnny Rosselli Story*. New York: Doubleday, 1991.

Reid, Ed, and Ovid Demaris. *The Green Felt Jungle*. New York: Pocket Books, 1964.

Roemer, William F., Jr. *War of the Godfathers*. New York: Ivy Books, 1990.

Sciacca, Tony. *Luciano: The Man Who Modernized the American Mafia*. New York: Pinnacle Books, 1975.

Turkus, Burton, and Sid Feder. *Murder, Inc.: The Story of "The Syndicate."* Cambridge, MA: Da Capo, 2003.

Chapter 3

FBI File. Electronic Reading Room. "Bugsy Siegel." http://foia.fbi.gov/foiaindex/siege.htm (accessed various times 2003–2005).

Reid, Ed, and Ovid Demaris. *The Green Felt Jungle*. New York: Pocket Books, 1964.

Turkus, Burton, and Sid Feder. *Murder, Inc.: The Story of "The Syndicate."* Cambridge, MA: Da Capo, 2003.

Yablonsky, Lewis. *George Raft*. New York: Signet Books, 1974.

Chapter 4

FBI File. Electronic Reading Room. "Morris 'Moe' Dalitz." http://foia.fbi.gov/foiaindex/daliz.htm (accessed various times, 2002–2005).

Kennedy, Robert F. *The Enemy Within*. New York: Popular Library, 1960.

Porrello, Rick. *Corn Sugar and Blood: The Rise and Fall of the Cleveland Mafia*. Ft. Lee, NJ: Barricade Books, 1995.

Chapter 5

Stenn, David. *Clara Bow: Runnin' Wild*. New York: Cooper Square, 2000.

Chapter 6

Jordan, Ted. *Norma Jeane: My Secret Life with Marilyn Monroe*. New York: William Morrow, 1989.

Summers, Anthony. *Goddess: The Secret Lives of Marilyn Monroe*. Reading, PA: Sphere Books, 1986.

Chapter 7

Stryker, Susan, and Christine Jorgensen. *Christine Jorgensen: A Personal Autobiography*. San Francisco: Cleis, 2000.

Chapter 8

Manchester, William R. *The Arms of Krupp, 1587–1968*. New York: Little, Brown, 1968.

Chapter 9

Brothers, Thomas, editor. *Louis Armstrong, in His Own Words*. New York: Oxford University Press, 1999.

Chapter 10

Clarke, Gerald. *Get Happy: The Life of Judy Garland*. New York: Random House, 2000.

Coleman, Emily R. *The Complete Judy Garland*. New York: Harper & Row, 1990.

Finch, Christopher. *Rainbow: The Stormy Life of Judy Garland*. New York: Ballantine Books, 1975.

Fricke, John. *Judy Garland: World's Greatest Entertainer*. New York: Henry Holt, 1992.

Chapter 11

Saxton, Martha. *Jayne Mansfield and the American Fifties*. Boston: Houghton Mifflin, 1975.

Chapter 12

Davis, Sammy, Jr., and Jane and Burt Boyar. *Sammy: An Autobiography*. New York: Farrar, Strauss and Giroux, 2000.

Exner, Judith, with Ovid Demaris. *My Story*. New York: Grove Press, 1977.

Chapter 13

Goldman, Albert, with Lawrence Schiller. *Ladies and Gentleman, Lenny Bruce!!* New York: Ballantine Books, 1974.

Chapter 14

Brown, Peter Harry, and Pat H. Broeske. *Down at the End of Lonely Street: The Life and Death of Elvis Presley*. New York: Dutton, 1997.

Nash, Alanna. *The Colonel: The Extraordinary Story of "Colonel" Tom Parker and Elvis Presley*. New York: Simon & Schuster, 2003.

Parker, John. *Elvis: The Secret Files*. London: Anaya, 1993.

Chapter 15

Hopkins, Jerry, and Danny Sugarman. *No One Here Gets Out Alive*. New York: Warner Books, 1980.

Chapter 16

Interview: Mark Rodney, 1995.

Chapter 19

Reid, Ed, and Ovid Demaris. *The Green Felt Jungle*. New York: Pocket Books, 1964.

Chapter 29

Fleeman, Michael. *If I Die . . .* New York: St. Martin's, 2002.

Chapter 30

Capote, Truman. *In Cold Blood*. New York: Random House, 1965.

INDEX